REMEMBER

REMEMBERING OCCUPIED WARSAW

Polish Narratives of World War II

Erica L. Tucker

NIU PRESS

DeKalb

© 2011 by Northern Illinois University Press

Published by the Northern Illinois University Press, DeKalb, Illinois 60115

Manufactured in the United States using acid-free paper.

All Rights Reserved

Design by Shaun Allshouse

Library of Congress Cataloging-in-Publication Data

Tucker, Erica L.

Remembering occupied Warsaw: Polish narratives of World War II / Erica L. Tucker.

p. cm.

Includes bibliographical references and index.

ISBN 978-0-87580-655-6 (original pbk.: alk. paper)

1. Warsaw (Poland)—History—Siege, 1939. 2. Warsaw (Poland)—History—Warsaw Ghetto Uprising, 1943. 3. Warsaw (Poland)—History—Uprising, 1944. 4. Poland—History—Occupation, 1939–1945. 5. Collective memory—Poland—Warsaw. I. Title.

D765.2.W3T83 2011

943.53'43841—dc23

2011016764

To my grandparents

Lydia Jane Johnson & Paul Tucker
and Elizabeth Grupa & James Burke

Contents

Acknowledgments

Many people have helped me with various phases of the project that have culminated in this book. I am deeply appreciative of all they have done to assist me in bringing this work to fruition. Responsibility for the interpretations I offer and any errors I make rests solely with me.

Most of all I am deeply grateful to my informants in Warsaw for generously sharing their memories, stories, and lives with me. It is my hope that in conveying their experiences to others, I can begin to return the gift they have given to me by fulfilling their wish that the times they lived in and their understandings of them will not be forgotten.

Many people have offered me various types of help over the duration of this project. Jack Kugelmass, Anatoly Khazanov, Margaret Beissinger, and Larry Breitborde have provided me with years of careful reading, constructive criticism, and encouragement. I am indebted to Ewa Miernowska for her role in helping me prepare for fieldwork and in gaining entrée into the community that is the focus of this study. Professor Zofia Sokolewicz at the University of Warsaw assisted me during my fieldwork in Warsaw. I have benefited from the excellent suggestions of Vieda Skultans and another anonymous reviewer, which have most certainly improved the quality of this book. For helping me navigate the world of publishing, I am grateful to my friends Sylvia Frank Rodrigue and Kevin Spicer and to Bruno Malisheski who helped me with the technical aspects of preparing the book. Many thanks to everyone at Northern Illinois University Press, as well.

Over the years I have benefited from the assistance of many friends in Poland. For helping me feel at home in Warsaw, I am grateful to Justyna Doboszyńska-Kowal, Joanna Doboszyńska, Dorota Franczyk, and Katarzyna Kozorys. Many thanks also to Barbara Szudra and Aneta Szudra Kram.

Finally, deepest thanks to my family for the generous and tireless support they continue to give me: Sandra and Terry Tucker, Marceli Tucker-Szudra, Robert Szudra, Nicole White, Danielle Matuschka, and Jane Tucker. This book would not have been possible without your encouragement.

REMEMBERING OCCUPIED WARSAW

Introduction

I WAS NEARING THE END of an interview with Hanna, an energetic professor emerita of classics in her mid-sixties, when she told me, "In general I do not reminisce." Given that we had spent the last two hours talking about her memories of growing up during the German occupation of Poland, the statement took me by surprise. "I'll tell you something more," she added, leaning closer and lowering her voice. "I asked my friend, 'Listen, have you been in that house where we were stationed?' And she said, 'No.' I haven't either." I was not surprised that Hanna and her friend had avoided the place where as teenagers they were stationed as medics and couriers for the Polish underground during the Warsaw Uprising of 1944. After all, a schoolmate had been killed there, and they had been forced to leave her body behind by the approach of German troops. Hanna and her friend were the only survivors of a battalion comprised entirely of girls under the age of eighteen. Then it struck me that the house must be nearby. Hanna confirmed that it was just around the corner. I had walked past it on the way there. In fact, it is the site of the shopping center, tram, and bus stop nearest to Hanna's house. "You've never been there since?" I asked in disbelief. Hanna, who when I met her walked with a cane, explained that a few times a week she went several blocks out of the way to do her grocery shopping, fill prescriptions, and the like. "I simply do not go there, maybe if I had to go or something, but, well, I do not feel like going. I would rather lock that history away."

On my way home I passed the house, thinking of Hanna. Elderly Warsovians have been known to protest if there is not a grocery store in their apartment building, which made Hanna's avoidance of the area all the more remarkable. Walking home that day, I began to think of the plethora of geographic details in my interviews. Before, they had always seemed like an unnecessary distraction. An informant would be in the middle of a gripping story and suddenly stop to explain that this happened at such and such a corner or break off mid-sentence to describe what the location looked like now. That day I recollected all those details on my walk home. The movie theater where *Titanic* was playing had served as a makeshift hospital where Olgierd Z——, one of my informants, had assisted in operations without anesthesia by candlelight. Janina, another informant, had transported the wounded on stretchers through the park. Down the street from my building was the house where the Gestapo arrested Wiesława for her activities in the underground. Around the corner, by the Rainbow Cinema, is the place where the first shots of the Warsaw Uprising were fired on August 1, 1944.

Drawing from ethnographic fieldwork and life history interviews that I conducted with older residents of Warsaw in the mid- to late 1990s, I probe the memory of World War II in Poland. My work examines how older ethnic Poles recollected and narrated the outbreak of war, the German occupation, and postwar recovery. My goal is not to reconstruct the past from these narratives but rather to understand the meaning that the past holds for those who lived it and how it influences their understandings of subsequent events, shaping attitudes and actions in contemporary Poland. In exploring these narratives, I offer arguments about factors that influence how residents remember the war and about the narrative frames they draw on to convey their experiences to others. At the same time I consider how they recovered from the rupture of war, suggesting that these processes were connected to efforts to reconstruct the city itself. Finally, I examine my informants' concern that, with the passing of their generation, this history will be deemed irrelevant or forgotten by younger generations. The overarching questions I explore all pertain to the relationship between memory and its narration, trauma, and place. How is remembering trauma shaped by individual and cultural factors? What is the role of place in these memories and in recovering from the violence of war? How are these narratives used to make meaning of suffering and to reinvest with familiarity places made strange and threatening by violence?

Poles of a certain age in any town or city could speak to these issues. However, Warsaw is unique not just among Polish cities but also among Nazi-occupied cities in some significant ways. First, Warsaw was the site of two major anti-Nazi uprisings: the Warsaw Ghetto Uprising of 1943 and the General Uprising of 1944, which is also known as the Warsaw Uprising.[1] Following the failure of the General Uprising, the city was emptied of its nearly one million inhabitants. Just as the Warsaw Ghetto was razed in the wake of the Warsaw Ghetto Uprising of 1943, so was the city of Warsaw systematically destroyed by Nazi troops in retaliation for the Warsaw Uprising of 1944. At the time of the city's liberation by Soviet troops on January 17, 1945, Warsaw lay in ruins, its populace displaced, incarcerated, or in hiding. An estimated 92 percent of the left bank, the cultural, economic, and governmental center of the capital, had been literally reduced to rubble (Borecka and Sempoliński 1985: 296; Roszkowski 1997: 138). Yet within days Warsovians began to return to the city. In the months that followed the liberation, thousands of former residents were drawn to Warsaw, making their way through the debris in an effort to survey the remains of their homes, to locate missing family members, and to begin the task of rebuilding their city and their lives. This history makes Warsaw an ideal place to examine not just memories of war but how people draw on memory and place to rebuild normalcy and reconstruct their lives.

But why pay attention to elderly Warsaw residents' memories of World War II? In a compelling essay written for the *New York Review of Books,* historian Timothy Snyder (2009) argues that our understanding of twentieth-century European history in general, and of the Holocaust in particular, has been skewed by histories focused largely on Germany and Western Europe. He cautions that while "the project to kill all Jews was substantially realized; the project to destroy Slavic populations was only very partially implemented" and remains little studied (ibid.). As a result of this void, many in the West are unaware that between 1933 and 1944 twelve million people, both Jews and non-Jews, in what is today Poland, Ukraine, Belarus, Lithuania, and Latvia were killed en masse as a result of Nazi and Soviet policies (ibid.). To fully understand World War II and the Holocaust we must understand the conditions that existed in the countries where genocide was carried out and how the inhabitants of occupied countries experienced the war and remember it today. Much has been written about Jewish experience and memory of the Holocaust. But to approach Eastern Europe as merely the setting for the Holocaust and East Europeans solely as walk-ons in the tragedy of Jewish suffering, sometimes aiding their Jewish compatriots, other times abetting the Nazis, all too often seemingly indifferent, is to risk oversimplification and misunderstanding. This can only limit our understanding of the past and its applicability to the present. In this book I use ethnographic research in an attempt to rectify, at least in part, this lacuna by illuminating Polish experiences and memories of the German occupation of Poland and their responses to it.

To be clear, I do not seek to make a case that the experiences and memories of ethnic Poles are more important than those of Jewish Poles or that the former group has suffered more than, or even as much as, the latter. Such claims would be inappropriate and erroneous. While a great deal has been written about Jewish Poles' experiences and memories of this period, relatively little has been written in English about ethnic Poles' memories of the same. In writing this book, I am suggesting that ethnic Polish experiences and memories of the war are interesting and valuable in their own right and that exploring them enriches our understanding of this period as a whole.

Żoliborz

Żoliborz, the Warsaw neighborhood where Hanna and the others reside, is unique in that it is part of that 8 percent of the city's left bank that was still standing in 1945. With many prewar buildings intact the neighborhood stands out as an island of continuity within a reconstructed city. As a result Żoliborz has much to offer to a study of memory, trauma, and place. The neighborhood has a degree of physical continuity with the past that is unusual in Warsaw. The current layout of the streets, the parks, and the center of Żoliborz is the same as it was prior to the outbreak of war in 1939. Moreover, schools, churches, shops, apartment complexes, and homes in the center of the neighborhood are those of the prewar era. Thus, a person who had been there before the war could recognize the place in spite of new additions to the landscape. This may seem commonplace; after all, only 60 some years have passed since the war ended. However, in Warsaw, where the majority of the city was built anew after 1945, this is the exception not the rule. In fact, only two other areas on Warsaw's left bank have this sort of continuity with the past, the Old Town, which is a historical reconstruction, and Mokotów. In terms of memory, Żoliborz has at least two advantages over both of these neighborhoods. During the war German troops displaced many of Mokotów's residents and forced them to relocate to other parts of Warsaw in order to create a German-only neighborhood. Thus, the vast majority of Mokotów residents experienced dislocation and the disruption of social networks as part of the wartime experience. While residents of Old Town were not forced out of their homes until autumn of 1944, the neighborhood was utterly uninhabitable when it was liberated in January of 1945, and the reconstruction of Old Town was not completed until 1953. As a result, residents of Old Town had no choice but to find housing in other parts of Warsaw or elsewhere entirely after the war. In contrast, Żoliborz residents experienced the war from the vantage point of their own neighborhood. After the city was liberated by the Red Army in January of 1945, many of the Żoliborz residents returned to their homes, found them intact, and took up residence. At the time of my research, some of my informants lived in the very homes they had lived in when they first moved to the neighborhood as children in the 1920s and 1930s. This gives Żoliborz both a physical and a social continuity with the past. Social networks tend to have deeper roots here than in areas that were completely rebuilt, like the neighboring districts of Old Town, Wola, or Muranów. Elderly residents of Żoliborz have enduring ties to place and community; thus the neighborhood and the city are not just the backdrops of their lives but also an integral part of their life stories, a repository of community and identity (Feld and Basso 1996). For this reason an overview of the neighborhood's cultural geography seems to be in order.

The vast majority of the people with whom I worked were born in the late 1920s, and their memories of Żoliborz reflect much of the prewar character of the neighborhood. Irmina, now an architect, moved with her family from the Old Town to Żoliborz in 1936 when she was six years old. She told me, "Here was this new neighborhood that was blossoming, and to me, a child brought up in the Old Town, it was a symbol of modernity, of new architecture, of wonderfully broad and green avenues, of great green gardens. So, I drank this all in with great satisfaction."

From an administrative point of view, Żoliborz currently consists of the three northern neighborhoods of Bielany, Marymont, and Old Żoliborz. However, longtime residents tend to use the name Żoliborz only in reference to "Old Żoliborz," a new appellation for an area that was developed in the 1920s and 1930s. As one informant explained to me, "That part which was founded after World War II is new and never was Żoliborz. That was Marymont, or Bielany, or Warsaw, or workers' housing because they were all subdistricts without character." Unless otherwise stated I follow my informants in using Żoliborz with reference to what is now called "Old Żoliborz."

Prewar residents in particular also distinguish between four different areas within the neighborhood that reflect both the history of the neighborhood's development and the social cleavages of those who resided there. These four areas are: Officers', Civil Employees', Journalists', and Workers' Żoliborz (Żoliborz Oficerski, Żoliborz Urzedniczy, Żoliborz Dziennikarski and Żoliborz Robotniczy). The first houses built in Żoliborz in 1922 were built for officers in the Polish army; thus the area became known as Officers' Żoliborz. Most of these homes are built in the style of the Polish manor houses favored by the landed gentry of the nineteenth century or are villas, though one also finds the occasional semidetached pair of homes.[2]

In 1923 ground was broken on the opposite side of Mickiewicz Street, the main artery running through Żoliborz, for a group of houses, also in the villa style, and apartment complexes for government employees. This area became known as Civil Employees' Żoliborz. The apartment complexes in this part of Żoliborz were often built cooperatively by employees of a given profession, such as the Teachers' Housing Cooperative on Słowacki Street. The apartments in this part of Żoliborz are spacious, the complexes usually three or four stories high and arranged in a U shape around a courtyard with the fourth side open to allow for better air circulation. These courtyards contain gardens, playgrounds, and occasionally small outdoor altars. Like oases in the city, the courtyards provide peaceful green space that is not only much quieter than the busy streets that surround them but also noticeably cooler in summer.

In the late 1920s and 1930s a number of journalists and writers built houses on the streets adjacent to the lower part of Officers' Żoliborz, and this area became known as Journalists' Żoliborz. The boundary between Officers' and Journalists' Żoliborz is the least distinct of the four areas, in part because there is no clear-cut geographical dividing line but also because both consist primarily of manor houses, villas, and large semidetached houses. The border has become further blurred due to the fact that in 1960–1961 twenty journalists created a cooperative, which has since disbanded, and built 20 houses on Kanionowska Street, one of the original streets in Officers' Żoliborz. The fourth district, Workers' Żoliborz, became the locus where a generation of young architects fused art with ideology to build affordable housing. As a result Żoliborz became the center for the avant-garde in Warsaw. This part of the neighborhood consists of large apartment complexes, four to six stories high, built primarily by the Warsaw Housing Cooperative (Warszawska Spoldzielnia Mieszkaniowa, commonly called WSM). Though intended as affordable housing for workers and their families, following the economic depression of 1929, the apartments were beyond the means of most workers, and the majority were purchased by members of the working intelligentsia (Mazur 1993). The architectural style inspired by Le Corbusier, the building materials, and the layouts of the complexes as well as the individual apartments all differentiate these prewar complexes from those built in the Communist era. In contrast, postwar apartment buildings tend to consist of large groups of identical high-rises, the likes of which can be found throughout the former Soviet bloc. Judging by appearances alone, the postwar buildings of the 1950s and 1960s tend to be in worse condition.

While many people who moved to Żoliborz after World War II do not distinguish one section from the other, prewar residents all emphasized the internal divisions within the neighborhood. As Olgierd B—— told me, "They were like four little worlds, and those four worlds make up Old Żoliborz. I think it is important to remember, because each of those worlds had different fates, developed differently."

While those living outside the neighborhood might be less aware of the particular character and history of these four areas, Żoliborz does hold a special place among Warsaw neighborhoods and a reputation far outside of Warsaw. In his memoirs of 1957–1961, *Letters to Mrs. Z*, Kazimierz Brandys (1964: 47) offered Żoliborz as an alternative to the "new man" that the state sought to create: "I have for you a certain proposition: Żoliborz. Please do not treat this in the residential sense; I know that you like your present address and do not intend to change it. I propose Żoliborz to you not as a neighborhood but as a worldview and lifestyle. It is a part of Warsaw settled for a long time by the working intelligentsia—a neighborhood of secular traditions, community oriented and democratic."

Brandys (1964: 47) describes Żoliborz residents (Żoliborzians) as a group with a well-developed consciousness of where they live: "A Żoliborzian does not live in Warsaw, but in Żoliborz, just like Mickiewicz [lived] in Lithuania."[3] In fact, there is an idiom still in use that illustrates this point. Literally everyone I spoke to cited it as evidence that Żoliborzians view their neighborhood as separate from the rest of Warsaw. As Olgierd B——, a retired journalist, explained, "It was a little like a big village in the sense that everyone knew each other. It was the so-called wonderful Province [of Warsaw]. Exactly as if it were separate. It was Warsaw, but at the same time not. The best proof of this is that sometimes we would say, 'I am going to Warsaw' although we were in Warsaw, and one always said, 'I am going to the city.'"

To appreciate why residents may have emphasized Żoliborz as a place apart, I turn to Jan Z——'s description of the neighborhood: "At the time when we moved in . . . [we were] the first one of a few hundred residents here in 1933. There were barely sixty houses here and nothing else. The nearest tramcar was on the outskirts of the so-called Jewish Ghetto.[4] You had to walk through the little wood, from here a little footpath over the railway lines, and then you got to the central square of Muranów, then you caught the tram car to take you to the city. So, it was FAR OFF [he yells for emphasis]! It was far out of the city."

While the neighborhood no longer can be said to be isolated from the rest of Warsaw and is now well connected by tram, bus, and a new metro line, Żoliborz residents still say, "I am going to the city." Moreover, as Brandys (1964: 46) points out, residents of Żoliborz have been christened "Żoliborzians," while residents of other neighborhoods are not known by similar appellations, illustrating the neighborhood's strong individual character. Accordingly, Brandys suggests that Żoliborzians have a lifestyle that is unique to them: "Żoliborz always had a concept of how to organize the country. It created its own original style of life, very European, but with nothing in common with imitation: a lifestyle of an engaged intellectual of humble means and of keen cultural needs, a reader, a discussant, a critical and conscious spectator" (ibid. 47).

Certainly with reference to the interwar era, most of my informants emphasized that the area was like a small town or village in that everyone knew everybody else. In fact, there were 50,000 residents of Żoliborz in 1939, so while it may have been possible to know all the residents by name or face in the 1920s, it would have been unlikely in the late 1930s. However, when one considers that most of my informants were school-aged children before the war and that there was only one secondary school for boys (Poniatowski) and two for girls (Aleksandra Piłsudska Middle and Secondary School and the Catholic school at the Sisters of the Resurrection), the basis for the perception that "everyone knew everybody" becomes clearer.

More than most areas of Warsaw, contemporary Żoliborz has a neighborhood feel to it. This sense of community may have endured after the war in part because many prewar residents returned to the neighborhood in search of family and, finding their homes intact, reclaimed them. As Brandys implies, Żoliborz may also attract a certain type of person, a member of the intelligentsia who sees herself as the successor to the neighborhood's progressive past. Indeed Brandys's description fits many of my informants.

Anthropological Fieldwork

Although I am writing on a historical topic, the research methods I use are those of a cultural anthropologist: fieldwork, participant observation, and in-depth life history interviews. Readers with a background in anthropology will recognize these as central to the field of cultural anthropology and may want to skip to the next paragraph. For those who are not anthropologists these terms may not be helpful in understanding the nature of how I work or how my research differs from that of a historian. For an anthropologist fieldwork entails living in the community that is the focus of our study, taking an active concern and interest in the daily lives of our research subjects, and recording the activities that are of interest in fieldnotes, which are in essence our data. This approach, called participant observation, is accompanied in my case by in-depth interviews about informants' memories of their lives before and during the war. These methods shape the types of questions I ask, the data I receive in answer, and the story that I present in the pages that follow. For anthropologists our professional ethics are focused on how we treat and represent the individuals with whom we work. Because our data are gained through active and intensive participation in and observation of people's daily lives as well as open-ended and, in my case, life-history, focused interviews, we gain our knowledge of the events and phenomena we write about in a relationship built on trust. The foundation of my relationship with my informants is their trust that I will present their experiences, their memories, and their lives fairly and empathetically. It would be neither appropriate nor ethical for me to judge their attitudes, behaviors, actions, or inactions toward each other or toward another group. Rather, as an anthropologist I seek to understand what my informants share with me in our interviews and conversations and what I observe within the cultural and historical framework in which those conversations occur. Anthropologists do not, however, treat their informants' accounts as sacred texts. In the pages that follow, I spend a great deal of time exploring the disconnect between what people say and what they do and in trying to tease out why people's memories of the past may differ radically from history. In doing so my goal is to understand these disjunctures in the broader social and cultural context. Additionally, as an anthropologist I recognize and write about how my informants' positions shape their narratives and influence their memories. I have not edited out informants' attitudes, remarks, or choices that may portray them in a negative (e.g., anti-Semitic or militaristic) light. I include such passages from their interviews in order to allow readers to draw their own conclusions.

I conducted my research in Żoliborz during the late 1990s, over a ten-month period, with shorter follow-up visits over several summers through 2008. Twenty-three of the twenty-five people I interviewed formally for my project were born in or before 1929 and have vivid recall not only of World War II but also of the interwar era. The older people who shared their life histories with me are all longtime, if not lifetime, residents of Żoliborz. For the most part their fathers were officers in the Polish army, engineers, doctors, and civil or municipal employees. Many of their mothers also held university degrees and worked before and after the war as educators, artists, doctors and dentists, or municipal employees. Equally important are their parents' political views and activities. As young people several of their parents were themselves active in the opposition to tsarist Russia, which ruled Warsaw and eastern Poland prior to World War I. Many of their fathers and a few of their mothers joined Piłsudski's Legions in the struggle for Polish independence at that time.[5] Later, some became members of the interwar-era Polish Socialist Party, which was very active in Żoliborz. It was of vital importance to my mentors that I understood that, while their parents were socialists, they were not communists either in the Cold War or in the contemporary understanding of that term in Eastern Europe. Joanna's comments illustrate these concerns well:

> Besides that, Żoliborz before the war [World War II] was still rather, how to describe it? A little leftist. Not communist! Absolutely not communist! But more socialist. There was even a housing development established that was called Jedność Robotnicza [United Workers] which was built for workers. It was part of Society for the Friends' of Children [Towarzystwo Przyjaciół Dzieci, known as TPD], which organized help, summer camps, those types of social things. So, they did not belong, God forbid, to a Soviet communist pattern, it was just Poland at its most progressive.

In terms of my informants themselves, 23 out of 25 of my informants have university educations, placing them by Polish standards in the intelligentsia. With two exceptions they are all ethnically Polish, and all but one were raised in the Catholic tradition, though adherence to those beliefs and practices varies considerably from person to person. In addition to their family backgrounds, level of education, and place of residence, they hold in common their participation in various underground organizations during World War II. In many cases their work in the underground culminated in their participation in the Warsaw Uprising of 1944.

I can make no claim to giving voice to a voiceless community. Such claims have received a great deal of scrutiny and some criticism: the most perceptive among them perhaps is that these are scholarly myths, stories that scholars tell themselves about their research (Andrews 2007: 41). The people with whom I worked are a highly articulate, literate, and well-read group. Theirs is a generation that has published numerous memoirs (not to mention some feature films) about the war, some of which were originally published outside of Poland due to censorship within. During much of the communist era, the government repressed public memory, muting their voices. This situation was already changing when I began my fieldwork. The problem was not so much that my informants did not have a voice but rather that they lacked an audience, scholarly or otherwise. Polish scholars on the subject are often presumed to be biased by their Western counterparts.

This is an area of history where scholars are often referenced with their nationality and religion as well as their discipline. Some of my informants expressed the belief that because I am not Polish people will believe me, suggesting that my scholarly interest and professional credentials might serve as a vehicle for garnering an audience. My aim is to give them a well-informed audience by offering readers the historical and cultural context with which to understand my informants' experiences and the meanings they have made of those experiences in later life.

As this is a study on narrative in which the author was the audience (and typically the sole member of that audience) for the narratives presented here, it would be worthwhile to consider how my informants perceived me. As I write this I am a middle-aged assistant professor at an American college, but my informants met me when I was a young scholar in my late twenties. In introducing myself I explained the goals and purpose of my research. They knew I was from the United States, and most were curious enough to ask whether I was of Polish heritage. I explained to them that one set of my great-grandparents is from Poland, but that I never knew them and that I learned Polish at university. Some responded to this information by declaring, "So, you are Polish!" Others responded, "Your Polish is excellent," upgrading their assessment of my language skills from mediocre to exceptional with the news that I learned it in school, not at home. A few probed further, taking an interest in my religious background: no, I am not Catholic. Others probed to see whether my name, Erica Tucker, indicated that I am also of German heritage. I explained that my remaining great-grandparents were from Ireland, Scotland, and England, pronounced my name as it is spelled in phonetic Polish, and then explained that the spelling I use for Erica means *heather* in Italian, which usually appealed to my informants and at least diminished the German connotations, which, as the reader will have gathered, were not helpful.

My fieldwork consisted primarily of life history interviews, but as I got to know my informants better, some invited me to attend birthday and nameday parties as well as commemorative celebrations. During my fieldwork I addressed all of my informants using the formal *Pan* for men or *Pani* for women. Some of my relationships with informants were friendly, but more formal. I met with Olgierd Z—— several times, but each time for one hour and one hour only. As soon as the tape recorder clicked off at the end of the second side, he would sigh and say, "Well, that's enough for this evening." Regardless of where we were in our conversation, at the end of an hour we concluded our meeting always with my request for yet another, which he invariably greeted with cordial acquiescence. My relationships with other informants were less formal. My meetings with Jerzy, for example, would sometimes go on for hours over tea and his homemade macaroons. Joanna would take time to show me whatever she was weaving or knitting at the moment. With some it was understood that when I came we would make a day of it and I would stay for supper, our conversations meandering onto subjects far afield from my research. I had daily contact with Sławka, Zosia, Basia, and Marek. While only a handful of these daily interactions are mentioned in the pages that follow, the conversations that we shared over meals, while grocery shopping, or after watching the evening news were of inestimable value in forming my understanding of how my informants view the world and how their past experiences color and shape their perceptions of the present.

I keep in touch with those who are still living through e-mail, Christmas cards, and the occasional visit. Now when I return to Żoliborz, my memories of my fieldwork are mingled with my informants' memories of their youth during the war, so that, walking through the neighborhood, I imagine myself as I was starting this project, and at the same time I hear their voices reminding me of what the neighborhood was like before the war and after. At every corner I remember something that one of them experienced there, and at the same time I remember sitting in their living rooms, studies, kitchen tables, always over tea, watching their faces as they recounted their lives for me. It was difficult to learn of all they had suffered and moving to learn of how they had endured, making meaningful lives for themselves in spite of devastating loss. It has been even more painful to learn of their deaths. I treasure our conversations and hope that I have done justice to all they have shared with me.

The Problem of Memory

Anthropologists of the early twentieth century recognized memory along with human behavior as the ethnographer's primary source, albeit one that is supremely elusive and complex (Malinowski 1961: 3). I approach memory as a social act, a dynamic process of association, negotiation, imagination, and narration through time. Memory and narrative are inextricably intertwined, in that narrative is perhaps the most direct path to accessing another's memories or of sharing our own memories with others. This is not to say that there are not a number of other ways to remember. Our homes, for example, may offer cues for our own memories through displays of pictures and mementos, photo albums, and scrapbooks. All these memory practices tell stories about who we were or are and what we have experienced, stories that are often unreadable and inaccessible to others without narrative. Issues of the role of narrative and identity in remembering, of kinds and functions of memory, and of public versus private production and control of memory are all at play in my research. In the pages that follow, I draw on a number of my informants' attitudes toward remembering that illustrate some of these current concerns in memory and oral-history research.

Many of my informants consider sharing their memories of the war with others to be, in their words, "a sacred obligation," both to those who died and to younger generations. This has motivated them to participate in a whole range of memory work beyond attending annual public commemorations. Such work includes volunteering at museums that depict World War II, leading school and scouting groups on historical tours of the neighborhood, compiling lists of those who were persecuted during the Stalinist era for their participation in the Polish underground during the war, erecting memorial plaques, caring for comrades who were disabled during the war, and even answering the questions of this anthropologist. All these forms of recollection are motivated by the conviction that this history should not be forgotten and that, as survivors of the German occupation, it is their duty to bear witness to others. Narrating memory as a testimony to suffering or as commemoration of those who perished is a well-documented impulse in scholarship on survivors of the Holocaust and other atrocities (Engelking 2001; DesPres 1976; Langer 1991; Lifton 1967; Levi 1989, 1995; Myerhoff 1978; Nałkowska 2000; Todorov 1996). Moreover, anthropologists have demonstrated persuasively that one of the primary ways that experience is brought to conscious awareness is through narrative and that therefore the ways we talk about our lives and our sense of self are inextricably intertwined (Ochs and Capps 1996: 21). This would suggest that sharing our life stories with others is as essential to human beings as our need for food, safety, and love (Myerhoff 1978: 271). It is what is shared, how it is shared, and the meanings conveyed in the recounting that are the central questions of this book.

Yet, while the elderly people with whom I worked felt a moral imperative to share their memories of the war with others, they also recognized the possibility that, at least for some, doing so was potentially debilitating. My neighbor Basia, for example, was careful to schedule our interviews when her husband, Marek, was otherwise occupied because she felt that he had an unhealthy preoccupation with the war—which for him had been extended in a sense due to a lengthy imprisonment in the Soviet gulag system—and that such conversations would only exacerbate the problem. If he attempted to enter the room while we were talking, she quickly changed the topic until he returned to his study. Similarly, Wiesława, a survivor of Majdanek, Auschwitz, and Ravensbrück, recalled that when she was editing a collection of memoirs written by Majdanek survivors, her husband, an Auschwitz survivor, complained that he could smell the smoke from the crematoria whenever he entered her study. She interpreted his comment as a concern that she not return to those times. I am not a psychologist and do not have the training to diagnose what has been called "survivor syndrome" or more recently "posttraumatic stress disorder" (Lifton 1967; Young 1993). While much of what we discussed in our interviews involved deprivation, loss, and violence, in other words *trauma*, most of my informants were not, I think, experiencing *traumatic memory* during our interviews. "Traumatic memory," as it is employed in the anthropological and sociological literature on memory, connotes memories that are intrusive, literal, lack a social component, and come unbidden outside the individual's will or control (Argenti and Schramm 2010: 10). Some argue that traumatic memory is distinguishable from narrative memory in that in the former individuals relive the event in the recounting as evidenced by the fact that the telling has a tendency to last as long as the event itself (Van der Kolk and Vander Hart 1991: 427, cited in Argenti and Schramm 2010: 9). Informants' concerns about the perils of gazing too long at the past suggest that, while remembering is a sacred duty, it is also one that they recognize as a potential snare that threatens to hold them in the grip of inconsolable grief, irreparable loss, and meaningless suffering.

Memory, of course, is not a stable medium with which to work for several reasons. Remembering is the process through which we understand our experiences and choose to recollect and relate them anew to ourselves and others (Thomson 1994: 8). How we do so changes over time with shifts in public representations of the past and with changes in how we perceive ourselves or want to be perceived by others (Lass 1994; Thomson 1994: 4). Thus, there is no memory of the past that exists in a pure or natural state waiting to be uncovered if only we ask the right questions or have the correct tools at our disposal (Cole 2001; Lambek 2006: 211). Our perceptions of events change over time as the following excerpt from an interview with Krystyna illustrates:

ELT: What did you think of the liberation?

Krystyna: Not very seriously, I thought very little about it at all then, but today I believe that it was monstrous. Right? Monstrous because people were killed. I recollect that I was in prison humorously, but others were killed in prison, right? And sent to Siberia, and those were terrible things. It wasn't a liberation. But those are my present-day reflections, and then I was young and foolish. Boys interested me more than—Well, I am speaking ill of myself.

Poland was liberated by the Soviet Red Army in 1945 but only after the Soviets waited on Warsaw's right bank of the Vistula River while German troops destroyed the majority of the left bank. Many Warsovians, indeed many Poles, see this as reason enough to regard the liberation with suspicion. However, Krystyna had more personal reasons to regard with distrust the Soviets and the Polish leaders they supported. Like many people who were part of the Polish underground during the war, she was detained for questioning in 1945 by the communist regime. Despite this the liberation itself failed to make a big impression on Krystyna at the time. As she explains in the preceding quotation, it is only as an adult that she sees the pattern of repression that she narrowly escaped, and she has come to feel through her own experiences, talks with others, and reading that the liberation of Poland from the Nazis only led to a different kind of repression by the Soviets.

The very term "liberation," though accurate in the sense that Soviet troops drove the German army out of Poland, masks the ambivalence that many Poles felt in being occupied by another foreign army that, as soon became obvious, had no intention of leaving. State-sanctioned memories of the liberation portray the Soviets as Poland's "friends," "liberators," even "saviors." Prior to 1989 many housing complexes made reference to "Soviet-Polish friendship" by naming streets in this way. This highlights the way that the state in Soviet bloc countries constructed official histories of events and public markers of them that often bore little resemblance to the lived experience of those who had participated in them, creating an enormous disjuncture between public and personal remembrance.

Though the preceding quotation does not do justice to her wit, Krystyna's observation that she chooses to talk of her imprisonment with humor highlights the significant role of identity in memory. Sometimes we choose to narrate our past experiences in very different ways than we initially felt about them. In our conversations Krystyna chose to highlight the humor in her situation and her own nonchalance in the face of danger. She considered this a matter of personal style, one that reflected her approach to life in general.

Krystyna's comment about her changing understanding of the liberation is pertinent in yet another way. It shows how difficult, if not impossible, it can prove to untangle lived experience from the interference of texts and other experiences. Clearly Krystyna's understandings of things she experienced personally, in this case the liberation, have changed over time, but it is impossible to point to the individual causes of her shift in understanding. What can be said is that subsequent events have colored her memory of the past. During the course of my research, I did have an opportunity to observe how media representations can influence personal memory. One of the most beloved and well-known residents of Żoliborz was the Polish politician Jacek Kuroń, who died in 2004. When I returned to the neighborhood a few weeks after his death, everyone I asked about him suddenly referred to him as "Jacek," rather than "Kuroń" as they had done in the past, suggesting a more personal connection than all but a few of my informants had actually had. Moreover, in talking about his contributions to Polish society, many of them offered the same examples, using almost identical phrases to describe his work. This would have struck me as odd had I not watched a documentary that had aired about him just after his death and that had described him in the same langauge almost verbatim. In this case, I believe my informants were, perhaps subconsciously, supplementing their own memories of Kuroń with those from the media in an effort to be a part of history and to draw themselves closer to a beloved public figure, one who, many felt, represented their own values. Anthropologist Andrew Lass (1994) has shown that individuals draw on whatever resources are available, not only in retrospect but also as events unfold, incorporating images, phrases, interpretations, and analyses into personal narratives. They do so in order to better understand personal experience in a wider context, to locate themselves vis-à-vis others, and ultimately to draw meaning from their lives. The way that my informants incorporated media-generated reflections about Kuroń into their own recollections of him illustrates the potential for mass media to have a homogenizing effect on individual memory.

Similarly, the past has resonance in the present shaping of our understandings and attitudes toward contemporary events. While conducting my fieldwork I rented a room in Pani Sławka's apartment, and she became one of my key informants. As is typical in Poland, the gas stove in the kitchen we shared had to be lit manually. At one point two out of every three matches in the box we kept on hand for this purpose failed to ignite. It was annoying. One day, watching me go through five defective matches in rapid secession, Sławka exclaimed in exasperation, "It's the PRL all over again!" During the Polish People's Republic (PRL) matches, it seems, were notoriously bad, something Sławka had experienced firsthand. The matches were so bad that they became a symbol for the inability of the system to meet people's daily needs. Tadeusz Konwicki enshrined such matches as an emblem of the failure of socialism in his novel *A Minor Apocalypse*, in which the hero is repeatedly thwarted in his quest to burn himself alive in protest of martial law by a lack of everyday necessities, among them matches. Were the matches resonant because of Konwicki's novel? Or did Konwicki use them because the experience would be recognizable to all? In this case it is hard to know if it is Sławka who draws on popular culture to lend power to her complaint, or if it was Konwicki who appeals to personal experience to create resonance in his novel. In any case, Sławka is clearly equating the early years of the post-socialist era to the PRL, on the basis that neither could produce a decent box of matches, suggesting that little had really changed. These examples illustrate that the division between personal or autobiographical memory and collective or cultural memory is highly permeable. Such memories also demonstrate that how we remember and narrate events to others matters—not as a matter of truth, but because how we remember and talk about the past colors our perceptions of events and shapes our understanding of the world and our expectations about how the world works.

Contested Memory

In much of Holocaust literature non-Jewish Poles are divided into three categories: rescuers, who comprise about 2 percent of the population (Prekerowa 1987); those who blackmailed Jews and who, for obvious reasons, were difficult to identify and quantify after the war—even though blackmailing Jews in Poland has been described as a profession by Holocaust scholar Israel Gutman (2003: 217); and the rest of the population, which is to say the majority of Poles who are summed up as "bystanders." The term "bystander" carries with it connotations of inactivity and indifference, in contrast to "witness," which, while it may not connote intervention on behalf of others, suggests seeing and being moved to tell others what one has seen. As Antony Polonsky has noted much of the literature on Polish "bystanders" is less concerned with what they did vis-à-vis Jews than with their lack of action and with speculation about how history might have been different had ethnic Poles taken a more active role in aiding Polish Jews (Polonsky, cited in Zimmerman 2003). Largely absent from the literature are sustained and objective inquiries into what the lives of "bystanders" were like.[6] It may be worth mentioning that few Poles perceive themselves as bystanders, not necessarily because they claim to have helped Jews or because they see themselves as witnesses to the horrific treatment of Polish Jews by the Nazis (and in some cases by their fellow Poles)—though many do see themselves in this way. They do not see themselves as bystanders because the German occupation impinged on their lives, brutally altering the composition and course of their nation, their communities, their families, and their own lives. In short, Poles view themselves as co-victims of Nazi violence.

And herein lies the problem because, while both ethnic and Jewish Poles suffered, Nazi policy targeted Jewish Poles for genocide and ethnic Poles for enslavement; thus, as communities their experiences of the war were qualitatively and quantitatively different. For example, both ethnic Poles and Polish Jews were given rations of food that were far below their nutritional needs, but Poles were allotted 669 calories while Jews were allotted 184. While some ethnic Poles lost their homes to German troops, only Jews (and Poland's Roma minority) were forced to move into ghettos and walled off from the rest of the population. Though the first Polish citizens sent to Nazi concentration camps were professors from Krakow's Jagiellonian University, the number of Jewish inmates later surpassed those of ethnic Poles. Furthermore while Poles were sent to German concentration camps during the war, they were deported to labor camps like Auschwitz or Majdanek, not death camps like Treblinka or Chełmno, at which inhabitants were killed within 24 hours. Moreover, because camps with a residential population like Auschwitz or Majdanek identified prisoners according to their ethnicity and nationality (e.g., Pole, Jew) or "crime" (e.g., political prisoner, homosexual), prisoners within the camp were treated differently, and Jewish concentration camp prisoners had a lower rate of survival than non-Jewish prisoners. Finally, while virtually all Poles that I know lost a family member to violence during the war, it is unusual to meet an ethnic Pole who lost his or her entire family. The same cannot be said of Polish Jewish Holocaust survivors. Many Poles have been blinded to the suffering of their Jewish compatriots by their own losses. In my view this blindness is rooted in experiences of loss, for on an individual level suffering is the same and what one feels first and foremost is the injustice, pain, and grief of one's own loss.

The conviction of many Poles that all Polish citizens suffered equally at the hands of the Nazis was quite naturally rejected by Jewish Poles, who themselves felt betrayed by their non-Jewish compatriots—if not literally denounced, then certainly disappointed in their expectations for assistance. Postwar pogroms, in which mobs attacked Jewish citizens in Krakow in 1945 and in Kielce in 1946, deepened this sense of betrayal, mistrust, and fear, leading many Jewish Poles to emigrate.[7] Similarly, the Polish government's efforts to purge the Polish Communist Party of Jewish leaders and Polish society more broadly of Jewish professionals in 1968–1969 led to the expulsion of the majority of Poland's Jewish population (Gross 2006; Michlic 2006). Doubtless these incidents influenced the image of Poles as co-perpetrators in Holocaust historiography, which at least until the late 1980s posited a positive correlation between the behavior and attitude of "bystanders" and the success of Nazi genocidal actions in Poland (Zimmerman 2003). These claims were reinforced by two more recent incidents, which reveal in different ways a great deal about the collective memory of the war in Poland. The first of these events was the controversy over the crosses at Auschwitz that began in 1984 with the erection of a papal cross by Carmelite nuns at a small convent in Oświęcim, which overlooks the concentration camp. This controversy erupted anew in 1996, when Eli Wiesel called for the removal of the crosses, and again in 1998, when what anthropologist Genevieve Zubrzycki (2006) has dubbed "the war of the crosses" began in earnest. The second incident is the subject of Jan Tomasz Gross's *Neighbors: The Destruction of the Jewish Community of Jedwabne, Poland* (2001), which describes the brutal murder of the Jews of Jedwabne, not by Nazi troops but by ethnic Polish members of their own community. The publication of *Neighbors* launched a prolonged, complex, public debate within Poland about Poles' treatment of their Jewish compatriots during and after the war (Polonsky and Michlic 2004). While the present book is not about how and why ethnic Poles and Jewish Poles remember and perceive the past differently, the reader needs to understand the broader historical context of twentieth-century Polish-Jewish relations in which the events that are the subject of this book took place, are recollected, and are narrated to others. Many of my informants believe that reports of events like postwar pogroms, the massacre of Jews by Poles in Jedwabne, and the debate over the crosses at Auschwitz have blackened the reputations of all Poles. They are aware that many outside Poland perceive Poles in general as anti-Semitic, a stereotype that many of them find not only undeserved but also painful because of the way it clashes with their own memories of the past.

Organization

In each of the following chapters, I put informants' narrated memory (remembering) to use in a number of ways to achieve three different levels of understanding. In some cases I use their narratives to understand something particular to the time and place of what was remembered, such as how the experience of the German invasion and occupation of Warsaw impinged upon the lives of my informants or what the experience of urban warfare was like for combatants, health-care workers, and civilians during the Warsaw Uprising. These narratives resonate as oral histories, offering us a greater understanding of a particular historical moment. Some narratives are useful beyond the history of Poland during World War II. These I analyze in an effort to enhance our understanding of war more generally, by drawing connections with studies of conflict in other places and times and drawing out larger patterns of the costs of war and how survivors recover from its destruction and live with its legacy. Finally, I put the narratives to use to understand something about memory and identity. I explore what happens when one's personal memories run counter to public and official representations of the past and how personal memories may be colored by subsequent events. The analyses I offer of these narratives illuminate the experience of recollecting traumatic experiences, as well as remembering youth from the vantage point of old age.

I begin by providing a history of Żoliborz, examining informants' narratives of childhood before the outbreak of World War II. In doing so I consider what it meant to be Polish in interwar Warsaw and how informants' notions of Polishness were shaped by socioeconomic class, ethnicity, and political identification. I then focus in chapter 2 on how older Warsovians narrate the disjuncture of war and the disintegration of the familiar. I draw on informants' life histories to identify patterns in how experiences, expectations about the war, as well as the narrative frames drawn on to describe them vary according to the age of the narrator. In contrast to their accounts of events that took place in 1944–1945, these narratives vary drastically according to the age of the speaker. The memory of trauma is an indelible feature in the narratives of those who were children in 1939. In contrast, those who experienced the war as teenagers remember and retell the same events in a way that embodies the enormous capacity for resilience and idealism that we associate with adolescence. Drawing on narratives from informants of a range of ages, I demonstrate that, rather than disappearing with the passage of time, these seemingly age-based variances in perspective have persisted in the ways that my informants recollect and narrate the invasion of Poland and the early weeks of the war. Interestingly, these age-based differences seem to diminish in narratives about the occupation itself.

The German occupation of Warsaw lasted from October 6, 1939, when the city surrendered, to August 1, 1944, when the General Uprising began. I begin my exploration of this time period in chapter 3 with a brief overview of Nazi policy toward various segments of the Polish population, giving special attention to the stance toward children and the intelligentsia, the class to which the majority of my informants and their families belonged. I also discuss Nazi policy vis-à-vis Polish Jews in an effort to illustrate how differential treatment divided Polish society, heightening preexisting divisions between the two groups. However, the primary focus of this chapter is on how the violence of the occupation impinged on people's everyday lives spatially, physically, mentally, and spiritually, as well as on their recollected responses to this disintegration of the familiar.

Poles have a rich history of resisting occupying powers, and like many Polish young people, my informants were determined to carry on this tradition. In the usage of my informants, "resistance" is a broad concept, encompassing a wide array of disparate activities. Drawing on a variety of theories of resistance, in chapter 4 I analyze their understandings of which activities did and did not constitute participation in the vast network of underground opposition organizations known as the "conspiracy." By exploring these activities I strive to arrive at an insider's understanding of resistance. I argue that, by seeking to develop intellectually and culturally, by serving others, and by remaining decent human beings, these young people ultimately sought to embody the values denied them by the Nazi occupation and to weave a web of solidarity that would allow them to preserve Polish culture. Though important aspects of resisting, these acts were only preludes to the enactment of the heroic ideals on which my informants had been raised. Above all else, these ideals celebrated sacrifice for the nation, for the continued existence of the Polish state and Polish culture. As is apparent in the narratives I present, the sacrifice sought was not time or energy, but life itself. However, though very broad in their use of the term, my informants' concept of resistance is one that fails to include the one activity that many Americans associate with World War II resistance: helping Jews. I address this disconnect in chapter 5 and explore why some other sorts of social activism and even self-help are considered resistance by my informants, while helping their Jewish compatriots was not. In doing so, I draw on informants' reflections and recollections of extending help to Polish Jews. I concentrate informants' beliefs about the extent to which ethnic Poles helped their Jewish neighbors and compare their notions with statistical data about help compiled by other social scientists. I then use informants' secondary accounts of help, stories in which other people—named and anonymous— are reported to have helped Jews, as well as personal accounts of help, to probe the disconnect between my informants' conviction that Poles helped Jews a great deal and the statistical evidence to the contrary. In doing so, I discuss the ways in which narrative frames operate to limit understandings of Polish Jews' experiences by obscuring the very real obstacles they faced in passing as ethnic Poles and thus reinforcing stereotypes about Jewish passivity. Too often we only find accounts of successful attempts to help or of help on a large scale, which creates the impression that people were either totally indifferent to human suffering or heroic rescuers. This leaves unexamined the spectrum of acts and attitudes in between. To fill this void I offer accounts of opportunistic, short-term, and long-term help in an effort to explore both internal and external constraints on action. These narratives reveal the qualitative and quantitative differences in suffering that rendered Polish Jews dependent on their fellow citizens for survival. These narratives also capture the range of difficulties that helping entailed and the fears and concerns that prevented many from ever trying.

Chapter 6 consists of narratives, both official and first person, of the citywide General Uprising of 1944, which I use to examine how Warsovians who witnessed and participated in the event understand it some 60 years later. Through informants' narratives I explore the Uprising of 1944 from a variety of individual perspectives as the lived and remembered experience of urban warfare. Rather than focusing on ideology or the military maneuvers of the uprising, I explore my informants' narratives about enacting their heroic ideals in a city populated by nearly a million people. I also examine the narratives of those who suffered the consequences, not as insurgents, but as residents of a war zone. In doing so, I focus on narratives from people who experienced the uprising from three different perspectives: as soldiers fighting in the streets, as health-care workers transporting and caring for the sick and the wounded in battle and in makeshift hospitals, and as civilians seeking shelter in basements. Finally, I look at narratives about escaping through the labyrinth of sewers beneath the city, an experience that is represented as the quintessential experience of the uprising as a whole, becoming the root metaphor of the so-called lost generation (Ortner 1973). In exploring these four perspectives on the uprising, I focus on my mentors' careful attention to place, arguing that Warsaw itself emerges in these narratives as a co-victim, the devastation of her buildings painstakingly recounted to others and, for them at least, imprinted on the contemporary cityscape as ever-present reminders of the past.

In chapter 7 I explore narratives of three key events in the lives of my informants and the history of the city: the Home Army's capitulation to the Nazis on October 2, 1944, which ended the uprising; the expulsion of those remaining in Warsaw and their deportation to various detention camps, which immediately followed; and their return to Warsaw following its systematic destruction by the Nazis and its liberation by Soviet troops on

January 17, 1945. Once the fighting stopped and survival was no longer a primary concern, how did people cope with the destruction of the familiar? How did they manage to rebuild normalcy, by which I mean daily life, when the city lay quite literally in ruins? I argue that returning to normalcy entailed reengaging the prewar past, remembering the city, life, and oneself as they had been, and imagining what they could be again.

Finally, in the conclusion I examine the competing visions of the past that have arisen in the communist and postcommunist eras. I explore my informants' concerns about various types of erasure of memory and their attempts to transmit their vision of the past to younger generations through a variety of memory practices. In doing so, I examine my informants' ideas about the place of wartime memories in their lives and the narrative frames they draw on to share their past with others. I argue that they compose their memories in such a way as to make sense of the past, constructing life narratives that are serviceable in bringing meaning to war and its losses but that are also helpful in navigating the present. In this effort the experiences, recollections, and ideas of these elderly Warsovians about remembering constitute more than a case study; they can also serve to illuminate how individuals relate to the past and put it to use in the present.

1   Identity Politics in Interwar Poland

THE OLDER WARSOVIANS WITH WHOM I conducted my research are members of the first generation of Poles in over a century to be born in an independent Poland. They grew up in a country struggling to define itself in order to maintain its newly regained autonomy. In contrast, their parents and grandparents grew up as members of a once powerful country that had lost its independence to its neighbors following the partitions of 1773, 1793, and 1795. As a result their parents had grown up with an awareness of being Poles and even of living on Polish soil, yet until 1918 they had lived under Russian, Prussian, or Austro-Hungarian rule. In 1918 Poland regained independence, and Poles who had lived in three different countries were once again reunited as one country. What did it mean to be Polish in this newly independent nation?

Ideas about which characteristics and beliefs were essential parts of Polishness shaped the attitudes of the individuals I interviewed, as well as the choices they made during the war. With this in mind, I examine how the Polish intelligentsia of the early twentieth century defined Polishness for themselves, the nation, and the world on the eve of the German invasion of Poland in 1939. In doing so, I investigate how their ideas about Polishness were inflected by class distinctions and ethnic and religious differences, as well as by political affiliation. While their sense of Polishness was influenced by all these factors, for most of them Polishness was defined by service to their country and support for a free and independent Poland. This was a cause tied to a long history of resistance to foreign oppression that I will also explore in the pages that follow.

The influence of socioeconomic class, ethnicity, and political affiliation on the identities of Żoliborz residents is not only evident in my interviews, as I will discuss momentarily, but is also visible in my informants' homes. In many of the residences I visited for my research, there is a corner or a wall in the living room decorated with old family photographs or a painted portrait and other memorabilia of bygone days. In one apartment, for example, two nineteenth-century swords framed a plaque of Marszał Józef Piłsudski, the charismatic military leader and cofounder of the Polish Socialist Party (PPS), who seized power in 1926 by military coup and who remains a national hero in the eyes of many Poles. While this sort of overt political statement was a bit extreme, many of my informants' living rooms featured subtler references to Piłsudski. For example, Olgierd Z——'s living room featured a display of family photos, including one of his father dressed in military uniform on horseback with Piłsudski's Legions. This and other family photographs were clustered around an icon of the Black Madonna of Częstohowa. In Pani Sławka's living room a long silken sash (*pas szlachecki*) printed in blue, gray, and silver hung next to the door. On the adjoining wall she displayed a collection of black-and-white photographs that included a photo of her father in Polish military uniform and others of family gatherings that had taken place before the Second World War. Two of the most interesting in the group are photographs of portraits of her mother and father that were painted by the Polish artist Stanisław Witkiewicz, also known as Witkacy. The only contemporary photo in this arrangement is one of Sławka and Basia standing in front of a manor house that had once belonged to their family. The photo was taken in 1997 on what they referred to as a "sentimental journey" to what was once their family's country home.

At first I thought of these displays simply as shrines to loved ones no longer living and to places lost to nationalization. As I got to know my informants better and came to understand more about the content of the decor and what it represented to them, I realized that the messages that informants sent through their choice of wall-hangings was much more complex. The Black Madonna of Częstohowa, for example, is the symbol of Polish Catholicism par excellence. Mary as represented in the Black Madonna icon is referred to as the Queen of Poland; hence the icon is both a representation of the mother of Jesus and a symbol of the nation. According to legend the icon saved Poland from invading Swedes in the seventeenth century. Thus, through its display, Olgierd is asserting both religious and patriotic values. Similarly Sławka's decor is a statement about herself that delineates a genealogy both personal and cultural, one that links her literally and symbolically to definitions of Polishness that are inflected by class, ethnicity, and political affiliation. I learned from Sławka that the sash is a replica of those worn by the Polish gentry (*szlachta*), who gave and accepted them in trade for entire villages. Thus, the sash is a symbol of her family's membership in the landed gentry, a group with long-standing ties to the struggle for Polish independence. The picture of Sławka and Basia at the manor furthers this association, with its allusions to life in the country, where her grandparents owned an estate where peasants worked the fields. The photograph of Sławka's father in the uniform of Piłsudski's Legions serves as a reference to her father's military service and to her own reverence for Marshal Piłsudski. Thus, the photo of her father is a testament to the family's longtime commitment to the struggle for an independent Poland and the ideals of the Polish Socialist Party. As a whole Sławka's decor signals an identity rooted in Polish tradition and the struggle for Polish independence, but one that is progressive in both taste and political affiliation. By invoking the symbols of the szlachta, the movement for an independent Poland, and the Polish Socialist Party, Pani Sławka presents her family, and by extension herself, as members of a political and social elite. For those who can read the symbols, the photographs and decorations in this room make a claim that she and her family are rooted in a specific tradition, one that is viewed by many as being quintessentially Polish.

The Szlachta

Prior to the nineteenth century to be Polish was to be a member of the gentry, or szlachta. In the golden era of the Polish-Lithuanian commonwealth, before Poland was partitioned, the Polish Diet was comprised solely of members of the szlachta, placing a monopoly of political power in their hands (Wandycz 1974: 4). In Poland 8 to 10 percent of the population were members of the gentry, a very large percentage in comparison with other European countries. This was a socioeconomically diverse group, ranging from the king, who was elected by parliament, to wealthy land magnates and petty noblemen with no land at all, but all of them had equal status and equal rights to participate in political life under the law (Steinlauf 1997: 12–13; Wandycz 1974: 5).

For a variety of reasons, the members of the szlachta often perceived other segments of society as less Polish. Part of this may be due to the fact that, although many nineteenth-century artists, writers, and politicians saw peasants as the exemplars of pure Polish culture and language untouched by outside influences (a view characteristic of most East and Central European countries at the time),[1] Polish peasants more often viewed themselves as belonging to the villages in which they lived, rather than to the nation (Jedlicki 1995). As a result their interests were often focused on local politics, which sometimes made them allies of the foreign rulers of Poland.

For example, in Russian-ruled Poland under the partitions, this was often evidenced by the peasants' willingness to report their szlachta landlords' anti-tsarist activities to the Russian authorities (Steinlauf 1997: 12–13). In 1846 in Austrian-ruled Galicia, Polish peasants joined with Austrian troops to put down an insurrection led by the Polish gentry, resulting in the deaths of an estimated two thousand landowners, their families, and estate officials (Wandycz 1974: 134–35). Perhaps it was in response to incidents such as these that in the late nineteenth century groups like the United Circle of Women Landowners (Zjednoczone Koło Ziemianek) established literacy programs, worked to improve health and living conditions in rural areas, and began taking steps to preserve (or cultivate) the Polish identity of peasant women (Ponichtera 1997: 18; for more details, see Rzepniewska 1995).

The peasants were not the only social group whom the gentry perceived as less than Polish. Many members of the szlachta saw industrialism in general, and capitalism in particular, as inherently un-Polish (Steinlauf 1997: 10–11). This was doubtless due at least in part to the threat that industrialism posed to the szlachta's traditional way of life, which was based on a semifeudal relationship between szlachta landlords and the peasants who served their country estates. Industrial growth at the close of the nineteenth century was shifting Polish society away from its agrarian base. This transformation had implications not only for the economy but for social relationships as well. Those members of the szlachta who were wealthy enough to enter into industrial enterprises were often seen as compromising the core values of Polishness. Many factories, however, were not solely owned by urbanized szlachta, many of whom were land rich but capital poor; many Polish textile and food ventures, for example, were financed by Polish Jews (ibid.). This marked a shift in another set of relationships: as members of the szlachta found themselves dependent on Polish Jewish investors for the financial backing of their businesses, once benign ethnic stereotypes were rendered potent as power became increasingly associated with wealth rather than social status (ibid. 14).

"A Very Tolerant People"

As early as 1386, when Poland and Lithuania formed the Polish Lithuanian commonwealth, Poland was characterized by a multiethnic population whose citizens professed belief in a variety of faiths and spoke several different languages. In addition to Roman Catholics, who were in the majority in Poland, the commonwealth was home to communities of Eastern Orthodox Christians, Jews, German-speaking Lutherans,

Polish Calvinists, Arians, Anabaptists, Armenians, Greeks, and Scots, as well as Tatar and Turkish Muslims. Tolerance toward these groups was guaranteed in the Confederation of Warsaw in 1573. The diversity and tolerance attributed to the commonwealth is remembered and often cited by contemporary Poles as counterevidence to claims of anti-Semitism. As historian Michael Steinlauf (1997: 2) suggests, it is a "key ingredient of modern Polish self-perception: the conviction that Poles are at heart a very tolerant people."

By the late nineteenth century many of Poland's minority groups had been absorbed into the dominant population through assimilation and intermarriage; however, Warsaw was still a diverse city with large Jewish, German, and Russian minorities (Wandycz 1974: 207). The treatment of Jews in Poland under the partitions differed from sector to sector but was particularly bleak in those areas ruled by tsarist Russia. In Russian-ruled Poland, Jews faced increasing restrictions from the government and were expelled from villages and cities (Steinlauf 1997: 8). In the late nineteenth century they became the victims of pogroms launched by groups with tsarist ties (ibid.).

In the interwar-era Republic of Poland, one half of the Jewish population of Poland resided in cities with over two hundred thousand inhabitants. Though Jews made up 10 percent of the overall population of Poland, the Jewish populations of large cities were often as much as 30 percent. Though the vast majority of Poland's Jewish citizens were workers or artisans, by 1921 60 percent of Polish business people were Jewish; by 1931 so were more than 50 percent of doctors and one-third of lawyers (ibid. 16–17). The textile and food industries were predominantly owned by Jewish Poles (ibid.).

Both socioeconomic class and ethnicity shaped ideas about what it meant to be Polish on both an individual and national level. This becomes clear when we examine the stance of the two main political parties of the interwar era on the question of citizenship. In order to do so, however, we first need to consider Polish history.

Resistance and Romanticism

Just as the images of the manor house and the silk sash are symbols of the landed gentry, the images of Sławka's and Olgierd's fathers wearing the uniform of the Polish Legions indicates active support for the cause of Polish independence. Both Sławka's and Olgierd's parents grew up in Warsaw, which was ruled by the Russian tsar. While Polish culture flourished in those parts of Poland ruled by the Austro-Hungarian Empire, attempts at suppressing Polish language and culture were the norm in those areas ruled by Russia and Prussia. Many Poles, both members of the gentry and the peasantry, found Russian rule intolerable and launched a series of armed uprisings aimed at freeing Poland from tsarist rule. The first of these was the November Uprising of 1830, which ended with the capture of Warsaw in September 1831. At that time Tsar Nicholas I suspended the constitution of the Congress Kingdom (in other words Russian-ruled Poland), confiscated the property of all officers who had served in the national government, drafted all remaining Polish soldiers into the Russian army for service in the Caucasus, and appointed the general who had led the fight against the insurrectionists as the military governor and "Prince of Warsaw" (Davies 1984: 166–67).[2] Russian field tribunals condemned an estimated 80,000 Poles, reputed rebels and their families, to walk to penal servitude in Siberia (ibid.). Though its consequences were disastrous, the November Uprising was followed by a series of armed insurrections staged in succession in 1846, 1848, and 1863. Each of these failed attempts to regain independence was answered by the tsar with increasingly severe repression for both the Polish fighters and the civilian population.

Nonetheless, the November Uprising and those that followed sparked the imagination of a generation of Polish writers. Adam Mickiewicz, Juliusz Słowacki, Zygmunt Krasiński, and Cyprian Norwid in poetry and prose transformed these military defeats into heroic battles for freedom. Words like "suffering," "blood," "sacrifice," and "resurrection" abound in these works, as do phrases describing Poland as the "Christ of Nations," crucified by the partitioning powers.[3] In Mickiewicz's later work Poles are portrayed as a "chosen people" who, despite entering the tomb of foreign domination, could look forward to the resurrection of their state (Sokolewicz 1991: 128–29). Through the mythologization of Polish history in poetry and drama, Polish romanticists imbued the nation's humiliation and suffering with meaning, all the while assuring readers that their own personal sacrifices for the cause of independence would not be in vain (ibid.). Glorified and popularized by the romanticists, the uprisings were mythologized, ensuring that the defeat of one uprising would only be revisited by a younger generation that, raised on romanticism, was ready to take up arms for the cause of Polish independence. In this way, though militarily, politically, and from every tangible measure unsuccessful, these insurrections mobilized many Poles to take up and continue the struggle for independence.

Barbara Tornquist Plewa (1992: 117), in her study of Polish social consciousness during the Solidarity era, dubs this phenomenon the "insurrection myth," which she defines as "the conviction, entrenched in Polish collective consciousness, that it is the fate and duty of each Polish generation since the fall of the state in 1795 to continually take up struggle (most often armed struggle) for the freedom of the fatherland." This sensibility is evident in letters and memoirs from the early nineteenth and twentieth centuries. Wanda Gertzówna, a woman who fought in the Polish units attached to the Austro-Hungarian army during World War I, recalled, "From my earliest years, my dream was to become a soldier in the Polish army. My father, an insurgent in 1863, lived with the hope of seeing an independent Poland. Insurgents often gathered at our home as well, spinning yarns about a free Poland. And I dreamed, brought up on stories of heroism" (as quoted in Piłsudska, ed. 1929: 49 in Ponichtera 1997: 1).[4] Defiance of Russian cultural domination and resistance to tsarist oppression not only motivated the fight to regain freedom but rendered it a moral imperative (Plewa 1992: 118); through their "moral grandeur and power of the spirit" the insurrectionists sought to crush the material strength of Poland's foes (Janion 1984: 119). The moral worth of these battles was not decided by victory alone. Rather, defeat was perceived as equally honorable and understood as an opportunity for the Polish insurrectionists to purify and perfect the world through the example of their fighting, suffering, and sacrifice (Plewa 1992: 124). In this way, no defeat was ever conceded as total and no battle considered futile; the mere fact that individuals gave their lives for the freedom of the collective was memorialized. This insured that the uprisings were remembered and inspired action on the part of subsequent generations (ibid. 118). Celebrated, sanctified, and mythologized by Polish romanticists, these insurrections became a part of Polish social consciousness, reminding the Polish people of what they had lost. In doing so, the uprisings and their retelling in poetry, novels, and plays kept the concept of a Polish nation alive in both memory and spirit.

After sixteen months of guerrilla warfare the January Uprising failed in 1864, resulting in the dissolution of the Congress Kingdom of Poland and its absorption into Russia proper (Davies 1984: 168).[5] In particular, residents of Warsaw were punished by the destruction of Żoliborz, one of the capital's most beautiful neighborhoods. Russian troops burned homes and palaces, and the governor levied a heavy tax on the residents of the city in order to fund the building of the Citadel, a fortress for Russian troops and a prison for Polish insurrectionists. Romuald Traugutt, the last surviving leader of the 1863 Uprising, was hung on the ramparts of the Citadel in 1864. This bitter reminder soured many Poles on revolt, and the insurrections as well as their szlachta leaders were the target of much criticism in the years following the failure of the January Uprising. The "Positivist" movement that followed attempted to refocus attention from dying magnificently to living rationally and praised the "heroism of a reasonable life." However, by the turn of the nineteenth century, the losses suffered as a result of the failed uprising had faded in the light of new repression that took the form of a Russification campaign (*Historia Polski* 1958: 3, pt.1, 437, quoted in Wandycz 1974: 207).[6] Just as a new generation of revolutionaries led by Piłsudski looked to the nineteenth-century uprisings for inspiration, so too did a new generation of authors and playwrights, such as Stanisław Wyspianski and Stefan Żeromski, draw from the themes of the romantics. The effect was to rekindle the desire not only to regain their nation's standing as an independent state but also to distinguish themselves in this struggle as heroes from a new generation of Polish young people. It was in this milieu that my informants' parents came of age.

Educated in the Romance of Heroism

Early twentieth-century Warsaw provided ample opportunity for young people to put their patriotic education into action in the numerous protests that took place against tsarist rule. School-aged children launched some of these protests. In the Russian zone, where most of my informants' parents lived, Polish children attended Russian-language schools at which the curricula were completely Russified (Wandycz 1974: 196).[7] This was also the case at the previously Polish university in Warsaw. As young people, many of my informants' parents protested the ban on their native language at school. On January 28, 1905, Polish students at six high schools began a boycott of their classes, vowing not to return until Polish was reinstated as the language of instruction (Ponichtera 1997: 20). The children were supported in large part by their mothers, who organized clandestine classes to educate children about Polish culture and history and to ensure that they did not fall behind in their education (ibid.). More than one informant told me with pride that their parents had participated in these school strikes. Indeed, with the help of their parents, my informants resisted Nazi attempts to suppress Polish education in a similar way.

The school strikes were, of course, just one part of a range of protests in Russian-ruled Poland, many of which were organized by the Polish Socialist Party (PPS). In some areas the demonstrations moved beyond marches and singing patriotic songs to bombing bridges, railways, and monuments to tsarist rule (ibid.). Similar incidents in Warsaw and across Congress Poland drove senior members of the Polish Socialist Party to develop the Combat

Organization in Kraków. In the summer of 1905, over one hundred men participated in courses on military drill, the use of firearms, divertive action, and orienteering that lasted from four to six weeks. Technically such organizations were legal under Austrian law, which permitted rifle clubs; however, in practical fact the rifle squads were an underground Polish army whose loyalties were divided between the Polish Socialist Party and the Nationalist Independent Camp (Garlicki 1995: 63). Funded by a series of bank robberies organized by Józef Piłsudski, the goal of the PPS in creating the Combat Organization was to prepare an armed force in the case of a European war or a Russian-led revolution that would loosen tsarist Russia's grip on Poland. By 1910, with Europe on the brink of war and Poland's partitioning powers in conflict with one another as a result of divided interests in the Balkans, the Combat Organization had evolved into the Union for Active Struggle, which had formed paramilitary organizations in Austro-Hungarian–ruled Galicia (ibid. 60). Membership in paramilitary units was not limited to men. Hanna proudly showed me portraits of both her parents wearing medals they had earned during the struggle to gain independence:

> My mother fought. You know we are an old PPS family . . . and my mother had to leave Warsaw when she was a young girl, because she took part in the conspiracy. There was a search and there was a weapon at my mother's home, so this Russian officer showed it to her and said, "Listen, you are so pretty, so—why? Do you know that you could be sent to Siberia?" My mother didn't say a thing; she just took her belongings and crossed from Congress Poland to Kraków through the woods. My father went to war in '14 with the legions. [Pointing to a portrait on the wall.] That, you see, is my mother, she has a medal of independence as well as the legionnaire's cross.

Between 1910 and 1912 three different combat organizations were opened for women with units in Lwów and Kraków (Ponichtera 1997: 22–23). Most of the women who volunteered for these units were university students trained in diversionary tactics, first aid, intelligence gathering, and as couriers (ibid.).[8] In October of 1912, when war broke out in the Balkans, Piłsudski was appointed commander of the riflemen and other paramilitary squads that later became known popularly as Piłsudski's Legions. In August 1914 Piłsudski's troops entered the kingdom of Poland in the hopes of rallying the populace to organize a joint struggle against Russia, only to find that, for the vast majority of Poles, independence was a nonissue (Chojnowski 1995: 30). Though disillusioned with their fellow countrymen, this event only served to affirm the troops' belief in the moral superiority and progressive nature of their own milieu, reaffirming their sense of Polishness (ibid. 31).

Political Affiliation

Photos of informants' parents in the uniform of the Polish Legions or portraits in which they wear medals honoring their service to Polish independence express the ideological commitments of their displayers, asserting a genealogical connection to a cultural elite that has been unflagging in its support of Polish independence. Its contemporary heirs are an elite, however, that for most of their lives has lacked economic and political power. This lineage does not stop with the attainment of a Polish state in 1918. Józef Piłsudski was also the leader of the PPS, a dominant force in interwar Poland. Any photo that references him by extension suggests that the displayer views the PPS favorably.[9]

The elderly Warsovians whom I interviewed took great pride in their parents' socialist views and activism in the interwar era, citing these as proof of Żoliborz's progressive character. Informants' recollections of school were some of the most telling in regards to the social diversity and political divisions of the neighborhood. Sławka remembers her school this way: "I went to a very good school just like my sister Basia, only she was in a higher [grade] and I in a lower. Szacht Majorowej, it was a private school, and we were very proud to go there, because Marszał Piłsudski's two daughters went there too." Clearly, Sławka and Basia attended an elite school and one whose student body was largely comprised of the children of Polish military officers. As the passage from my interview with Irmina demonstrates, this was far from being the only choice:

> When I had to go to school I could choose from the closest school, which was just a few steps away, and [another] which was situated at a little further distance and so there was a discussion in our family. This neighborhood where we were living [and where she still resides in the same building] was the so-called Officer's Żoliborz. Here there lived many military families with various ranks and their children. I did go to this preschool here, but my father, who was a true democrat, believed that it was up to him to send his child to the kind of school where there were students from all social groups. As a result I went to a school a little bit further away from home, and that school had, really, a very socially diverse element. The majority were new residents of Żoliborz, well Żoliborz was altogether a new neighborhood . . .

and the school had a certain social activism on behalf of the whole region, because in Żoliborz there was still this area where poor people lived, and that school really took on a caring function in relation to the pupils, especially to those impoverished ones. They all received breakfast and were surrounded by care, they and their parents, their brothers and sisters who were really small children. My mother and other ladies came to school to give breakfast to the poor children. The enthusiasm for that school was enormous, among the city's intelligentsia as well. The neighboring school was very exclusive, the children who went there were mostly the military children. A little further was a school that had a completely different orientation, a left-wing orientation, that was the Worker's School of the Society of the Friends' of Children on Plac Wilsona where the movie theater is now. Further on, there was a school run by nuns where there was—well, there was a very different environment. The neighborhood was very diverse but there was not a single—it was just that parents simply had various political views, and schools were directed along the lines of certain political or social concerns.

The core of the PPS believed that social change was only possible once independence was achieved and that, once free of tsarist oppression, an independent Polish state would be better able to remedy the ills of poverty and inequality. Those members of the party who sought to put socialism first were viewed as lacking in patriotism and marginalized. For members of the Polish Socialist Party, Polishness was about being a member of a community that shared historical and cultural values, above all the ideal of achieving an independent Poland (Steinlauf 1997: 13). PPS supporters maintained that those who carried the positive traits of Polish national character were not members of a single social class but rather a group whose ethos had been shaped by the struggle for independence (Chojnowski 1995: 36; Jedlicki 1995: 12, 13, 19). Such individuals could be found among landowners, members of the bourgeoisie, the proletariat, and the peasantry (Chojnowski 1995: 36). For members of the PPS, the outward expression of Polishness was participation in the struggle for independence. Once this goal was achieved, they turned their attentions to the development of a pluralistic society, the alleviation of poverty, and the furthering of social justice. For members of the PPS, social service and unflagging conviction to the ideal of Polish autonomy became the highest expression of the virtues of Polishness.

The Polish Socialist Party's definition of Polishness included Poland's minorities, provided they supported independence and thought of themselves as citizens of Poland. This inclusive view of Polish citizenship was not embraced by all of Poland's interwar political parties. In fact, the PPS's main rival for power, the National Democratic Party (ND or *Endecja*), took the view that only those individuals of ethnic Polish descent were Poles, a view that was linked to Roman Catholicism. The leader of the National Democratic Party, Roman Dmowski, was convinced that an ethnically heterogeneous nation was a weaker one and launched a boycott of Jewish-owned businesses even before the nation gained independence in 1918. The ND party viewed Jewish influences as a threat to the moral and cultural health of the nation. This led them to launch an anti-Jewish propaganda campaign, reputedly in the hopes that this would increase Poles' sense of themselves as members of a distinct cultural group superior to others, an attitude that historian Andrzej Chojnowski (1995: 30) has dubbed the "national egoism" (see also Jedlicki 1995). A major component of the ND party's campaign was the argument that ethnic Poles were the underdogs in a battle for the political and economic dominance of Poland (Steinlauf 1997: 14). Although Polish Jews lacked political power, from the perspective of the ND party Jews were formidable opponents because their economic power at the turn of the century was undeniable.

When Poland gained independence in 1918, the nationalistic sentiments of the National Democrats and their supporters were only intensified. While at this time other parties made appeals to Catholic values in intellectual and moral life, what distinguished the National Democrats was the conviction that Poland was an absolute category in which membership could be readily defined by ethnicity and religion (Chojnowski 1995: 33). To this end the party's propaganda depicted Poland as a homogenous population, when in reality 30 percent of the population was not ethnically Polish (ibid.). The National Democrats increasingly dedicated their efforts to isolating Jewish Poles by portraying them as either capitalist exploiters and usurers or as rival applicants for jobs and promotions in an increasingly depressed economy. National Democrat propaganda also accused Jews of attempting to influence Polish society through the spread of communism, as well as through the dissemination of the liberal values of progress and democracy (ibid.).[10] Jews were not the ND party's only target. In the late 1920s party members began to speak openly of the need to Polonize Ukrainian and Belorussian minorities in Poland and demanded that Germans be deported (ibid.), goals that went unrealized. Freeing Polish society of these "foreign" or "cosmopolitan" influences became the ND party's primary goal in the 1930s.

I had the opportunity to become acquainted with one of the National Democrats' proposed deportees on an evening in June of 1996. I had already heard a great deal about Doctor Jan S—— in previous interviews with people who remembered his work at a makeshift hospital in Żoliborz during the Uprising of 1944. I had anticipated spending the majority of the evening talking about the uprising, but to my surprise he started by explaining to me how he had come to view himself as Polish. What followed was an account of his family history and his own personal struggle with the question of identity that illustrated the complexities and fluidity of personal identification over time. Jan described his great-grandparents as Baltic Germans (*Baltendeutsche*), the descendents of German immigrants, who lived in a small town near Riga in Latvia. Indeed, his surname is a common German name spelled in phonetic Polish. Although it was a long-standing tradition in his family that the eldest son be sent to study at a Lutheran seminary, Jan's great-grandparents broke with the tradition and sought what, according to Jan, was the much healthier career of forestry for their son Edward, Jan's grandfather. After finishing his studies in Saint Petersburg, Edward married a young woman named Katarina, whose father was also a Baltic German but whose mother was Russian and Russian Orthodox. At that time in Russia, couples of different faiths could only be married in the Russian Orthodox Church, with the non-Orthodox partner converting to Orthodoxy and both vowing to raise their children in the Russian Orthodox faith. Edward and Katarina complied, just as her parents had. After his marriage Edward found work in the forests of Białowieża near Białystok, in Russian-ruled Poland. As a result Jan's father, Piotr, grew up in Poland and was baptized in the Orthodox Church. According to Jan, his father spoke German at home, Russian at school, and Polish with his friends. After studying engineering, Piotr married a Russian woman, so the language of his marital home was Russian. Of his father's attitudes toward Poland, Jan told me, "They Polonized, already in my father's generation. They already knew the Polish language, they sympathized with the Polish nation and believed that a wrong had been done to the Polish nation, and in general they were anti-tsarist."

In 1908, the year of his birth, Jan was baptized in the Russian Orthodox Church, just as his father had been. Jan spent his early childhood in Minsk during World War I. After the war the family returned to Białystok, which had become a part of the Republic of Poland. Jan explained:

> My father had a lot of friends from school who were Polish, and they knew that he had always been a friend and a leader against the tsar, and all that, and he immediately got a good position working for the railroad. He didn't have any troubles with work. And at school, if it came to a question about

nationality, Father wrote "Russian" because that is what he had written before, so in general nobody was going to force him to assimilate [*przystosowywać się*]. Since my father answered that way, I wrote that my national religion was Russian Orthodox and my nationality, Russian. But I became increasingly like a Pole. Just as we can say the *Baltsdeutsche* Russified, in the same way our family Polonized.

Of course, in independent Poland the language of the classroom was no longer Russian but Polish. Thus, Jan became as fluent in Polish as his father had become in Russian. After completing medical school in Warsaw, Jan married a Polish Roman Catholic woman, and Polish became the primary language of his marital home. When we met in 1996, he still spoke with a discernible Russian accent; however, Polish is clearly his daughters' native tongue. "Now . . . I feel more and more like a Pole," he told me.

Jan's identification with Poland as his home, indeed with Polishness as a key component of his identity, is not solely the result of marriage to a Polish woman or a lifetime lived in Poland. Under different historical circumstances he might well have lived his days as a Russian, a citizen of the Soviet Union, in permanent residence in Poland or, indeed, as a German. As Jan explained to me nationality was for him a conscious choice:

> In regards to documents, until the war broke out I wrote "Russian" because—I'll keep this simple. Honestly, I would say at the moment when war broke out, it was clear that those Russians who admitted to knowing the Russian language were not so oppressed by the Germans. What is more, the Germans tried to pull [us] into collaboration. And I had it even worse because I had German blood too, and so they wanted to make a *Volksdeutsche* out of me, right? So, then, in order to best spurn those problems and to clearly illustrate my position on who I am and on whose side I was, from that moment on I have been a Pole.

For Jan the decision to declare himself Polish at the crucial moment of the outbreak of war was the culmination of what he viewed as a natural process of Polonization that had started before his birth, with his grandparents' move to Poland. In this way, becoming Polish publicly and officially in 1939 was the final step in a process made all the easier by his desire to break ties with the Germans, who occupied his home country, and the Soviets, who at that time were their allies. At the time, Jan lived in Żoliborz where the PPS was strong and an inclusive definition of Polishness was dominant. His acceptance as being Polish was certainly aided by his enlistment and service in the Polish army as a surgeon. Thus, he was perceived by his Polish neighbors and colleagues as both honorable and patriotic, if not ethnically Polish.

Similarly, for Polish Jews Polonization was not always an obvious choice. The wider Jewish community did not perceive Polonization positively, nor did the wider community of Poles always accept and acknowledge it as legitimate, as the National Democratic Party's policy shows. The difficulties of this situation are captured poignantly in the diaries of young Polish Jews that were collected as part of a contest sponsored by YIVO (Yidisher Vissenshaftlikher Institut) in Vilnius in the 1930s. The diaries, which were submitted to the competition in 1932, 1934, and 1939, address the complex issues of identity while also dispelling the common misperception that Jews in Poland lived distinctly separate lives from their ethnically Polish contemporaries.[11] For instance, Zygmunt Horwitz (No. 128, dated 1934), a young man from the mountain resort town of Zakopane, wrote, "Aside from Zionism, I really had nothing in common with Jewishness. I considered the Hebrew language a hobby and I thought only in Polish, I got to love this nation and its language, its history. Even today, Sienkiewicz's trilogy gives me the most immense pleasure. . . . Jewish history, on the other hand, represented distant events, something smacking of legend, at least for me who had been brought up far from the atmosphere of Jewry and Jewishness. I was partially assimilated and the organization converted me" (quoted in Cała 1994: 52).

Of the seventy writers who chose to write in Polish rather than Yiddish, Zygmunt is one of only six who came from assimilated families (ibid. 42).[12] In contrast to Zygmunt, who seems to have been quite comfortable thinking of himself as a Pole by virtue of his language and the culture he grew up in, Abraham Rotfarb ("A. Harefuler" No. 245, 1939) is clearly in conflict and finds it impossible to be both a Pole and a Jew. In the passage that follows, the young man wrote about how he discovered Polishness at his Jewish school, Khinukh Yelodim:[13] "I am a poor assimilated soul. I am a Jew and a Pole, or rather I was a Jew but gradually, under the influence of my environment, under the influence of the place where I lived, and under the influence of the language, the culture and the literature, I have also become a Pole. I love Poland. Its language, its culture, and most of all the fact of its liberation and the heroism of its independence struggle, all pluck at my heartstrings and fire my feelings and enthusiasm. But I do not love that Poland which, for no apparent reason, hates me, that Poland which tears at my heart and soul, which drives me into a state of apathy, melancholy and dark depression. . . . Poland has brought me up as a Pole but brands me a Jew who has to be driven out" (quoted in Cała 1994: 52).

Following the death of Piłsudski in 1935, incidents of anti-Semitic propaganda and action were on the rise, and the liberally inclined prime minister M.Z. Kościałkowski failed to take effective measures to stop the economic boycotts and pogroms (Melzer 1989: 128). In 1936, along with its political allies, the National Democratic Party began an active campaign supported by the government to "Polonize" Polish commerce. The program encouraged Poles nationwide to join in a boycott of Jews in the realms of both business and social life (ibid. 133–34; Tomaszewski 1989: 153–54). In response to the boycott, Prime Minister Felicjan Sławoj-Składkowski, a longtime member of the Polish Socialist Party, commented that he opposed violence against the Jews but believed the boycott was justified (*Sprawozdanie Stenograficzne Sejmu Rzeczypospolitej,* June 4, 1936, col.7, cited in Polonsky 1989: 125). In the same year Cardinal August Hlond, primate of Poland, issued a pastoral letter condemning racial hatred and violence against Jews as un-Christian but supporting what he deemed the moral struggle against the "Jewish vices" of atheism, Bolshevism, pornography, and fraud and suggesting that nonviolent means, such as boycotts of Jewish businesses, be used in place of outright attack (Steinlauf 1997: 21). Like all pastoral letters, this one was intended for dissemination from the pulpits of churches across Poland. Although the left opposed any kind of struggle against the Jews, economic or otherwise, the boycott continued until the outbreak of World War II.

Commitment and Resistance

Although they were born in the independent Second Republic of Poland, my informants were educated in the ideals of Polish independence and service to their country. In times of peace, this meant active participation in civic life, which often took the form of campaigns aimed at the alleviation of poverty and social injustice. In wartime this same commitment to one's fellow citizens met with social approbation. However, resistance, in particular armed combat, not only was a duty but was also perceived as the highest expression of belonging to the nation by those who embraced the ideals of the PPS. During the war many young people subscribed to this ideology, rooted in nineteenth-century romanticism that, through literature, the arts, and political discourse, encouraged armed opposition to foreign domination, valorizing sacrifice for the nation and sanctifying defeat. Warsovians did not learn this brand of patriotic action only in school but also at home, where they heard accounts of their parents' own involvement in the movement for an independent Poland. Such recitations clearly suggested to their children that resistance was a well-established and legitimate family tradition. That many of their parents both supported Piłsudski and had served in the Polish military demonstrated to them that military action was honorable and in fact a duty when the nation was threatened. It is this education in heroism, based on Poland's history of struggle, the popular literature of the times, and their own family histories, that in part motivated them to join the underground movement against the Nazis and eventually to take up arms in the Warsaw Uprising of 1944. Studies on the effects of war and political violence on children caught up in more recent conflicts suggest that children whose parents are ideologically committed to a cause appear to be buffered by the stress of violence if they have knowledge of their parents' beliefs, something that was clearly the case for all of my informants (Protacio-Marcelino 1991; Punamaki 1996). This effect is increased if the children also take part in actions organized to protest or resist the oppression they face (Punamaki 1996).

Another factor motivating their participation in underground activities was the brutality of the German occupation. In this way the enormous enthusiasm of the general public and the participation of so many of Warsaw's youth could be interpreted as an internalization of violence and the desire, bred by oppression, to reflect it back on their oppressors. As Polish historian and longtime Żoliborz resident Krzysztof Dunin-Wąsowicz (1981: 199–200) wrote in his monograph about the neighborhood during World War II: "It must be clearly stated that the longing for active battle with the enemy, nurtured through the five years of occupational night, was in Polish society enormous. Every layer of society wanted open armed battle which would at last bring vengeance to the hated enemy." Sławka also recalled the overwhelming hatred she and all the young people she knew in the underground felt for the Germans and their desire to drive them from the city, even if it cost them their own lives.

In this way Poland's uprisings can be viewed as the enactment of what James C. Scott (1992: 58) has called the "hidden transcript," which he defines as "those offstage speeches, gestures, and practices that confirm, contradict, or inflect what appears in the public transcript." The hidden transcript stands in contrast to the "public transcript," the term Scott uses to describe the ways in which subordinates such as slaves, serfs, the untouchables, and discriminated-against minorities conduct themselves in the presence of dominant members of society where to respond according to their true feelings would bring about reprisal (ibid.). To use Scott's terminology, during the war it was the Germans' ability to systematically *"frustrate reciprocal action"* on the part of Poles that led to the hidden transcript of resistance that culminated in the Warsaw Uprising of 1944, a sort of acting out of the fantasy of rage and reciprocal aggression. As Scott describes it, "The frustration, tension, and control necessary in public give way to unbridled retaliation in a safer setting, where the accounts of reciprocity are, symbolically at least, finally balanced" (ibid. 64). Conspiratorial activities are a sort of prologue to the enactment of the hidden transcript, which outlines a reversal of fortunes in which the oppressed take up arms against the occupant and free their city. In this way the uprising can be understood as an attempt to realize both the hidden transcript as well as my informants' education in heroism by making it a model for public action.

Inspired by Roger Callois's comparison of war in contemporary society to feast times of the Middle Ages, Polish scholar Barbara Engelking suggests that ethnic Poles experienced World War II as "time out of time," not as a holiday in the English sense but, rather, as holy or sacred time. This meaning is implicit in the Polish word for holiday or feast day, święto, which is related to the word "holy," święty. Engelking argues that, while war completely transforms society, cutting it off from peacetime, at the same time war is all consuming and "no individual matter can survive it—neither artistic activity, nor happiness, nor even fear. No one can remain on the sidelines and occupy themselves with something else, because war will find employment for everyone" (Engelking 2001: 25). Engelking draws a further distinction between "occupation-time" and times of actual fighting. While life under occupation differs from the everyday, times of fighting are characterized by the reversal of social norms, or war as carnival, and by feelings of exaltation, excitement, and social solidarity (ibid.). In this way, regardless of how they experienced it, Warsovians recollect the uprising as a time of sacred struggle for the restoration of Polish independence. As a result, death in the course of that battle is interpreted as (if not initially felt to be) part of a common, national martyrology (ibid. 27).

What Engelking describes is heroic memory: the war is remembered as an active struggle against the Germans in which all of Polish society took part, while the Warsaw Uprising is venerated as the culmination of that struggle (ibid.). Indeed, feelings of exaltation, excitement, and solidarity abound in my informants' narratives. However, anthropologists Deepak Mehta and Roma Chatterji (2001: 206) remind us, "As people narrate their experiences we see not what happened but rather how the imagination of violence and relief work comes to be sedimented in language."[14] In the pages that follow, much of what is remembered lacks this heroic quality. Heroic memory is the public face of informants' memories of the war; however, it is far from being the only thing recollected, imagined, or captured in their accounts. In the narratives I present there are different types of memory at work. They not only differ from one individual to another, but a given individual may also vary the way she or he recollects and retells the uprising, sometimes remembering the heroic, other times the tragic, the absurd, or the mundane.

Carolyn Nordstrom (1992: 269) suggests that, for people who live in areas devastated by war, the most readily available system of knowledge that provides a model for action is "the politicomilitary one, in which force is equated with right and violence is seen as instrumental to power," which leads civilian victims of terror "to absorb and, more dangerously, accept fundamental knowledge constructs that are based on force." In wartime Poland not only was the politicomilitary system of knowledge ever present, permeating all aspects of life, but despite the consequences it had been the dominant system of knowledge and a model that had been valorized and turned to again and again for more than one hundred and fifty years.

2 Memories of the Invasion

Irmina: There were all the bombardments, well, all the fear. I remember that once we were sitting in a shelter in 1939, and there was shooting and shooting. I remember that I fell asleep for a moment . . . and dreamt, I dreamt about something funny: a picture of a green meadow, a house drawn like a child would draw, a white house with windows and with a blue sky. I remember that it was so funny, I saw this funny sugary picture, it was so silly and at that moment the shooting started again, and I woke up and started to cry because that fairy-tale house was not real, only a dream, and this was reality.

Bogumiła: And you've remembered that, all these years, as a symbol of something that you had lost.

Sławomira: I guess it must have been the last day of August when we returned to Warsaw, because school was about to begin. Indeed I remember the radio alarms of the first of September. The first explosions, the first bombardments, the first terrible attacks, except that of course we (my sister Basia and I) didn't grasp the threat of it. And because we had been raised on lessons that were very, shall we say, patriotic, in which it seemed that each war was something wonderful, Basia and I were as a result very interested in it all. My mother was in despair because she knew what war meant.

DURING THE COURSE of my fieldwork I interviewed 20-some people who ranged in age from 65 to 90 years old, a difference of 25 years between the oldest and the youngest informants. The experiences dividing a 65-year-old and a 90-year-old may be lost on those of us who have not yet found ourselves in that group, which our society labels with the blanket terms "senior citizens" or "the elderly." However, there is a world of difference between the perspectives and understandings that separate a 9-year-old from a 34-year-old, their ages in 1939 when the war began. I must confess that initially I viewed all my informants as "older people," and when I imagined them during the war, I tended to picture them as roughly the same age as myself at the time of our interviews, that is, in their late 20s. While this might be attributable to lack of imagination on my part, or perhaps overidentification, I think that it was also due to the fact that, especially in interviews about later periods of the war, I found that informants' experiences were often quite similar to one another, regardless of their age, with even the youngest's experiences mirroring those of adults.

However, there is one place in the narratives I have collected in which the difference in the ages of my informants is unmistakable, and that is in their recollections of the invasion of Poland. The quotations from Sławomira and Irmina that open this chapter illustrate two of the clearest distinctions in these narratives: those of perspective and expectation. As evidenced in the example of the mother's despair and her children's anticipation, narratives about the invasion of Poland and the early days of the war vary drastically according to the age of the speaker. In this chapter I will discuss the ways in which my informants remember the early months of the war, addressing the issue of what people of different ages expected war to be and how they perceived events as a result of these expectations. I will also address the persistent and troubling question of how war impinges on the lives of children and young adults, shaping and sometimes changing the trajectories that those lives take and the possibilities that these people see for themselves in later life.

Differences in the content of what people remembered and described become increasingly less apparent when one examines narratives focused on later periods of the war. What is at work here is more than the natural passage of time and the maturation of individuals. The conditions of the occupation, a topic I will discuss in greater detail in the following chapter, caused children to suffer (and justifiably so) anxieties about their personal survival and that of those closest to them, and in some cases they were forced to take on the responsibilities of adults. Moreover, in their efforts to re-create a normal life during the occupation, young people became implicated in the resistance activities of adults. The longer the war went on, the more personally involved they became. As a result, the experiences of young people became more and more similar to those of adults as the war continued (see Gross 1979), something that becomes evident when one compares narratives on the invasion with those focused on 1944 or

1945. It is not, however, just the content of the narratives about the invasion that differs according to age. In the following pages I examine the narrative responses of people who in 1939 were children, adolescents, and adults. I do so in an effort to illustrate how striking the differences are between people of different ages in terms of attitudes toward the very idea of war, responses to the invasion, and expectations of how war might change their lives, particularly with regard to issues of Polish nationalism, ideology, education, social action, and heroism.

The German Invasion of Poland

When the Nazis invaded Poland on September 1, 1939, they made little distinction between military and civilian targets. As one historian commented, "From the very moment German armies plunged across the vulnerable Polish frontier, it was apparent that they were not waging a conventional war, that is, a war against the Polish government and its armed forces. Instead, the Germans waged war against the Polish people, intent on destroying the Polish nation" (Lukas 1986: 1). Using incendiary devices, the Luftwaffe bombed and strafed civilians, aiming not only at military targets but also at roadways, sanitariums, hospitals, and apartment buildings, as well as peasants working in the fields (ibid.).

After signing the Molotov-Ribbentropp pact, the Soviets invaded Poland from the east, on September 17, 1939, partitioning Poland for the fourth time.[1] Prime Minister Sławoj-Składowski claimed powerlessness against the combined forces of the Soviet Union and Germany and gave a general order for Polish troops to retreat to Romania and Hungary (Roszkowski 1997: 90). The Polish government and high command escaped to Romania, and on September 30 they formed a new government in France under the leadership of General Sikorski. Made up of a coalition of parties, including the Polish Socialist Party, the National Party (Stronnictwo Narodowe), and the People's Party (Stronnictwo Ludowe), who opposed the rule of the Sanacja government imposed after Piłsudski's coup, as well as a few members of the postcoup government, this so-called government-in-exile was located first in France and then in London (Davies 1984: 65; Roszkowski 1997: 99–100). As Polish soldiers poured into France from Romania and Hungary, the government turned its attention first to the reorganization and training of Polish military units. Joined by Polish French volunteers, the Polish army in France grew to number 84,000, while five Polish naval units joined forces with the British (Roszkowski 1997: 100).

The Siege of Warsaw

Despite the flight of the national government, residents of Warsaw defended the capital from September 9 to September 29. Mayor Stefan Starzyński and General Walerian Czuma remained in the city throughout the siege in order to provide the people of Warsaw with the services that they so desperately needed. Through radio broadcasts the mayor rallied citizens to come to their own defense. As a result, virtually every apartment building was mobilized as an antiaircraft defense unit, and volunteers were organized to distribute food. Since the city's police force had been mobilized for battle, Starzyński created the Citizens' Guard to take their place (Gross 1979: 216). Organizations like the Capital's Committee for Social Assistance (*Stołeczny Komitet Pomocy Społeczny*) and the Warsaw Workers' Committee for Social Assistance (*Warszawski Robotniczy Komitet Pomocy Społeczny*) were established to aid refugees from western Poland who poured into Warsaw, fleeing the advancing German forces (ibid.). Political leaders and other prominent Warsovians, previously divided by political ideology, joined together on the Citizens' Committee, which gathered at Prince Zdzisław Lubomirski's residence to discuss policy matters (ibid. 217). The Polish Socialist Party was highly successful in organizing volunteer detachments into the Workers' Volunteer Brigade of the Defense of Warsaw, and when Starzyński broadcast an appeal to form the Battalion of the Defenders of Warsaw, several thousand people reported to the designated spot within the half-hour (Bartoszewski 1968: 38). Girl Scouts were also active during the siege, working with the Red Cross to staff "help points" where they and other volunteers provided the elderly, the wounded, and women with young children with shelter, first aid, meals, and child care (Zawadzka 1998: 99–101). Girl Scouts also worked at hospitals during the siege as nurses' aides and helped with the removal of rubble from bombarded buildings (ibid.).

The volunteer organizations created during the siege laid the groundwork for underground social-service networks during the occupation. The two paramilitary groups, the Workers' Volunteer Brigade of the Defense of Warsaw and the Battalion of the Defenders of Warsaw, became the foundation for the Armia Krajowa, or Home Army, an organization that many of my informants joined during the occupation. Thus, the institutional framework for opposition to the occupation was already in place when the Germans captured the city. Equally important was the symbolic significance of the three-week battle, which not only revealed the mutual dependence of one citizen on another that lay hidden during peacetime but also offered proof that in solidarity resistance was possible (Gross 1979: 222, 223).

Children's Perspectives

Irmina: Well, in the third grade the war broke out. As a result there was a lot of destruction here in Żoliborz, although not as much as in the center of the city. Among others, my friend, who lived on Plac Słoneczny, was killed—a very close girlfriend.

Bogumiła: But that was during the uprising, wasn't it?

Irmina: No, that was in 1939! . . . I'll tell you that for me memories of 1939 are the worst of all my wartime recollections, because for me normal reality was entirely broken. Everything that was certain, peaceful, everyday became foreign and threatening. When we returned to our damaged house, there were no panes in the windows. Please imagine what it means to live in an apartment without window panes. . . . That first winter of the war, that was a terrible winter, in 1939 there was a terrible frost, it was below freezing— and everyone in this destroyed Warsaw nested in, in what were generally miserable conditions.

Irmina's account was not unusual; these narratives tend to focus on the trauma of wartime. Several of the people with whom I spoke, who were not yet in their teens at that time, shared the view that 1939 was an especially difficult period of the war. The sudden break with normal everyday life as well as the unprecedented conditions and demands of the Nazi occupants were recalled as a turning point by those who were children at the war's beginning. Many adults comforted themselves and their children with the idea that France and England would quickly defeat Germany; as this hope was soon disappointed, the first few months of the war were bitter indeed.

During the siege of Warsaw, the Germans destroyed 12 percent of the buildings in the capital and killed 60,000 civilians (Bartoszewski 1968: 18). Irmina speaks to the growing atmosphere of fear created by the bombardments, the sensation that one was trapped in a city destined for destruction. Pani Sławomira's initial excitement and patriotic enthusiasm, noted in the opening lines of this chapter, were at least temporarily extinguished by the difficult circumstances in which she and her family found themselves.

ELT: I have a question about the first year of the war, when you were in Warsaw, I know that there wasn't school, so what did you do every day?

Sławomira: I don't even remember that well at this time. I remember that I spent a lot of time at home reading books, because—one must say that one life ended very precisely. That time which was a period in which I was happy, at peace, safe, surrounded by love, where good was good, and bad was bad, and good always conquered—that ended. That was the end of one world. I remember that first period of the war, that first year when I didn't go to school, when I was at home, I remember that as something terribly sad. First of all, at home it was cold. There was no coal, which was very bad, so one burned very little. It was chilly at home. During the bombardment the window panes were blown out, and they were only repaired [some time] later. In addition it was like this: my father lost his job. He didn't work, so doubtlessly that had an effect on that first period of the war. He looked for gainful employment in order to earn something. Fortunately, my mother worked because she was a dentist, and her clinic functioned, but not right away because the clinic was damaged and had to be remodeled. In general life changed diametrically. A peaceful life became a life that was wholly different. I remember that most of all I sat at home, because even going out then was special. Winter was very difficult. That winter was snowy, heavy, there was hunger because, well, you know, there wasn't any food.

At twelve years of age and on the doorstep of adolescence in 1939, Pani Sławomira's reflections on the war encapsulate both the remembered fears and discomforts reported by those who were slightly younger, as well as the curiosity and excitement that I have found to be characteristic of those who were in their teens when the war broke out.

Adolescents' Perspectives

Rather than viewing the onset of war as a threat with very real implications for themselves, their families, and their communities, as did adults, or with unmasked terror and confusion, as did younger children, many adolescents viewed the war with great curiosity and a spirit of adventure. This is best exemplified by the quotation from Sławomira at the opening of the chapter. Pani Sławomira's enthusiasm surprised me, and so I was eager to learn if others had felt the same curiosity about the war or if they had held the same belief that wars were patriotic and therefore somehow good. I did not have to look far to find others who shared Sławomira's initial excitement. When I told Olgierd Z——, a retired physician who had been 17 years old and preparing for his final year at secondary school when the war broke out, about her comments and asked him if he had felt the same way, he told me: "Those days were gray, of course, but because one was young, one was curious about everything, everything was of interest, and all of it was a great adventure. I would not change anything that I've gone through—

every moment, the whole history. It was wonderful, especially the uprising, well—in general, each day starting with the beginning of the war in 1939."

Embedded in these descriptions of the war as something wonderful is an assumption of invulnerability. Though later in the war both Olgierd and Sławomira experienced personal danger and the loss of friends and family members, at least in the above quotations they seem to see themselves in the retrospective light of memory as untouched by the violence around them, as if still unaware of the potential for the war to bring suffering into their lives. As the occupation stretched on from weeks, to months, to years, the harsh realities of life under German occupation and personal loss tempered the initial excitement felt by many young people. Yet, for some an enthusiastic and committed activism on behalf of others or in the name of a free Poland transformed both their initial expectations of adventure and later experiences of grief, a subject I will discuss in greater length in the following chapters.

One of the most common attitudes reflected in the narratives of those who were in their teens in 1939 was the sense that war brought with it exciting opportunities. Chief among these was the chance to prove themselves as full adult members of society, to enact the heroic ideals on which they had been raised, and to play a role in the latest act of Poland's struggle to remain an autonomous and independent state. Perhaps it is for this reason that adolescents' narratives of the early days of the war often read like adventure tales with the narrator as hero, a feature that is somewhat diminished in their accounts of later events. In the following passage, for example, Jan R——, a retired engineer who was 22 years old in 1939, assigns himself a Cassandra-like role, seeing the inevitability of war long before his elders:

> Well, all this is my very personal history. So, as I said, I studied at the Polytechnic, and it so happened that in 1938 I was on vacation with the Society of International Students, "Oliga." I received an internship abroad in Hitler's Germany, and I went to Hitler's Germany, to Berlin, to work on the building site of a new housing complex. I lived in a dorm called the Charlottenberg with German students. Moreover, because I was in scouting [*harcerstwo*], I made contact with the Hitler Youth, with the leadership of the Hitler Youth. A remarkably delicate game was being played by the [Polish] scouts with the Hitler Youth. It had to do with saving Polish scouting troops in Germany. The Germans owed us cooperation, which was nonexistent, and it was just that we wanted Polish troops in Śląsk [Silesia] and Mazuria to be able to exist. And I went to the Hitler Youth looking for cooperation, but I got their organizational materials and was able to talk with other people.

I became convinced in 1938 in August that there would be war. I sent the materials to the Polish embassy in Berlin and to the Society for International Students in Poland, and here I had a meeting with them. I said, "Listen, in my opinion, looking at the preparations of youth and the schooling of the Hitler Youth, there will soon be war." That was not popular. In Poland, the thinking was—they looked at me as if I had somehow changed, as if I wasn't as I used to be. "You'll see," I told them.

In the interview excerpted above, Jan R——— alludes to a mission, for which he was the envoy, to regain the rights of Polish young people living in (then German-controlled) areas of Silesia and Mazuria to organize and participate in scouting troops. Though ethnically mixed, Germany governed these areas and expected the Poles living there to Germanize. As a result, German policy banned Polish young people from forming their own organizations, and Poles were not welcome in the German youth organizations like the Hitler Youth and the *Bund deutscher Madel*, organizations that were not only anti-Semitic but also anti-Slav. Thus the purpose for Jan R———'s mission was one of importance for Polish young people. Even so, Jan R——— also gives the impression that he alone foresaw the mobilization of the German populace and the growing threat of war. When Jan first told me of his "mission," I pictured him frantically going from office to office, telling anyone who would listen of all he had observed in Germany, showing them the literature produced by and for the Hitler Youth, only to have his concerns dismissed and his evidence declared child's play. I imagined his growing frustration, his desperation as the leaders dismissed his warnings and showed him the door. In his narrative he is the young hero of the story, wise beyond his years, ignored by foolish adults who are blind to what is to come. These leaders, with whom he has entrusted vital information about German preparations for war, have fallen short of his expectations, betraying his trust and at the same time revealing that the world for which he holds them responsible is not as it should be (see, for example, Elkind 1967, 1985). Yet while the International Student Organization might have dismissed his concerns about the Hitler Youth, and it is not at all difficult to imagine that the Polish embassy in Germany may have declined to discuss the issue with a college student, those in power were not in doubt about the very real threat of war. Indeed, the question of whether there would be war was very much on the minds of many Poles. Some argued that Germany was a cultured nation and, after the failure of the last war, unlikely to try conquering Europe again. Given Hitler's demands for a "corridor" through Poland along the Baltic to East Prussia and his incursions into Czechoslovakia and Austria, others saw the war as inevitable. How, then, is one to understand Jan R——'s account of his mission?

While it would be easy to dismiss the story of Jan's mission as a deliberate exaggeration designed to impress a scholar from the States, I think there is more to it. Jan R——'s account of his mission suggests that one way that young people coped with the threat of violence was not only through activism but by constructing narratives about the things they did that show them behaving with foresight, wisdom, courage, and even heroism. According to Raija Punamaki-Gitai, a scholar of the effects of political violence on young people, older children tend to be less traumatized by war in general than their younger counterparts. Older children, she found, also use more active means to cope with political violence than younger children (Punamaki-Gitai 1990). Thus, while Irmina, who experienced the war as a child, recalls primarily the trauma of war and things that happened to her or to her family, adolescents not only took action—something difficult, if not impossible for younger children to do—but also constructed narratives of that action, narratives in which, even if unsuccessful, they are empowered.

In this way, despite the fact that the interpretation that Jan R——ascribes to the indifference of Polish officials is rather unlikely (i.e., that they were shocked at the mere suggestion that there would be a war with Germany), the narrative is in its own way compelling because it demonstrates one way in which young people coped with the threat of violence. In turn, by endowing the narrator with an element of personal agency, to say nothing of bravery and intelligence, coping through the construction of narratives encouraged greater activism, in that the narratives not only suggest that control is achievable but also demonstrate that resistance is possible. Clearly the perspective that Jan R—— presents in this narrative is not one influenced by the hindsight of decades nor by a greater understanding of how the adults he encountered might have viewed the warnings of a young man about what was, in essence, a group of German Boy Scouts. However, the fact that some 50 years after the event Jan R—— is able to describe it, perhaps not as he experienced it at the moment but most probably in a way he came to think of the incident shortly after the war began, testifies to the resilience of memory as well as to the tenacity and power possessed by the stories that we construct and repeat about ourselves over time. Developmental psychologist David Elkind (1967, 1985) suggests that adolescents see themselves through a lens in which they are unique and immune to the rules that govern the rest of society—and invulnerable to the consequences that come from breaking those rules. He describes this worldview as "personal fable" and suggests that it is precisely these personal fables that enable young people to take risks by simultaneously blinding them to very real dangers. For me what is fascinating about Jan R——'s story is that his personal fable has been transformed from a story that he told himself and (if I am any indication) others to give meaning to what must have been a humiliating experience to an enduring statement about himself as a person of vision.[2]

While Pan Jan R——'s story about his mission in Germany is perhaps the clearest example of adherence to a personal fable several decades after the event it enshrines in memory, other narratives of those who experienced the war as adolescents also seem to have this quality. In response to my questions about the early days of the war, many of the men I interviewed in this age group told me about their efforts to enlist. The following passage is an example of one such account and is an excerpt from a rather unusual interview. Arranged by my neighbor Pani Basia, this was my first interview with her dear friend and fellow combatant, Pan Jurek. During the interview Stefan, an old friend visiting Warsaw from Paris, joined us and took part in the conversation. The three friends knew these stories so well that they felt comfortable interrupting to remind the speaker of details left out, pertinent information missed.

> **Jurek:** On the second or third of September, just as we had all agreed (or almost all of us friends who were at military training camp), [we] reported to the barracks on Konwiktorska Street, to a voluntary company of convoy sentries. We went there in our uniforms, and they gave us coats, they gave us rifles and the like, and we were enlisted in the army as volunteers. Except that our parents' permission was required.
>
> **Stefan:** I had to make a special trip to my father, because father—
>
> **Jurek [interrupting]:** So, if a buddy had difficulties with their parents, then one signed the permission for the other. Well, and we were quartered there in normal army barracks on Konwiktorska Street. And that's how it was until September seventh.
>
> **Stefan:** On the seventh they woke us at five in the morning.
>
> **Jurek:** Because on the seventh of September this officer, Colonel Umiastowski, who worked with the military press and information, made—well—a mistake maybe because he announced on the radio that all men able to carry arms should leave Warsaw and travel to the east. It was simply about not staying here under German Occupation. Well, nobody, of course, had any idea what would happen next, right?

Chaos ensued in the wake of Umiastowski's order as many men left Warsaw with their families in tow. With the hope that they could regroup and form a force strong enough to push back the Germans, they headed eastward on roads already crowded with refugees from western Poland.

> **Jurek:** And it was macabre. Because not only those from Warsaw but, after all, people [from western Poland] were retreating east through Warsaw from the Germans. So, the roads were crowded. Well, the Germans murdered people with their airplanes. The planes were flying at our heads. They shot at cattle and people and, in general, at whatever showed itself in their path.
>
> **Basia:** And they shot—
>
> **Jurek [interrupting]:** They shot at cattle and people and in general at anything that showed itself.

On September 17, 1939, the Soviet Union invaded Poland from the east. In the wake of the advancing Red Army, hundreds of people living in Kresy, the Polish Ukraine and what is now Lithuania, fled westward. In the chaos of the second invasion, all hopes of a counteraction were crushed, and those Warsovians who had traveled east in the hopes of organizing military units there were forced to flee. Many Warsovians I spoke with referred to the evacuation east and their journey back to Warsaw with the ironic term *wędrówka*, which is a diminutive for the noun "wandering."

The younger people I spoke with saw their "wanderings" as a sort of misadventure. Although their goals of enlisting in the east were thwarted, their journeys provided the makings of a good adventure story.

> **Jurek:** Well, the first days we wandered as a whole company, but before [we got to] Siedlice, it became dangerous on the roads, and later we wandered in groups. Well, unfortunately we weren't needed. Stefan managed to wander far to the east and escaped from imprisonment in Russia because on the 17th of September the Russians crossed the border. Stefan was on a train and was captured by the Russians, but he escaped and returned to Warsaw and on the way took part in the last battle of September. That means at the Battle of Kock, with General Kleeberg. When he told me about it later, as far as combat, there wasn't much to speak of because he was lying in a furrow in a potato field [he starts laughing], and there was just the whistling of bullets strafing the ground, and there really was not much to shoot with nor anyone to shoot at. So, that's the hopeless truth.

In regards to his own "wanderings" home, which were far less eventful than Pan Stefan's, Pan Jurek focuses not only on the hospitality of the peasant family but also vividly recalls the comforts of their home.

Jurek: We stopped near Grużyca, near Jasienica, there Władek Walczak and his family had a small farm and there they greeted us.

Basia [overlapping]: They welcomed you, fed you, clothed you.

Jurek: They sent us to this huge marital bed, two of us slept in one direction and the third between us in the other direction. All of us covered up with a thick down comforter, and we laid in that bed in those fresh, clean sheets. In the middle of the bed, they placed this big bowl of scrambled eggs, and bread, and village bread at that. Listen, it was something fantastic!

Basia: The best scrambled eggs in the world.

Jurek: And with that milk, listen when we had finished eating . . . we didn't even thank them, instead each of us fell back into the bed and woke only the next afternoon. So, it ended well for us, and later on our way back to Warsaw by cart, we were able to organize some food because—

Basia [interrupting]: Well, there wasn't any in Warsaw.

Jurek: So, we didn't return empty-handed. Andrzej's father came with money, and we bought cabbages, potatoes, if you please, bread, eggs—

Basia: All the necessary things.

A common theme in tales about the "wanderings" is the kindness of strangers, particularly Polish villagers, who often gave displaced Warsovians food and a place to stay. In the case of Pan Jurek, the peasants also gave the boys clothing and disposed of their uniforms so that, upon returning to Warsaw, they would not be immediately recognized by Germans as soldiers, which would have led to their arrest. Individually, accounts such as this one illustrate the ongoing ties between city-dwelling szlachta and the peasants, a relationship characterized at least in these narratives by loyalty and hospitality. Collectively, these accounts suggest a spirit of social solidarity in the face of assault that allowed the disputes and disagreements of peacetime to be, at least temporarily, put aside. Memories of food, particularly meals consumed after or during a period of scarcity, came up in many people's recollections, not just of the invasion but also during the Warsaw Uprising of 1944. Here, it is not just the meal and the comforts of home that Jurek and his friends took pleasure in but also the ability to bring provisions back to their families in Warsaw. In doing so, the boys claimed a measure of adult responsibility from their otherwise wasted wanderings, asserting not so much independence from their families as much as a new, if only temporary, status as provider within it.

Sociologist Jan Tomasz Gross (1979: 167) argues that the war caused many families to disintegrate as parents disappeared or were unable to cope with the economic difficulties brought on by the occupation. This forced many adolescents to take on the role of supporting the family. Gross suggests that, in their attempts to cope with German occupation, young people turned away from their families in search of more successful role models, thus cutting short their childhood under pressure to adapt to the environment of German occupation. While my research supports Gross's assertion that young people were forced by the circumstances of daily life to confront worries and dangers that ideally even adults would not have to face, my research does not support his assertion that families disintegrated under the pressures of the German occupation. Certainly some of the people I spoke with lost parents during the war; however, I would argue that, rather than resulting in disintegration and social atomization, family bonds were often strengthened as a result of the occupation. Family members in these circumstances viewed themselves as increasingly dependent on one another for both emotional and material support. While it is true that many teens worked (in fact they had to, in order to avoid deportation to work camps in Germany), none of the people I worked with used their meager wages to eke out a living independent from their families. Rather, the pattern I have found is that they contributed to the household income, taking pride in their ability to show themselves as mature and responsible members of the family. Finally, in an environment where trust and loyalty were questions of life and death, family ties were some of the most important social bonds.[3]

Adults' Reflections

Only five of the people I interviewed had completed their studies and were in their thirties in 1939 and thus can be said to have experienced the entire war as full-fledged adults in the eyes of Polish society. Dr. Jan S—— and Pani Maria were both married with children in 1939. Pan Stefan W—— was also married as was Pani Janina K——, whose husband spent the majority of the war in a POW camp. Pani Eugenia, like Janina K——, was a teacher in Żoliborz. All recalled feeling anxious about family members, society as a whole, and the future during the opening weeks of the war, though initially these fears were somewhat tempered by their memories of the German occupation of Poland during World War I. The narratives of Eugenia and Janina, both of whom enjoyed careers as teachers before and after the war, tended to focus on their work in schools, their thoughts about the young people they taught, and their own involvement with charitable organizations. Work and activity play an important role in their narratives, perhaps because work, paid or voluntary, gave them a sense of control and purpose. In helping their students and others, they ultimately helped themselves re-create a sense of normalcy amid the radical change brought about by the invasion. I will discuss their activities during the occupation in more detail in the following chapter.

As a military doctor Jan S—— had a very different experience from the two women. However, his narrative of the early days of the war also concentrates on his experiences working in a field hospital. Jan S——'s unit consisted of 50 horse-drawn wagons (*formanek*). By the time the hospital was mobilized, the Germans had already started bombing, and the field hospital was ordered to evacuate to the east. According to Dr. Jan, the hospital traveled ("We really overdid it," he confided) past Wołyn, almost to Pińsk, before they were forced to turn back to avoid being captured by the Soviets. By that time chaos reigned, with much of the Polish army having fled to Romania where, if captured, they were interned as prisoners of war. Hoping to join the troops of General Kleeberg (a Polish general), who were moving from Lublin toward Warsaw in order to defend the capital, the field hospital took a westward course across the "green border," or in other words, through the woods. In the following excerpt from an interview with him in 1996, he explains the hospital's necessarily slow and cautious means of maneuvering patients in wagons through the forests. Jan S——'s narrative is an account of his unit's "wandering" back to Warsaw. However, unlike those of Jurek and Stefan, Jan's recollections of this event focus on the hardships brought about by the demands of duty.

> So, then we consulted about what to do and we decided—that means our commandant decided—and I thought then, "Shouldn't we rather . . ." because after all, it was clear that sooner or later we would be caught between the Germans and the Soviets, because after all Hitler had his plans, and Stalin needed Ukraine and the Caucasus, and so on, so I thought, "Wouldn't it be better at the moment to stay, and wait, and not go fight with the army?" But our commandant told us that "an army doctor's responsibility is to be where the battle is. The battle at the moment is at Warsaw, Warsaw has not fallen, so our duty is in the direction of Warsaw." So we started out for the battle. . . . Well, that was really suicide because one was going toward Warsaw, and Warsaw was already lost. We hadn't been commanded there, but it was our duty to go.

Notice the contrast between Jan S——'s pragmatic attitude, the reluctance to join a battle that was already virtually lost, and the statements made by Sławomira at the beginning of the chapter. While the latter brim with an idealism that seems to blind the speaker to the very real danger of war, the former seems bound in duty. Jan displays what those working in the field of developmental psychology have dubbed "postformal thought," which is qualitatively different from the thinking style of adolescents. This "adult" thinking style is more flexible, adaptive, and relativistic (Sinnott 1998; Labouvie-Vief 1990). It often arises in response to a crisis that challenges a black-and-white view of the world, enabling adults to transcend a single logical system, such as a political ideology, and to reconcile or choose among conflicting ideas or demands (Sinnott 1998.) Thus, although Jan clearly suspects that little good will come of joining the battle, he submits to the call of responsibility. Yet, at least in retrospect, he does this not with the sense of heroic sacrifice common in the narratives of many younger people but rather with a sense of the futility of the situation and with regret that the demands of duty must be met regardless of the cost. Jan continued:

> So, how did we travel? We were in a situation in which the Germans only had control of the roads for cars and tanks, but the forests and those types of areas were not under German control yet. A curfew (police hour) had been announced, and after that hour no travel was permitted. Traveling at night on horses with the wounded in carts, the doctors would go from village to village, seeking out General Kleeberg's army on the Lublin-Warsaw Road. . . . At night, various German cars flew down the wide road, sports cars and tanks, but at night a car could be seen from ten kilometers away. They were not afraid of lighting up the sky to see, right? So, we crouched down in the bushes that lined the road, and when the road was dark in both directions, then we would cross the road on horseback and [ride] into the forest, from the road to the forest. And whenever we saw lights, then halt! Everyone retreated to the bushes, so that the car passed right by while we sat in the bushes.
>
> But at the very end we made a mistake. There were the last four or five wagons [on one side of the road], the last ones, and we saw the light, and we should have [gotten off the road], and I said, "Go! Those five wagons will make it across." It was too late, but we jumped across, and evidently they saw us . . . headed for the forest, and those cars stopped near the place [where we had crossed], and they searched with flashlights. We had already started down the road, and they were stopped, but we made it to a village and had started to feed the horses—well, you had to feed the horses—when a peasant came running to tell us that the Germans were there.
>
> The village was divided into fields, and all around the fields were woods, and we went out and looked around, and there they stood with machine guns. Ohh! And we were surrounded. Well, we raised the Red Cross standard, because we were a hospital, right? And everyone who had a pistol

or something threw it into the well. The cashier gave everyone money. Well, they appeared and we had good fortune. . . . Luckily it was not an SS patrol, it was just a normal unit of Germans mobilized and sent to the front. They came to us by car and saw that we were a medical unit. Very elegantly they disputed that those who—I spoke German, a few of us started to argue with them. They ordered us to get into the carts and to form columns, and we rode to Radom. And at that time Kleeberg had his battle at Kock.[4]

In the preceding quotation Jan describes in detail the difficulties of moving the field hospital toward the battle. Though he does not dwell on it, he clearly takes the responsibility for giving the command to cross the road even after the headlights of the German cars had been sighted. The language he uses here suggests neither embellishment nor a sense that he felt that any of this was particularly heroic.

Jan S—— and his unit were sent to a prisoner-of-war camp in Radom. In the following passage he describes the conditions he encountered there.

Nothing was allowed, tools weren't allowed, and everything was the death penalty. On general principle, anything was punishable by death. . . . At the same time I saw that they clearly treated doctors a little better in that camp. That means, for example, that most of the prisoners of war were out in a field surrounded by guard towers, machine guns, and it was not permissible to go near the barbed wire; they shot those who got close to the wire, and they did so in broad daylight. But the doctors were divided from the rest, and they put us up in a small villa of sorts, in any case we had a roof over our heads. That was the first difference for the doctors, that we had a roof over our heads while they treated the others illegally . . .

I had my medical bag with me, and in that bag I had a small, stiff knife. And I, you know, seeing that they treated doctors differently and that knife to me was a remembrance of my grandfather who gave it to me, and I felt terrible about losing it. So I thought to myself, "After all, they probably wouldn't kill a doctor," and I kept it and had it in my bag. They came to us and told us, "Now, Doctors, we are opening a hospital for wounded Polish prisoners of war. Who wants to go there?" Well, everyone volunteered, of course, and they took us, around ten doctors, to a hospital in the Apollo Cinema in Radom. And it looked this way: the hall was destroyed and all the chairs were thrown out, and on the floor there were rows of straw and cannon fodder was brought in, all in a terrible state, on all sorts of vehicles after the battle of Kock. Well, terrible things, you know. And in the camp, the staff were SS men. So, it was different in this way: the entire area of our hospital was surrounded, we had a roof over our heads, because the hospital was in the movie theater, and we were surrounded by barbed wire in the Warta [*sic*] (Apollo) Cinema. The guards walked there. In reality no one was allowed to leave, right? . . . And again they brought this German, some SS man, and with great irony he showed us that hall and said, "Well, doctors go to your task, fulfill your responsibilities."

Common Themes

While the perceptions of and expectations for the war held by individuals vary drastically according to age, as does the content, there are many themes in the interviews I conducted about the early days of the war that occur throughout informants' narratives regardless of age. Among these are accounts of encounters with the enemy and stories in which the narrator narrowly escapes capture or death. Recollections on these themes were not confined solely to interviews about the invasion, of course, but rather they appear in interviews about all periods of the war. Memories about brushes with death are worth exploring for what they reveal about how people make sense of traumatic experiences. What is interesting in the case of narratives of the enemy is how static and uniform these descriptions are.

Narrow Escapes

Memories of the "wanderings," in particular, tend to focus on narrow escapes, moments when the narrator and her or his companions were nearly caught by German or Soviet forces but by wit, stealth, sheer luck, or divine intervention managed to escape. The following excerpt from an interview I conducted with Sławomira is an excellent example. In accordance with Umiastowski's order to mobilize in the east, Sławomira's father, along with her mother, herself, and her older sister drove eastward by car to join family members in Lwów. They had only been there for a few days when the Red Army invaded.

> The Germans besieged Warsaw and Warsaw defended herself. But on the 17th of September, the Bolsheviks crossed the Polish border and, in accordance to an agreement that they had with the Germans, at a certain moment attacked Lwów. The Germans withdrew and the city fell to the Bolsheviks. That was terrible. I was twelve then, and I still have always before my eyes this scene which made such a terrifying impression on me: I saw a Polish soldier, walking with his hands in the air, and behind him a Bolshevik prodding him on with a rifle. That was awful!

And here begins again, shall we say, a Polish odyssey like many others—because the first outcome of any Bolshevik rule was, in principle, a mess of cosmic proportions. My father grasped that it was absolutely impossible to stay in that place because, for one, we would be immediately arrested and carted away, and what would happen to us no one knew, and for another, he understood what a terrible way to govern communism was, and that we could all find ourselves in Siberia. So, in light of that, we decided to return to Warsaw across the green border—the green border is an illegal crossing. We say this because one goes through forests, fields, rivers, well, in a word across the terrain, not a border crossing, but around it. Somewhere, I don't remember now, but sometime at the beginning, they decided—father along with some other Warsovians—that we would all rent a wagon and cross near Zamość. So we went, and a Polish guide showed us the way. Unfortunately, we were caught by Ukrainians. There was a Soviet post on the edge of the forest, and they led us to the Soviet commandant with their rifles drawn. I remember how they surrounded our wagon and yelled, "Ruki wierch!" That means "hands in the air." And they led us to the post. At the military post a miracle took place, if I can say so. At the base there was one officer, who was of Georgian descent. Georgians have always liked Poles. My mother spoke Russian very well. She was a very handsome and elegant lady, and she started to explain that we are returning, that there are other children at home. You know, she lied a little, but it was understandable, and the officer said, "Well, go on, go ahead and go back to Lwów." But that Ukrainian stepped in and said, "What do you mean? We caught these people who want to escape from the happiness of the Soviet Union [this she cannot say without laughing], from the care of the Soviet Union and you let them go!?" The officer said to us, "Well, register at Zamość with the war commandant," and he let us go. We were relatively fortunate, because just a bit earlier, before us, they had caught some unfortunate people who were sent to Zamość to the war commandant under the watch of a convoy of soldiers. As a result that officer (the Georgian) was left alone, so he was not afraid that someone would reveal that he let us go. So, in that sense it was a miracle. At that moment we absolutely did not realize that we had been saved from being transported deep into Russia because all those who were caught were immediately packed into transports and sent deep into Siberia, where they died in masses and so on.

In this excerpt, Pani Sławomira describes the scene with a sense of being part of a larger history, which she calls the Polish odyssey, a new chapter in the nation's journey, in which the country is again partitioned by its old foes, losing independence once more. Though even at the time of their flight her parents sensed the potential for disaster, she is careful to note that it was only later that the family discovered and fully comprehended the danger they were in when captured by the Soviets. Thus the initial sense of relief at escape takes on even greater meaning when the fate of others who were not so fortunate is learned. In her memory the fact that the Georgian is left alone at the outpost is no mere coincidence, or even a result of circumstance, but nothing short of a miracle, ensuring their survival for things yet to come. This could be interpreted as an unstated need to find meaning in the fact that she and her family were saved from deportation and death from exposure and starvation in the gulag. Devoid of an answer as to why they were saved and others were not, suffering, and by extension, life and death themselves become arbitrary, taking on an unbearable insignificance. In this way the Georgian officer's leniency is interpreted as an act of brotherhood, while the coincidence that he is nearly alone at the outpost is transformed into a miracle engineered by the divine, imbuing both survival and life with meaning. Note also that Sławomira is very specific in noting that the nationality of the officer who helps them is not Russian. It is no coincidence that Pani Sławomira recollects and views as salient that the officer who allowed her family to go free without an escort was Georgian. As a member of a nation that, like Poland, suffered tsarist domination yet carried on a struggle for independence prior to being incorporated into the Soviet Union in 1920, Georgia is a nation with which Pani Sławomira and other Poles can identify. In marked contrast she remembers the Ukrainian soldiers as flunkies of the Soviets, blinded to the point of absurdity in their devotion to Soviet ideology and unsympathetic to Sławomira's family, and by extension to Poles. Ukraine was not just the subject of Russian and Soviet imperialism, but as mentioned in the previous chapter, it was the target of the Second Polish Republic's attempts to Polonize minority groups within their borders, which at that time included parts of what is now Ukraine. Later in the war many Warsovians would again encounter Ukrainians during the Warsaw Uprising of 1944, where they made up the Fourteenth Division of the Waffen SS, which took part in Nazi efforts to "pacify" the city (Rybarczyk 2000). Many Warsovians associate the massacres of unarmed civilians that took place in the neighborhood of Wola with this Ukrainian division.

In the following passage Dr. Jan S——relates his near escape from certain death in the German prisoner-of-war camp in Radom. As he explained in the following excerpt from this same interview presented earlier in the chapter, rather than turning it in as ordered, Jan kept a small knife that had been a gift from his grandfather. When faced with the state of the movie theater and the need to make it fit for the soldiers wounded at the battle of Kock, he found the knife useful.

> And I thought to myself, "Well, the hell with it, someone has to do it and it might as well be me, so what should be done?" What had to be done was to tear the boards from the walls, to cut coats into strips in order to bandage those suffering broken bones, you understand. So, I thought to myself, "Damn, I have that knife. I can do this with the knife," and I set to work with it. In general they did not bother us, and they did not approach us, just watched over us. But, sometime—either the second or third day of that work, I was standing before the washbasin, and suddenly someone grabbed me and kicked me in the behind and yelled. I had that knife simply laid out in front of me on the edge of the sink because I was washing up, and he saw me and saw that I had a knife, and we were not permitted to have those, because we had been forced to give them up when they brought us into the camp. That means that I concealed a knife, you understand. Well for that—oh [the death penalty]!
>
> And so now we begin, proszę Pani [if you please], a very emotional experience. He took me to the guard house and there was a table, and around that table sat a few of those guards, there was an older noncommissioned officer who was their superior, and he stands me with my face to the wall, and I stand there with my face to the wall, and on the left is a window from which I can see the entry to the hospital and what is going on in the neighboring street. They are discussing what to do. One says, "Well shoot!! What is there to think about, after all immediately you catch him, immediately you execute him. That's the regulation. So shoot!" And another one explains that as there is a hospital next door, with the red cross hanging, where the wounded are lying—in other words he was trying to get out of it.
>
> They started bargaining among themselves about what to do with me, right? Then, at last the leader said, "Well, do it this way, in order not to do it [execute him] here in the hospital, take him to the camp and shoot him there." Well, I heard it all in German, and I could understand, and my knees went soft. But I looked out the window and a car was coming. An elegant German officer jumped out of the car, and he went to the hospital. Five minutes or so went by, and that officer appeared in the room. It was a captain, surname Zeifert. Later I found that out. And he asked, "What do you want from this man?" The leader told him that mine was a heavy crime: "He had a knife and we've been ordered to shoot," and all that. And the captain said, "Well, yes, but I need him." And that commandant, that guard he had a lower rank, right? He started negotiating, "Sir, you are a captain and he must shoot him,

and if he doesn't shoot him, he'll be fined because, as you know very well, sir, in times of war you either shoot or in the best case send him to the front lines." I would rather have my behind, right?

So, in a word, they did not want to give me up, but Zeifert said that I was necessary to him. And the captain, Zeifert, had a higher rank, and they went to the table and "Aufsteien!" that means "Stand!" And then when I stood, he came and took me by the arm and led me out.

So, what had happened? It happened that when Zeifert arrived at our hospital he immediately met with our commandant [that is the Polish POW's] who organized the German hospital and who was from Poznań; he spoke perfect German and at the same time he belonged to some German organization, and he saved my life because he immediately appealed to that German captain. He told Zeifert that five minutes before they had taken one of his doctors, and why, and that they intended to shoot and—in a word, he defended me. But, unfortunately, they scented him [the Polish officer] out and within a short time they somehow checked his documents, and they came and took him away, and so in all likelihood, he certainly was killed. In any case, one can say that he gave his life for mine. It's only because of him that I am alive.

Proszę Pani, well, what else? That is, you see, one example of cultural unity. He [the German captain] took me by the arm, and he took me down the stairs and he said, "Please do not worry sir, now you are under my command. I could not do anything to harm you." Because he was the doctor who had come in order to take command of the German hospital, that German doctor Ziefert, our lives—if he had come by car five minutes later we would not be talking today.

Well, if you please, contradictory things started to happen, because he had, of course, under his command German soldiers and Polish prisoners of war. . . . They gave us tools, medicine, and their medics who I would say "took care" of us there—guarded us, but they were ordinary people, you know. . . . I didn't speak German too badly. Now it's a lot worse, now I have forgotten a lot, but when you spoke to them, they were ordinary people, and they would drink a little vodka, and they would say, "Where the hell is that leader of ours taking us? Where is this all going to end?"

Jan S—— is clearly ambivalent about the Germans he encountered as a prisoner in the POW camp. Through a dispassionate recitation of the conditions of the general camp and those of the hospital, he condemns the system itself as illegal and inhumane. Yet the individual Germans receive varied treatment in his account. The soldiers who guarded against his escape on a daily basis he recalls as ordinary people, troubled by the war itself, yet continuing to follow orders. Although it was a German soldier who beat him when he found Jan with the knife, and a group of German officers who pushed for his execution, it was also the German captain Zeifert who, acting on the appeal of a Polish officer, intervened to save his life. In contrast to the camp officials, who come off as both brutal and absurd (one after all wants to execute him but feels it would be in poor taste to do so in the vicinity of the hospital), he remembers Zeifert as elegant, compassionate, and swift to action. Zeifert enters the scene at the last moment like a hero on a white horse. If he had arrived a few moments later, Jan feels certain that his fate would have been quite different. Still, it is the unnamed leader of the Polish doctors (who, like Jan, is of German descent) whom Jan credits with saving his life. Jan sees the Polish doctor's disappearance some weeks later as somehow connected to his intervention on Jan's behalf and feels that from that point onward he must redeem the other man's death through his own life. Once again, as in his recollection that it was he who gave the order to cross the road leading to the discovery and arrest of his unit, Jan takes on the burden of responsibility for the death of another. This despite the fact that nothing he said in our interview would indicate that the Polish doctor's arrest was connected with his appeal to Zeifert to save Jan's life. Jan S—— also felt indebted to Zeifert, and after the war he tried to locate him in Germany in an effort to thank him and renew their acquaintance. While he was successful in finding the officer's family, Zeifert himself never returned home and was presumed to have died on the eastern front in the battle of Stalingrad.

In his study of Hiroshima survivors, *Life in Death,* psychohistorian Robert Jay Lifton (1967: 489–90) found that "no survival experience . . . can occur without severe guilt"; what is more, survivors' feelings of responsibility for another's death are often transmuted to feelings of actually having caused the death of that individual. Jan's feelings of responsibility for the ultimate death of the Polish doctor would suggest that he suffered from what Lifton has dubbed "survivor's guilt," something evident, though to a much lesser degree, in the quotation from Sławomira. Because Jan feels indebted to the Polish doctor and to Zeifert for his own life, this guilt takes on the added weight of obligation toward the dead. This is a common theme in narratives in which near misses with capture, arrest, and death are recounted, and it seems to occur in the narratives regardless of the informant's religious views. Few informants interpreted survival under such circumstances as owing merely to chance, perhaps because of the horrible arbitrariness of suffering, of life and death, that such a perspective would imply.

To borrow Lifton's term, Jan "formulates" meaning from this experience through the notion of redemption. The anonymous Polish doctor of German descent died, in Jan's view, because he intervened to save Jan's life; thus Jan feels he must live his life in such a way as to make the lost man's sacrifice one of value. A major part of the process of "formulation," as Lifton describes it, is re-creating a sense of connection with people and places that have been broken or damaged by a rupture in human experience, as well as reestablishing the sense of cohesion and significance of his or her life that would include a transcendence of the trauma (ibid. 367). In his work with Hiroshima survivors, Lifton has found two basic patterns to making meaning out of trauma, "psychological non-resistance" and "special mission." Those who view their experience as being beyond comprehension and description—or as arbitrary, in other words, as a sort of mystery—fall into the former category. Lifton argues that the inability to convey their experience to others may enable "psychological non-resistors" to create a view of the world that allows them to see beyond their immediate suffering and reassert a sense of connection, integrity, and development with their prewar selves (ibid. 369). Those, like Jan and Sławomira, who fall into the pattern of seeing survival as a "special mission" tend to view their survival as the result of a miracle, fate, or luck (ibid. 372–73). In the preceding quotations Pan Jan S—— and Pani Sławomira both credit their survival to a miracle. Like many who fall into this pattern, Jan feels that it is his responsibility to fulfill some deeper purpose, as if in repayment to those whom he feels died in his place (see also ibid. 383, 385).

At the close of this interview, Jan reflected on his own longevity and told me, "In general, throughout my life I have had exceptional luck, you know. Somehow, to a large extent due to providence, it has brought me to this age which is not very nice at all at the moment, but I have survived various oppressions. I must have died a few times, and how I stayed alive borders on the miraculous because how else would I have been saved from these situations?" Here, it seems that simply being alive at the age of 89 is cause for reflection on how it is that he has survived not only the "various oppressions" of the war that have been described here but also those brought by old age. Again, at a time when he was approaching the end of his life, Jan found himself surviving while others did not. Are elderly people who survive many friends and family members plagued by the same sense of survivor's guilt that leads them to question how it is that they are still living when so many of the people they knew and cared about have died? If Jan is any indication, it would seem that, at the very least, such circumstances are cause for wonder and reflection.

Memories of Others

For Jan S—— the distinction between enemy and ally was perhaps ambiguous, not only because he felt that Zeifert was instrumental in saving his life but, as I have discussed in the previous chapter, Jan himself is of German descent. German was Jan's second language, and he asserted throughout the interview that he was not ashamed of that part of his heritage but strived to preserve and respect it as a marker of ethnic identity. Notable in their absence were similar remarks about his Russian heritage. Russian was Jan's first language, the language he spoke both in his childhood home and in his early years at school. On his documents, he told me, he always wrote "Russian" in the space for nationality and "Orthodox" in the blank for religion, as had his father. In fact, until the eve of the war, Jan continued to do so. When compared to his earlier remarks about the Germans he encountered as a prisoner of war, the passage that follows below is quite a contrast, considering that the two armies were at that time allies. The difference in his description of these enemies is rendered all the more intriguing by Pan Jan's cultural and familial ties to both groups.

> Proszę Pani, at the moment when they [the Soviets] came, that means when the fighting died down a bit, it was already clear that almost all of Poland was occupied. Only Polesia there by the Bug River [was not occupied by Germans], which was already People's Poland, so not really Polish terrain then either because the Russians had already invaded. This being the case we held a meeting. Early in the morning we were sitting in the forest with the wagons hidden (and they had piled a lot of dirt on them, the jerks!), and we look and there are tanks coming, and entirely different tanks from those of the Germans because the German tanks had the black cross and were so fast and clean, you know. And this was a gigantic movement and dusty. People were walking in a column, people with long coats, and rifles on their backs, well, in one word that Soviet army gave the impression that here was something wild.

While Jan's recollections of the German soldiers and officers he encountered at the camp are quite varied and in that respect different from those of many of the people I interviewed, his description of the Soviets is not unique. Typically, informants recalled members of the Red Army as wild, unpredictable, given to theft and rape (a topic mentioned and as quickly as possible dropped by my informants), and more often than not inebriated. When we spoke in 1996, it seemed that Jan S—— did not identify with his Russian cultural heritage in the same way as he did with his German ancestry. This may have been the result of his wartime encounters with the Red Army but may also have resulted from the impressions of Soviet-style communism formed during the communist era. Germany occupied Poland for five years during World War II, yet some older Poles view the communist era as 45 years of Soviet occupation. I did not discuss postwar-era politics with Jan S——, but I cannot believe that he would subscribe to this view. Perhaps forgetting for a moment that I am not Polish, he was shocked to learn that I do not speak Russian and told me he thought that the abandonment of required Russian language classes in primary and secondary schools was a big mistake. Jan S——'s daughter, Bogumiła, told me that very late in his career he joined the communist party and later regretted it. She did not elaborate, and I did not feel comfortable asking him about it at what, due to illness followed by his death in 1997, turned out to be our first and only meeting. Perhaps 50 years after the war it was easier for Pan Jan to come to terms with his German heritage than with his Russian roots. What is interesting about these narratives of the enemy is that the representation of the Soviets and the Ukrainians has been shaped by events that took place later in the war or by the communist era.

Conclusions

In this chapter I have sought to demonstrate key differences in the expectations and attitudes with which people at different stages of the life cycle met the outbreak of war. I had expected that some 50 years after these events even those adolescents who initially viewed the war as "something wonderful" or "a great adventure" would bracket these feelings with phrases denoting a change in point of view stemming from experiences of loss later in the war. However, this was not the case in the interviews I collected. Rather than disappearing with the passage of time, these seemingly age-based variances in perspective have persisted in the ways my mentors recollect the invasion of Poland and the early weeks of the war. In the chapters that follow, this trend holds true despite the increasing similarity in the life experiences of adults, adolescents, and children. That the life histories I have collected differ so greatly according to the age of the informant, five decades after the events they describe, raises questions about the ways in which memories of things experienced at different stages of life are recalled decades later. It seems that traumatic events experienced during adolescence may in some way be impervious to the passage of time in that they seem less colored by subsequent events, by changes in political climate, or even personal growth and self-awareness than similar events experienced a few years earlier or a few years later in life. It seems as though the enormous capacity for resilience and idealism that we associate with adolescence has persisted in memories of things experienced while an adolescent.

Yet at the same time my informants who experienced the war as adolescents persisted in their views of the war as a "great adventure," even in the face of later personal loss; they would also tell me of habits and fears of wartime that stayed with them still, explaining them with the comment that "some things cannot be scrubbed away." So, too, did people who experienced the war as children. This indelibility of the memory of trauma experienced in adolescence and childhood seems to be preserved in these memories much as they were originally experienced or at least as first formulated for the retelling.

With the end of the siege of Warsaw on September 27, 1939, and the capitulation of the city, people returned from their wanderings to Warsaw to begin life under the new conditions of the Nazi occupation of the capital. Unable to keep the occupation from encroaching into their private lives, the experiences of children and adolescents became progressively similar to those of adults, while the recollected meanings assigned to these experiences seem to vary along the same lines as the initial expectations for the war that I have described here. How these expectations were impacted by the experience of the occupation and how the experience of occupation shaped responses to the occupation are the questions that drive the next two chapters. In these chapters I will return to the topic of Polish nationalism and the ideology and education that prepared young people for a life of social activism, even heroism enacted. How this ideology shaped the choices they made during the war is a question that threads its way through the entire book, and no less so in the following chapters, where I will explore the relationship between political violence and ideological commitment.

3 Memories of the Occupation

Sławomira: You know, at this moment I'm not able to imagine it, but I think that it was such a big shock for everyone to begin to construct a new life. Most of all I escaped in books. Also, no one realized what the German occupation was going to be like because one could say that we had contact with Germans during World War I, but they weren't these Germans, who were so cruel.

AS SŁAWOMIRA NOTED, MEMORIES of the Great War and Prussian rule in the nineteenth century influenced how many Poles imagined what the German occupation of the Second World War held in store for Poland. Similarly, some sixty years later, my informants found remembering the occupation to be fraught with its own difficulties due to the nature of events that they had experienced. Beginning with the physical presence of a foreign army on the streets of Warsaw, followed by the incursion of Nazi policy into the daily routines of life and the growing sense of fear brought about by arbitrary violence, normalcy quickly became nothing more than a thin veneer that was all too easily torn away. The cohort of people who came of age during the war and experienced the occupation firsthand is known in Poland as the "tragic" or the "lost" generation. The sudden and brutal end of childhood, the loss of family and friends, displacement from their homes, and the destruction of their city marked the lives of this "tragic" generation. The occupation interrupted the lives of the members of this generation at a crucial time in their personal development, limiting and altering their possibilities for the future as well as their ability to fulfill the ambitions of youth. In this chapter I will draw on informants' recollections about how the Nazi occupation impinged upon their lives and on their recollected responses to this disintegration of the familiar. This chapter focuses on memories of daily life in German-occupied Warsaw from October 6, 1939, when the siege of Warsaw ended with the surrender of the city, to August 1, 1944, when the Polish underground launched the General Uprising. Drawing primarily on documentary evidence, I will briefly outline Nazi policy toward various segments of the Polish population, with special attention to the stance toward children as well as the intelligentsia, the social class to which the majority of my informants and their families belonged. I will also discuss Nazi policy vis-à-vis Polish Jews in an effort to illustrate how differential treatment divided Polish society, heightening preexisting cultural differences between members of each group and creating new ones.

Writing this chapter was a three-part process that involved taking apart the interviews I had conducted with each individual informant and extracting information about the occupation, then comparing these narratives with other informants' attitudes and experiences of similar events, and finally imposing a sort of order on their recollections, one that does not occur naturally or spontaneously in the original telling. In remembering the situations described in the pages that follow and imparting those memories to me, my mentors did not stick to a chronological retelling of events. Rather, I would pose a question, and in answering it, my informants would recall and tell me about other incidents that came to mind, incidents that were out of sequence and sometimes seemingly off topic. In writing this chapter, I have tried to preserve the original flow of thought and to make clearer the almost imperceptible connections of one recollected moment of life to another while constructing an overarching narrative that renders these individual memories comprehensible to the reader.

German Policy toward the Polish Populace

One of Hitler's goals in occupying Poland was to turn the country into a German colony, or as he referred to it, living space (*Lebensraum*) for the German Aryans. According to this policy, Poles were to be a source of cheap and ultimately expendable labor (Lukas 1986). As a result German policy toward the populace of Poland during World War II was, as Sławomira mentioned in the opening quotation, much different than in previous eras, when the goal had been to Germanize the Poles through the privileging of German language and culture. Moreover, as Jan Tomasz Gross (1979: 226, 228) points out, it is important to consider that the Nazis made no attempt to legitimize to the Poles their presence in Poland or the treatment of its citizens; thus no alternative to coercion as a method of social control was ever developed. Along with Jews[1] and Gypsies,[2] the Nazis considered the Slav "race" to be *Untermenschen*, or "subhuman" (Lukas 1986: 4), and Poles, as the most degenerate of the Slav race, a base but dangerous enemy of the Reich (Macardle 1951: 65). As one postwar aid worker noted, a common saying among the German troops in Poland was "living room for Germans means death room for Poles" (ibid.). However, while Nazis considered Poles to be a threatening and inferior group, they did not consider them to be parasites or social bacilli. Only Jews and Gypsies were put into this group. The "Polish problem" for the Nazis, then, was how to transform an independent nation, with its own language and cultural traditions as well as a demonstrated history of political, social, and military opposition to foreign rule, into a nation of submissive servants. Such a transformation required not only far more than the occupation of space alone but also a domination that permeated the daily lives of Polish citizens. Thus, rather than systematic extermination, the Nazis planned to enslave the Poles through ethnocide, a policy that required the elimination of the elite, who might impede this process, as well as the reduction of the Polish populace itself through such methods as Germanization, execution, forced labor, and the lowering of the birthrate (Lukas 1986: 5).[3]

Just as German Jews saw their civil rights eroded under Hitler's regime, Poles also saw their legal rights disappear one by one. In contrast to Germany, where this took place incrementally over the course of several years, the Nazis barraged Poles on nearly a daily basis with new decrees that limited their activities. By October 31, 1939, the SS had been given sole jurisdiction over all cases that it viewed as "anti-German" in nature. According to a decree issued on the same day, such acts were broadly defined to include such things as insubordination and failure to report a misdemeanor and were to be considered capital offenses (Bartoszewski 1968: 20). In this way the Germans deemed even small acts of resistance, such as defacing German propaganda posters, as sabotage and punishable by death. This was the fate of a student named Elżbieta Zahorska who was arrested for tearing down a poster depicting Chamberlain against the background of the Warsaw ruins with the caption "England, this is your work." The Nazis executed her by firing squad in November 1939 (ibid. 22). Such executions provided the most compelling evidence that the German occupation of 1939 was operating under rules and assumptions that were entirely different from those of the previous war.

In October of 1939, the first official notifications of executions carried out in Warsaw appeared. Sławomira describes an execution that took place in December of that year:

> The first enormous shock for Warsaw and all its residents, including children, was an execution that took place in Wawer. Imagine, sometime around Christmas, the first wartime Christmas (i.e., of 1939), two German soldiers were in a bar in Wawer; they argued, and one shot the other. But it was just between the two of them: one shot the other. The Germans used this as a pretext. [They said] that they were killed by Poles, and, therefore, they (the Germans) went to Wawer in the night, they surrounded a huge number of houses and from those homes they took all the men. For example, there was an acquaintance of ours, a nice lady who lived there; both her father and her husband were taken. She was left with her little son. All of those people [who were taken] were shot, it was an immediate execution, do you understand? They arrested those men and shot them immediately. This was an enormous shock because it uncovered the face of the German occupation.

The Germans murdered 75 people on the spot in the incident Sławomira describes (ibid. 32). This type of execution became known as "reprisal killing." As was the case in Wawer, a reprisal killing took place following the murder of an individual or group of Germans or someone collaborating with them, and in response, the Germans arrested not (or not only) the person or persons responsible for the murder, but, depending on who had been killed, a number of people at random. The first such reprisal killing in Warsaw took place on November 22, 1939, when all the residents of the tenement house at 9 Nalewki Street were arrested and executed in retaliation for the murder of a Polish policeman in German service who was shot at the same address on November 13 by Pinkus Zylberryng, a young ex-convict just released from prison (ibid. 24). The individuals executed in the first three months of the occupation included both ethnic Poles and Polish Jews with professions such as scholars, artists, army officers, landowners, civil servants, students, artisans, workers, and schoolchildren (ibid. 27). Meted out at random, collective punishment provided further evidence that the Nazis' goals in Poland amounted to a program of radical social change, one intended to create a new sort of human being, with a new morality, and a new set of social relationships (Gross 1979: 211).

Poles experienced arbitrary violence in other ways as well during the first year of the war. The "first great manhunt" in Warsaw took place on May 8, 1940, when, in compliance with Himmler's orders, the SS murdered an estimated 6,000 people (Lukas 1986: 9). According to one underground paper, *Polska Żyje* (*Poland Lives*), German troops rounded up some 6,500 men and boys and drove them "like cattle" to a barracks from whence they shipped them out to concentration camps at night (Bartoszewski

1968: 36). Later that month the Germans launched Operation A-B or *AuBerordentliche Befriedungsaktion,* a policy of "extraordinary pacification" toward those Poles described as political and spiritual leaders. In order to transform Poland into Lebensraum, Poland had first to be stripped of its leaders, the intelligentsia. The Germans executed this plan on several fronts simultaneously: from the physical occupation of Poland to the occupation of the bodies and minds of Poles. Hans Frank, the governor of the General Government, described the objective of the program in this way: "to hasten the liquidation of the seditious politicians, most of whom are in our hands, and other politically suspect persons, and to put an end to traditional Polish lawlessness. I frankly admit that this will cost the lives of some thousands of Poles, mainly from leading members of the Polish intelligentsia. The times enjoin us all as National Socialists to pledge ourselves to ensuring that no resistance develops among the Polish people. . . . Suspected persons are to be liquidated immediately. . . . We cannot saddle the Reich concentration camps with our problems" (quoted in Bartoszewski 1968: 37–38).

Occupation of Place

> Jan R——: Well, I remember my first impressions when we saw German soldiers marching to an orchestra in Śródmieście (i.e., City Center). I was sitting with a certain lady, an engineer who is now deceased, who when she saw those German boots, and that march: their legs thrown so high just like Germans, so stiff; and the orchestra, well, she burst into tears. It was so sad that they . . . [his voice trails off].

When the siege of Warsaw ended on October 5, 1939, many residents of the city were still making their way back to the capital from eastern Poland, where they had fled in the hopes of organizing a force that could counter the German attacks on the city. The journey to Warsaw was a perilous one: refugees fleeing in both directions risked shelling by the Luftwaffe and arrest by both Soviet and German troops. Warsaw, too, damaged by air raids, shelling, and organized burning, was no haven. In fact, the German offensive on Warsaw destroyed 12 percent of Warsaw's buildings and caused the deaths of 60,000 civilians (Bartoszewski 1968: 18). Military losses were even greater. In the siege of Warsaw alone, the Germans killed an estimated 70,000 officers and soldiers, wounded an additional 133,000, and took an estimated 420,000 prisoners (ibid.).

After the surrender German troops occupied the majority of the country, including Warsaw. Immediately the Germans made their presence known through displays like the one Jan R—— described. Though the marching style was familiar, "just like Germans," the troops were still, as Sławomira recalled in the quotation at the beginning of the chapter, an unknown commodity. When I asked my informants about their first impressions of the city after the siege, like Jan R——, what came most readily to people's minds were memories focused on the occupation of place, in other words on the physical presence of German soldiers on the streets of Warsaw. Far from invading political space alone, the Germans took over public space with demonstrations of German military power in many public squares and the posting of propaganda posters around the city. Public spaces were Germanized in an effort to efface the past by giving it a German face. Thus, the occupying forces gave new German names to streets named in honor of famous Poles and destroyed monuments honoring Polish heroes like Tadeusz Kościuszko and Józef Piłsudski or Polish cultural figures like Frederyk Chopin and Adam Mickiewicz. In the case of statues of Copernicus (Mikołaj Kopernik), like the one that stood before the gates of the University of Warsaw, the Germans replaced the plaques with new ones that declared the Polish astronomer to be German (Majdaczyk 1970: 341–42).[4]

Sometimes the German occupation of space was literally an occupation of Polish homes. For example, after Sławomira's family returned from eastern Poland and then back to Warsaw, they discovered the extent to which the German occupation had penetrated into private living spaces and personal allegiances:

> My mother's sister, Aunt Jadzia, and our servant stayed in our apartment [during the evacuation]. Our servant was from the Poznań area, and when the Germans came her German sentiments were suddenly awakened and she signed the *Volksliste. Volksdeutsche* were people who suddenly claimed that they were German, that they had German ancestors, or something like that, and because of that they had certain privileges. She had invited a bunch of [German] soldiers, who simply were living in our house. So it happened that, you know, no matter how good a servant she was before then, it turned out that she was a very indecent human being. For example, she took my mother's jewelry, and she was not at all ashamed of it. When my mother said to her, "Jadwiga, you have taken my jewelry," she said, "Yes, but there is nothing you can do because I can tell them who has been visiting you," and because in my parents' house there were often people from the government, because they had friends and people connected with the government and the resistance, they [the Germans] would have immediately arrested my father. So, of course, my mother didn't say anything, but fortunately not much later

the soldiers were given orders to leave Warsaw, and that Jadwiga said, "Well, I'm going with them." When she left the house the groundskeeper came and said, "I'll go unregister her!" And he went and right away had her taken off the list of residents for our building. It turned out to be a very wise decision because the next day she came back, because she had thought it over and decided she would rather stay here [in Warsaw]. At that Mama said, "Well, Jadwiga you are no longer registered here, and you know one cannot live where one is not registered." You see, one had to be registered, the Germans really enforced those things then, so that if one was not registered at a certain place, one didn't have the right to be there, and so on. So, she left. She went away and, happily, disappeared from our lives. She took the jewelry with her, but that was already just a trifle. I mean she didn't take all the jewelry but the majority of it, but that was such a trifle and, in general, became unimportant.

Jadwiga seems to fulfill some sort of expectation about Polish collaboration with the Germans, a topic mainly discussed in relation to the betrayal of Polish Jews rather than each other. Jadwiga's actions seem to be opportunistic and motivated by a mixture of ethnic identification with the German soldiers (she was from a part of Poland that had been under German rule of one form or another from the time of the partitions until the end of World War I) and a desire to be on the side of those in power, to say nothing of economic gain. It seems worth mentioning that although Jadwiga's request to rejoin Sławomira's family was quite understandably denied, she neither attempted to blackmail herself back into the home, nor did she follow through with her threats to reveal all to the Gestapo. Nonetheless, I do find myself wondering whether this, presumably her first foray into blackmail, was also her last or whether she turned her hand to easier targets. This incident reveals less about Jadwiga and her motives, of course, than it does about the occupation and the way it impinged upon private spaces and private lives that Sławomira, at least, recalls most vividly.

Sławomira also described more mundane ways in which space was controlled and daily life curtailed through German policy in Warsaw:

Life was limited above all by the police hour (the curfew). Sometimes the hour was earlier, sometimes later, depending on the period of the war. If there had been an attack on a German, on [SS Brigadefuehrer Franz Kutschera, for example], the Germans set a very early curfew, and then everyone had to sit at home from a very early hour of the evening until five or seven in the morning. It varied. Those were very changeable things. One burden on everyday life was that, in the name of saving energy, the Germans turned off the lights. For example, one day they turned off the lights on one side of the street and the next day on the other. But that was set; one knew that on Mondays, Wednesdays, and Fridays, even-numbered buildings went without light, and on Tuesdays, Thursdays, and Saturdays the odd numbers did. As a result one spent one's evenings by kerosene or carbide acetylene [*karbidówki*] lamps. Carbide acetylene lamps gave a comparatively bright light, only that they were very unpleasant because of two characteristics that aren't very nice. First, they smelled awful, the smell of acetylene was disgusting, and it also happened that from time to time they would explode, which wasn't very pleasant either. But somehow people got used to all that because human beings have the ability to adjust to many things.

Though the family did indeed adapt to these and other limitations on their activities in and out of their homes, Sławomira's apartment was not free of German occupants for long. Situated in the Warsaw neighborhood of Mokotów, near Belvedere Palace (the home of Poland's presidents during the interwar era), Łazienki Park, and Polish Parliament, their apartment was in a desirable location, one that soon became a neighborhood designated for Germans only.

In the meantime, we were thrown out of the German neighborhood. We lived on Chopin Street. The Germans created a German neighborhood there because that was a very beautiful part of Warsaw. As a result, that neighborhood was set aside for Germans. And on Chopin Street there was a little palace where Frank, the Governor of the General Government slept when he came from Kraków to Warsaw. Well, first, they took part of the apartment for quarters. They moved a German officer in with us. He was from some place in East Prussia, but I must say that he behaved very decently. This was a man from the Wehrmacht, a captain from the Wehrmacht and he was very—he was polite, pleasant and, after all, we even made use of his presence quite a bit because he had a radio. He had a key to the house, but when we listened to the radio we bolted the door and locked it with the chain so that he couldn't come in unexpectedly. Then we could listen to the radio, one could listen to London then, so that was wonderful. He didn't really bother us. But at some point some Volksdeutsche turned up; they saw the apartment—it was a very nice apartment—and decided that they would take it. Even the German officer—he was named Scheberber—he even went to some German commandant to say that he wanted to stay, that he lived well there, and to ask them to allow us all to stay, but they told him that he would be given other quarters and that the ones who suddenly [appeared and asked for the apartment, would be given it]—Volksdeutsche, those were people who decided suddenly that they were Germans. They had a German grandfather, grandmother, or uncle, and suddenly they felt that they were Germans, and they had certain privileges from that. So, they simply threw us out of that apartment. The furniture was put into storage, and we moved to our cousin's on Inflancka Street, here near Żoliborz. She [the cousin] had gone somewhere outside of Warsaw because she had found some sort of work, and so we moved to her tiny apartment. Well, at least we had someplace to go to live.

In creating the German neighborhood in Mokotów, the Nazis displaced Polish (and I use the adjective in its pluralistic sense) families, giving their homes to German officers, German businessmen, and Nazi officials, as well as to Poles of German heritage who, like Jadwiga, had taken an oath of loyalty to the Reich. The creation of the German neighborhood was one of many in which the occupation of space was used to transform social place and by extension society, in an effort to implement Nazi racial ideology.

In Warsaw the most striking example of the transformation of place as a means of social engineering was, of course, the creation of the Warsaw Ghetto in what was then the predominantly Jewish neighborhood of Muranów. The Germans introduced repressive laws targeting Polish Jews as a group distinct from ethnic Poles prior to the creation of the ghetto. As I have discussed previously, the issue of whether Polish Jews were Polish was a matter of ongoing debate within Polish society at the time. Nazi policy toward the Jews of Poland, however, was quite clear on the issue: Jews and Poles were two different races presenting different threats to the Reich and were thus to be dealt with differently. As Sławomira told me:

> Everything changed, because father recollected how it had been before, during the time of the first war, and here was a second war but everything was different. The persecution of Jews had begun. Jews were required to wear an armband with a Star of David. You know, they began to create the ghetto. At first it was open, not closed, but still a Jewish quarter. My parents had friends [*przyjaciół*] who were Jews, and they were friendly with many others, so of course there were, shall we say, attempts. After all, at the beginning the Jews themselves were not aware that going to the ghetto was the beginning of the end. And many people would tell them, "Wait, don't go to the ghetto at all," but they decided [to go] because they were simply afraid of what would happen if they didn't follow [the order].

As Sławomira's narrative illustrates, long before they attempted a physical segregation of Polish Jews from ethnic Poles, the Nazis made distinctions that psychologically distanced one group from the other. In November 1939 the Germans introduced in Warsaw the armbands mentioned by Sławomira. Immediately these armbands became the most well-known means by which Jews throughout Europe were distinguished from their fellow citizens. Another way of dividing the population was to foment fear. For example, before the ghetto appeared in the cityscape as an area walled off from the rest of the city, notices posted at the entrances of streets that would later demarcate its boundaries warned passersby that the neighborhood was infected with typhus,[5] thus creating fear of contagion (Szpilman 1999: 58). In early 1940 the Germans required Polish Jews to register with the Jewish Council (*Judenrat*) for transportation to so-called work camps, and in the fall of 1940 they forced Jews to move to the ghetto. In his memoir, *The Pianist*, Władysław Szpilman, a onetime resident of the Warsaw Ghetto, wrote about how the establishment of the ghetto was presented to the wider public by German authorities. Szpilman sardonically describes how, according to a report in the sole Polish-language German daily,

> not only were Jews social parasites, they also spread infection. They were not, said the report, to be shut up in a ghetto; even the word ghetto was not to be used. The Germans were too cultured and magnanimous a race, said the newspaper, to confine even parasites like the Jews to ghettos, a medieval remnant unworthy of the new order in Europe. Instead there was to be a new quarter of the city where only Jews lived, where they would enjoy total freedom, and where they could continue to practice their racial customs and culture. Purely for hygienic reasons, this quarter was to be surrounded by a wall so that typhus and other Jewish diseases could not spread to other parts of the city. (Ibid. 58–59)

While the majority of Muranów residents before the war were Jewish, this is not to say that all the Jews of Warsaw lived in Muranów. On the contrary, the Germans forced thousands of people from other Warsaw neighborhoods, as well as from towns and villages surrounding Warsaw into the ghetto, and later they crowded Jews from other occupied countries into it as well. Not all of those who were required by Nazi law to live in the ghetto saw themselves as Jewish, as Sławomira explained to me:

> **Sławomira:** At the same time, of course, the criteria were awful, because it was enough to have one grandparent on the mother's side or father's side who was Jewish or of Jewish descent to be classified as a Jew. So, well, you know, terrible things, because that was a racist law, right?

ELT: Was it a shock to you or your family that the Germans were so anti-Semitic?

Sławomira: We somehow knew about it because before the war we got news from Germany, but that it [anti-Semitism] took that form, of course, it was a shock. A person cannot comprehend. But you know, in general, reality was terrible for them and to us in equal measure. Those who were in the worst situation were those who were completely Polonized. It absolutely did not occur to them that they should feel Jewish, and here all of a sudden the Germans labeled them as Jews, and they simply could not defend themselves. Also, I think that if a person is brought up in a law-abiding way, one follows certain regulations because it does not enter one's head that one should not, and only later with time one learns that one cannot do it because of the threat of certain sanctions.

On November 15, 1940, the Germans sealed the ghetto. As Szpilman recalls, "Half a million people had to find somewhere to lay their heads in an already over-populated part of the city, which scarcely had room for more than a hundred thousand" (Szpilman 1999: 59). Sławomira, who was then living with her family in her cousin's apartment on Inflancka Street, one of the streets that overlooked the ghetto, recalled her parents' concern for their Jewish friends on the other side of the wall:

So, when the Jews were shut up in the ghetto, the ghetto was already closed, of course sometimes one had success in crossing to the other side. Among other things, I haven't forgotten that a friend of my parents came to us, Mr. Borman. At that time his wife and his mother-in-law were in the ghetto. He came in order to make arrangements [for his family to go into hiding], and my parents proposed to arrange for him a hiding place on the Aryan side, but his wife's mother said that she wouldn't move, and they stayed in the ghetto and were lost [killed]. There were a lot of incidents like that, a lot of similar incidents.

If they did not die first from starvation, exposure, disease, or execution, the fate of the majority of people who, in compliance with German orders, registered as Jews with the Judenrat and moved to the ghetto in 1939 was deportation to the extermination camp at Treblinka, where they died in the gas chambers within hours of arrival. Armed with the knowledge of their ultimate fate, many people now question why residents of the Warsaw Ghetto obeyed, why only a few resisted, and why resistance came so late. Often this is explained in terms of fear of the consequences of disobedience or out of respect for authorities. In other words, this is explained as a sort of occupation of the mind, an explanation that Sławomira put forth when she said, "I think that if a person is brought up in a law-abiding way, one follows certain regulations, because it does not enter one's head that one should not, and only later, with time, one learns that one cannot do it because of the threat of certain sanctions." However, in the quotation above, she recalled that Mr. Borman stayed in the ghetto, not out of some (misplaced) sense of trust in the Nazis but out of deference to his elderly mother-in-law and, it would seem, an understandable unwillingness to divide the family by leaving her behind.

Sławomira recalls the Warsaw Ghetto through her parents' largely unsuccessful attempts to persuade friends not to go or to arrange for them hiding places on the outside. Her knowledge is limited by what her parents knew from their friends, by what they were willing to say in the presence of their younger daughter, and by what she was able to glean from meetings such as the one with Pan Borman. Because they were ethnic Poles and non-Jews, the Germans did not force any of my informants to move to the ghetto. However, as residents of Warsaw in general—and of Żoliborz, which borders on Muranów, in particular—the ghetto was part of their wartime experiences and their recollections, too. For ethnic Poles living in the shadow of the ghetto's walls, the ghetto represented more than an occupation of space but also an occupation of the imagination as well (see Nałkowska 2000). Like most people her age, indeed, like most ethnic Poles, Sławomira's knowledge of what went on there is that of an outsider; while hearing noises from the other side, the fate of those within was left to the imagination. The influence this had over people's perceptions and experiences, or at least over their memory of those perceptions and experiences, of the occupation is perhaps best illustrated by this exchange between Irmina and myself.

> **ELT:** Could you tell me how your everyday life changed during the occupation?
> **Irmina [indignantly]:** Did everyday life change? Well, of course it did! Of course it changed, if only due to the state of constant threat. And after all, Warsaw was under occupation, and with the ghetto a terrible thing was created. We were conscious that terrible things were happening there, that people were locked behind walls. In general, no one knew what was going to happen to them; we didn't know. But just the fact that people had to live behind walls was something so horribly depressing that it was clear that something awful was going to happen there.

Irmina is, I believe, the only person I interviewed who recollected the ghetto when asked about how *her* daily life had changed. Many of my informants spoke of the ghetto when they recalled traveling from Żoliborz to the center of the city, a route that took them past and sometimes through the ghetto. As Irmina recalls,

> During the occupation the tram ran across the viaduct, turned on Muranowska, to Krasiński Place. I remember exactly that when it passed that terrain, which the Germans had closed off with high walls—those walls were three meters high, and behind those walls was the Jewish neighborhood [i.e., the Warsaw Ghetto]. The tram went crazily fast, because as long as it—sometimes it stopped—and sometimes people would jump on, and save themselves [by riding out of the ghetto]. One time the tram came and I remember that some people jumped on and were saved. I saw that they were transporting children. Only I knew from my parents that I was not supposed to watch, that I was not to let it be understood that the person who got on the tram was in any way out of the ordinary. In general, one absolutely had to pretend that one saw nothing, that one knew nothing.

Janina K——was in no doubt about the treatment of Jews in the ghetto. She recalled the following incident:

> You went around the walled ghetto, and from time to time in the wall at the bottom, there was a small crack, a place where a brick or two was missing so that water could flow to the sewer on the non-Jewish side, out of the ghetto. One went by tram. So, I was standing at the back, and I saw through that opening two slight, very thin, and correspondingly dirty legs of a child. A German saw the same, he ran, pulled the child out, [he was] this small [she makes a gesture indicating the child's height at a little over two feet]. Well, maybe he was three years old. He [the German] grabbed him by the legs, and ripped [the child apart]. That is how they [Jews] were treated.

Pan Olgierd Z—— came by his knowledge of the ghetto through firsthand experience. Like all young people he was required to work in order to have legal identity papers, which were crucial, though not a guarantee, to avoid deportation to labor or concentration camps. As he planned to study medicine after graduating from secondary school, he found work in a pharmacy, mixing medicines. In this excerpt from an interview I conducted with him, he recounts some of his memories from his work in the ghetto.

> **Olgierd:** The pharmacy was called Pharmacy under the Star, on the corner of Twarda and Szenda.[6] Now there is only an empty square there, the house

[where the pharmacy was located] no longer exists. It was burned. It was a Jewish pharmacy, because in the beginning the Germans took all the pharmacies from the Jews and reassigned them to Poles; that means the Polish administration took over pharmacies, clinics for employees.

ELT: The pharmacy was in the Jewish Ghetto?

Olgierd: The pharmacy where I worked at one moment was in the Little Ghetto, because before then it wasn't. I went to work as usual, and one day I remember that exactly around the pharmacy in the middle of the night the Germans had built a wall, right, and so the pharmacy was in the ghetto. At the beginning we had passes. Working in the pharmacy we received passes, we [were permitted] to come to work because we had them.

Both the Little Ghetto and the Big Ghetto were walled off from the rest of the city, but Jews and German soldiers could travel from one part of the ghetto to another by crossing a pedestrian bridge over Chłodna Street. The Little Ghetto was the home of many Jewish intellectuals and artists who had lived in the neighborhood prior to the war and so had, until that point, continued to reside in their own homes. In contrast the terrain covered by the Big Ghetto had been a staunchly working-class neighborhood for some time. Olgierd continues:

We immediately began to actively help the Jews who were there because we carried correspondence, letters [to and from the ghetto] because they weren't allowed to write anything—and even if they had been, everything was censored, and we also carried packages if someone asked for something. And, of course, we did it for free, none of us thought of compensation, because it was just the normal humane thing to do. Well, I really experienced that time strongly, because as a young boy working as a courier, who prepared medicines in the pharmacy, I had contact just with those who were poor, thrown out on the streets, on Twarda and Szenda streets. I saw that small children were lying [in the streets] hungry. It was a terrible scene, and no one did anything about it. The Germans were contemptuous. We had some possibilities [to help], but at the same time they were limited possibilities, but if somebody needed something there—I have a photo that I'll show you later, because one day an order came that we were to give the pharmacy back to the Jewish owner because they lived in a house just opposite the pharmacy. That house where the owners lived still exists. They [the Germans] ordered us to give back our passes to the ghetto, and we weren't allowed to go there any more.

Well, not much later that so-called Little Ghetto was liquidated by the Germans, and everyone was thrown into the Big Ghetto. Of course, the pharmacy was destroyed later, during the time of the Ghetto Uprising when everything else was. My memory [of the ghetto] has faded because that's been so many years, but nonetheless I remember the worst—[interrupting himself] I remember this actor who I often met on the street there just outside of the pharmacy. Zynicz. He was this prewar actor, Zynicz, a very good actor. He always went on walks. Later I saw there people who came on transports from Belgium and France—Jews who truly thought they were going on some sort of vacation. At that time they were sent temporarily to the ghetto, and then they sent them to camps: the ladies were elegantly dressed in furs. You could see they wore jewelry. All, of course, that was all. They were all murdered.

So, yes, for such a young boy as me that was an enormous thing to live through, watching those people dying in agony on the streets. And there was nothing to be done, right—except what I had in the pharmacy. Of course, one had to watch out because if the Germans saw that something was helpful, they took it away, so one had to be very, very careful. But fortunately, somehow, I was never searched, never. I had a bag that was not very large, and I always had letters, and I could bring things. Of course, [what] the Germans [did] with those Jews who worked there—I don't know. Because after that, after the Ghetto Uprising, I never met them again.

The conditions of his work in the ghetto and later his inability to gain entrance limited Olgierd's opportunities to help Jews. In this passage Olgierd also referred to the so-called resettlement of the Little Ghetto. On Wednesday, July 26, 1942, the Germans used Ukrainian troops to clear nursing homes, veterans' homes, and overnight shelters where displaced Jews from shtetl towns surrounding Warsaw, from Germany, Czechoslovakia, Romania, and Hungary, had taken up residence upon their arrival at the Warsaw Ghetto.[7]

The liquidation of the Little Ghetto had a direct effect on Pani Sławomira and her family as she explains,

> You know the ghetto changed. First it was comparatively large in area. One [part] was called the Little Ghetto and [the other] the Big Ghetto, which were connected to each other by a bridge. Later the Germans ordered all the Jews to move from the Little Ghetto to the Big Ghetto, and there [in the Little Ghetto] they cleared [evacuated] those houses; that means that those houses became—well, those houses were empty. Among other things they began to give apartments in those houses [in what had been the Little Ghetto] to those who had been thrown out of the German neighborhood, for example. Among others, we were given one of these apartments. That was terrible, you know? When we entered that apartment, it was horrible because it was such

a terrible image! It was maddeningly sad. In general that we had something like that, but we didn't have a[n alternative] place in which to find shelter [because] that cousin was returning, and we didn't have anywhere else to go.

So, it was like this: a Mezuzah still hung by the door, that sacred scroll from the Torah. Throughout the entire apartment there were stacks of photographs scattered on the floor and an enormous amount of feathers, because the Germans looked for treasures there, so they had shaken everything out; they tore apart the down comforters and the pillows, and everything was covered with those feathers and those photographs. Well, those photographs were gathered up and put into a box [with the thought that] well maybe someone, someday, will look for them, and they were packed away and carried to the basement to keep them safe. Well, of course, during the Uprising [of 1944] it was all burned anyway, so that settled that. Surely those people also [had perished] earlier.

The transformation of place resulted in the displacement of residents from their homes in an effort to create ethnically segregated "sectors" of the city and, more important, to isolate those classified as Polish Jews from the rest of Polish society. Closing the ghetto marked not only an occupation of space for those who witnessed it, to say nothing of those who experienced life within its walls, but also an encroachment on the imagination. Just as the condition of the apartment insinuated the violence done to its Jewish occupants, the mere knowledge that a place like the ghetto existed, that people were living locked behind walls, as Irmina recollected, created fear for those living in the ghetto and also for themselves because if the Nazis were capable of creating a place like the ghetto, what did they have in store for the rest of Polish society? The existence of the ghetto penetrated categories of thought as well. As the implementation of a racial policy that categorized Polish Jews as something other than ethnic Poles, it imposed an answer in brick and mortar to preexisting but unresolved debates about who could claim Polish identity.

The occupation of place was one of the most dramatic outward manifestations of the Nazi occupation of the capital, and it is an aspect of the occupation that in many ways remains with the city to this day. In the late 1990s, traveling from Żoliborz toward City Center, one rode the tram lines over the viaduct, with the reconstructed Old Town on the left and Muranów, with its dreary Stalinist-era apartment blocks on the right. There, in between various housing complexes, is an open expanse of space that is empty save for Nathan Rapaport's monument to the Warsaw Ghetto fighters and a few memorial stones marking significant sites in the ghetto, as well as the path to the *Umschlagplatz,* where residents of the ghetto were forced into cattle cars bound for Treblinka. I remember standing in front of the monument in March of 1989 in the rain, trying to formulate some sort of opinion about the memorial. The empty space seemed effective, as if speaking to an irreplaceable loss, which seemed appropriate but problematic too, given that the memorial revealed so little about the nature of that culture and its people, except the way in which they were destroyed.

Occupation of the Body

Though its legacy is the most visibly enduring in the present-day cityscape, the transformation of public space was far from being the sole way in which the Nazis set about dominating the residents of Warsaw. Under the rubric of the occupation of space, I have discussed the ways in which private space, freedom of movement, and comfort were adversely impacted by the occupation, but the Nazi's occupation of the physical bodies of Poles also included attempts to control food and the consumption of alcohol, sex, and reproduction in an attempt to cull the populace and limit population growth. Hitler himself viewed the reduction of the birthrate of Slavs, in general, as a necessary step in transforming Poland into Lebensraum and the Poles into slaves. He suggested that "by doing this gradually and without bloodshed, we demonstrate our humanity" (Hermann 1939, cited in Macardle 1951: 65). In Poland these so-called nonviolent means ranged from systematic malnutrition to overt attempts to discourage reproduction. In the effort to starve the city into submission and decrease the population, the Germans issued ration cards for food, as Pani Sławomira describes:

> There wasn't anything to buy food with, everything had become so expensive. The Germans introduced [ration] cards. With the cards, the food rations were very small because they were—at this moment I can't tell you, but you can find it somewhere in the literature, right? In any case it was not a great deal of black, disgusting bread; marmalade made from beets—Well, you know, everything was gone. There wasn't any tea, there wasn't any coffee. At home one drank this sort of tea made from dried apple peels that were boiled and what remained was a something that was supposed to imitate tea. There was no sugar, only saccharine—you know, suddenly life changed completely.

In June 1941 a Warsaw worker earned 120–300 złoty a month, yet it cost 1,568 złoty to feed a family of four (Hanson 1982: 22–23, cited in Lukas 1986: 30). Pan Stefan W——, who worked in the underground throughout the occupation recalls:

Ahhhh, my ex-wife [but not yet ex in 1939] worked before the war in the Ujazdowski Military Institute's Hospital [*Wojskowej Instytucji Szpitalu Ujazdowskich*]. During the occupation she worked there . . . it was a military hospital before the war and after the war, too, for prisoners of war, for Germans, and so on and so forth. Well, the salaries there were very small. She made forty złoty a month and a bottle of vodka, I'm just giving an example, cost around a hundred złoty—and that wasn't expensive either, but that's all the Germans paid. They gave miserable rations: six dekagrams of sugar, some marmalade, some sort of margarine, and once a month a half-liter [of vodka], because the Germans nourished Poles on vodka, half a liter of vodka. And that's how it was until the uprising broke out.

The difference between being classified as social parasites, as were the Jews, as opposed to simply subhuman, as were the Slavs, becomes clear when one examines the specifics of Nazi rations for these groups within occupied Poland. In 1941 the average daily food allotment to Warsovians was 669 calories to Poles and 184 to Jews, while Germans received an allotment of 2,613 calories (Duraczyński 1974: 69). Next to Jews, Poles had one of the lowest food rations in German-occupied countries, with a monthly 4,300 grams of bread rationed to Poles and 9,000 to Germans; 400 grams of flour, barley, and macaroni to Poles and 2,000 to Germans; and one egg to Poles and twelve to Germans (Hanson 1982: 28, cited in Lukas 1986: 30). These figures are powerful, but they say nothing about the difference in the quality and nutritional value of the food the different groups received. For example, according to several of my informants, bread for non-Germans was baked with little flour and much sawdust. By limiting access to food, the Germans conducted an occupation of the body, yet people found a number of ways to supplement their meager rations. As Sławomira recalled:

In addition, the Germans introduced the death penalty for everything, right? For buying white rolls, for—well, you know, for everything. There was no meat, there was no coal—you understand, life ceased to exist in its old form. At the same time, it happened that people were enormously enterprising and had a tremendous will to live and an enormous ability to adjust to these conditions because they started to create. It was simply that different groups of people, in wanting to survive themselves, made others' survival possible. One of these very typical characters was the so-called smuggler. That is someone who smuggled food from the village to Warsaw. He made money on that, but at the same time put himself at risk. If he were caught, then, depending on the humor of the guards, they would beat him, or take all of his goods, or kill him on the spot. We could say it was a lottery.

But listen, those smugglers saved the city from hunger! Also, sometimes it was funny, and they immediately appeared in Warsaw's songs. All those old ladies who rode [to Warsaw] wrapped in lard, sausages, and the like— fat like I don't know what, because they couldn't smuggle it any other way. The Germans allowed milk, so they had canisters of milk on their backs and between the canisters they also had different things. So, in some sense [normal life] was rebuilt.

At the same time it happened that my mother earned money then. One could say that the Germans oppressed doctors relatively less. For example, Mama received *spirytus* [medical grade, 90-proof alcohol] for medicinal purposes. After all, the Germans very consciously encouraged the consumption of alcohol [*rozpijali*], so they gave very large rations of 90-proof alcohol.

In our house in Gołgów, outside of Warsaw, there was also help because first we spent the summer there, and there was an excellent pool there, and our lessons, and our harvest, and so on, and secondly, in the garden flowers grew, potatoes, there were lots of fruit trees, so there was fruit. So, our house outside of Warsaw enhanced our possibilities for food. We could bring potatoes, fruit, preserves, and that always gave our normal diet more variety.

Of course, the price of meat and other contraband smuggled into Warsaw was such that it may well have been cost prohibitive for people of lesser means than Sławomira's family. Access to a country home and the goods available there was also limited by socioeconomic class—and, of course, after the creation of the ghetto, it was virtually impossible for the Jews who resided inside its walls to gain access to either source of additional food. Yet, for those who could afford it, this constituted a means of resisting hunger and the occupation of their bodies that it represented.

By severely limiting the amount, type, and quality of food that Poles ate, the Germans hoped to starve the populace into submission through hunger. But hunger was more than an end in and of itself; it was also an attempt to limit population growth. Such efforts did not stop at the dinner table but extended into the bedroom as well. A German decree issued on October 10, 1941, limited legal marriages between Poles exclusively to those between men over 28 years of age and women over 25 and required a special license (Macardle 1951: 65). The decree also declared that, married or not, if a woman under the age of 25 gave birth the child was to be taken away from her (ibid.). Following the policy of the Racial Political Office, Himmler issued an order on May 15, 1940, for the removal of Polish children to Germany and for the annual "sifting" of children between the ages of six and ten into those who were deemed racially valuable and nonvaluable (ibid. 75). By February of 1942, the abduction of small children had begun under the auspices of the so-called *Lebensborn* program, under which the SS abducted an estimated 20,000 children from Poland and, after determining whether the children were racially worthy, sent them to orphanages in the Reich for reeducation and subsequent adoption by German families (Hrabar 1981: 206).[8] Thus, by systematically removing the youngest members of Polish society from their homes, the Germans were able to curtail social and cultural reproduction.

It is hard to imagine a discussion of the occupation of the body without a discussion of rape. The incidence of systematic rape, as a weapon of war, is an area that has received little attention with regard to World War II. My own research does little toward illuminating the issue. Early on, I decided against asking my informants about rape, primarily because I felt that asking any given individual about it in relation to their own experience would be too much to ask. As a result there are only a few references to rape in the narratives I have collected. Without exception, in these cases rape is discussed as something that happened to someone other than the speaker, and it is mentioned almost in passing, in the telling of another overarching event. In other words, talking about the rape itself was not the point of the narrative. Moreover, these accounts of rapes witnessed are not situated during the occupation but rather after the capitulation of the Home Army in October 1944, during the evacuation of the city. They seem to reflect not a systematic policy of rape so much as opportunism on the level of individual or small groups of German soldiers. Yet, a 1942 Save the Children Fund's publication entitled *Children in Bondage* describes a camp in the town of Helenowo near Łódz where German soldiers repeatedly raped Polish girls with the intent of impregnating them. If the girls did become pregnant, they were sent to Germany to give birth, after which the children, if found fit, were given to German families (Save the Children Report, cited in Macardle 1951: 70). Carole Nagengast reminds us that the use of rape as a method of torture "both creates and punishes Otherness" (Nagengast 1994: 121). In the case of Helenowo, the abducted girls were not being raped in an effort to extract information from them or from family members, nor was Poland a society where male honor was associated primarily with the virginity or sexual purity of the women of their communities. In this case Otherness appears as a by-product of an effort intended to ensure that the reproduction of the Nazi Self would not be outstripped by that of the Slav Other.

Virtually all of my informants mentioned some sort of physical privation in their recollections of how the occupation altered everyday life, and among these hunger and cold figure the most prominently, followed by the curfew, which curtailed their ability to move about the city. Of course, controlling a people's ability to move freely, to provide food for their families, to marry and have children, imposes more than a burden on the physical body; it is also a powerful tool in the occupation of the mind and spirit.

Occupation of the Mind

In an effort to transform Poland into, to quote Hans Frank, "an intellectual desert" (quoted in Lukas 1986: 10), the Germans set out on a campaign to Germanize, destroy, or erase from memory Polish cultural heritage. Thus, the Germans banned the works of fifteen hundred Polish authors, as well as political or ideological works, and books in English and French (Macardle 1951: 77). Similarly, they banned compositions by Chopin, Szymanowski, and other Polish composers as well as Polish folk music and the works of Polish playwrights from public performance. Indeed, throughout the occupation Germans barred Poles from publishing books, plays, and music (ibid.). Those publications that the Germans sold in Polish were either entirely propagandistic or were, as aptly summed up by one scholar, "of a trivial and erotic type" (ibid).

Germans confiscated Polish art collections, both public and private, and sent them to Germany on the grounds that there was no such thing as Polish art. If one believes Hans Frank, then, as of 1942, very few works of art were left in Poland, as at that time he bragged that 90 percent of Polish collections in the General Government had already been sent to Germany (Lukas 1986: 11). Eager to acquire historical documents that established German claims to Polish territory or that demonstrated German cultural influences in Polish society, the Germans also plundered Polish archival collections, most of which were housed in Warsaw (ibid. 10–11). When the records proved to be of little use for these purposes, as was frequently the case, the Germans often discarded or destroyed them. According to one account, all the Polish archives combined lost 92 percent of their collections: the Archives of the Age of Enlightenment as well as those of the Treasury and Municipal Archives were completely destroyed, while the Archives of Recent Records lost 97 percent of its collection, the Central Archives of Earlier Records 90 percent, and the Archives of Earlier Records 80 percent. Commenting on these losses one archivist stated, "No Tartar invasion of the Middle Ages had resulted in such devastation" (Stebelski 1964: 5–34).

The Germans treated research laboratories similarly, as Pan Olgierd Z——recalled:

I went to the school of Docent Jan Zaorski, which was located on the terrain of the University of Warsaw. It was a private school, and unofficially it offered the first, second, and third year of medical school. One day the Germans threw us out of there. So we had to take a few hours to move the school. I remember the moment when we had to carry all the teaching aids and research equipment that we were able to the apartment of Professor Przewęski from the physiological chemistry department who lived opposite the university, and there at his place in one room we packed it all, because it was all about having the equipment.

The Germans' attempts to occupy the minds of Poles by erasing evidence of their nation's history and artistic, cultural, and scholarly achievements was not limited solely to the destruction of material culture. On the contrary, efforts to recast Poland as an intellectual wasteland began with an assault against the intelligentsia itself. On November 6, 1939, under an anti-Polish directive, the SS arrested nearly 200 professors and fellows of Jagiellonian University and the Polytechnic in Kraków and sent them to a concentration camp at Sachsenhausen, where many of them died before their release. Thus, Nazi violence against the Polish intelligentsia, a group that included people from a variety of ethnic backgrounds, predates Nazi actions targeted specifically at Polish Jews. Far from being an aberrant action, the arrest of the Jagiellonian faculty was part of a systematic campaign to eliminate the Polish elite. As Hans Frank told his officers, "The Fuhrer told me: 'What we have now recognized in Poland to be the elite must be liquidated; we must watch out for the seeds that begin to sprout again, so as to stamp them out again in good time'" (Poliakov 1979: 269). The Nazis' definition of intelligentsia encompassed "Polish priests, teachers (including university lecturers), doctors, dentists, veterinary surgeons, officers, executives, businessmen, landowners, writers, journalists, plus all persons who have received a higher or secondary education" (Nuremberg Document No. 2325, "Die Frage der Behandlung der Bevolkerung der ehemaligen polnischen Gebiete nach rassenpolitischen Gesichtspunkten," Dr. E. Wetzel and Dr. G. Hecht in their minutes of November 25, 1939, cited in Bartoszewski 1968: 16). In this way, all but two of the people with whom I worked were considered by the Nazis to be members of the intelligentsia on the basis of their own occupations or level of education, or their parents' professions and levels of education, as well as their own academic and professional aspirations.

A week after the arrest of the professors and fellows in Kraków, the remainder of Polish universities and institutions of higher learning and scholarly societies, along with secondary schools (*liceum*) and middle schools (*gimnazjum*), were also closed to ensure that the next generation of Poles would grow up without the benefit of an education. From a chronological point of view, the people with whom I worked experienced the repression of the intelligentsia as a select group to which they belonged before they witnessed the repression of their Jewish neighbors. However, chronology is not always the guiding principle of recollection, nor is it the organizational principle of this chapter. Sometimes it is the emotional intensity that colors an event that brings a particular memory to the forefront of our thoughts. Irmina B——, for example, listed the creation of the Warsaw Ghetto and other actions against the Jews first among those things that impacted her daily life, although these events could not have been the first things she experienced. For most of the people with whom I worked, however, the closing of Polish schools was one of the first things they told me about when our conversations turned toward the topic of the occupation.

Pani Eugenia, a teacher before, during, and after the war at a public secondary school for girls in Żoliborz, recalls in the passage beleow the school closures:

> I must still tell you that our school during the siege of Warsaw, which was—Do you know the history? The siege of Warsaw was in 1939 when the Germans were conquering Warsaw. Then on the 13th of September, our school was bombarded. An air raid cut it in half from the top floor to the basement. But I must say the officers' cooperative, whose building it was, rebuilt it exceptionally quickly so that already in the middle of November—no, actually at the beginning of November, the fourth, we could begin lessons. From the 13th of September to the 4th of November, it was completely rebuilt. We started lessons in a normal school just like before the war. The children were so glad. Those who returned from vacation were very happy. Proszę Pani, on the 16th of November they [the Germans] closed our schools. They closed our schools so we had only twelve days of lessons. They closed the schools because, they said, that there was typhus and that they had to close them. But it was all in order that the general education schools would not exist, so that secondary schools would not exist, so one would feel that one was under German rule.

In occupied Poland children attended school from the first through the seventh grade but with a drastically limited curriculum, as the Germans banned core subjects such as Polish literature and language, Polish history, and foreign languages, with the exception of German.[9] Not only was it forbidden to teach Polish literature and history, but textbooks for these subjects were confiscated. Gimnazjums, which most closely resemble junior high schools in the U.S. system, were truncated to two years and turned into vocational schools for sixth and seventh graders, where students were to be taught how to measure and weigh things, to sew, to cook, and to speak a bit of German. In other words, the Germans intended these schools to prepare Polish children for low-skill jobs in the service of Germans. Yet, even in primary schools and gimnazjums, teachers resisted the Nazi decrees by creating false walls in their classrooms to hide tiny rooms in which children in small groups would study forbidden subjects. In the passage that follows, Sławomira recalls the establishment of the clandestine system of education:

> That went through very easily, because, I think among other things, that in Poland there was in general an enormous tradition of underground schools—if one can express it that way, because during the time of the Russian [partition] or the time of the German [partition], Poles always tried to educate in [secret] schools, or additional lessons, so that [underground schools during the occupation] began to function very quickly, and very well. Actually, in some senses those schools were really at a high level because, for example, university professors who had lost their positions often taught in such schools. We had excellent lecturers. I remember that school with enormous sentiment and enormous gratitude, because I learned a great deal at that school.

Eugenia gave me the following information on the secret classes within vocational gimnazjums:

> In '39 from the 16th of November until the end of vacations in June '40, we taught in secret. In *komplets*. Seven or eight persons in private homes studied together. Later, slowly, as the children returned from vacations from those various wanderings—well, one could simply find oneself on the other side of the border—the komplets were formed. One of the first komplets that was organized was for girls in higher grades where there was a *matura* that had to be [taken] earlier. . . . So, I also worked in clandestine education. Namely, along with the director, I organized the secret schools. The main director was our late Mrs. Lubeska. She was the principal, but we teachers ran various secret schools. Primarily, we pretended that the school was a vocational school for tailors and seamstresses, or we pretended that it was a school for embroidery, or weaving, or leather working, but they were all gimnazjums, right? So I ran the school for seamstresses because I had finished my studies at the Institute for Handiwork. So I ran the seamstress school, and the embroidery school,

and the weaving school. I operated as the director, but on the ground it was really about arranging identity cards [for the students] because the Germans tolerated the vocational schools. Vocational schools had the right to exist. Only general educational schools did not, so in this way we received identity cards for our students, both for those who were in the schools and those who learned in the secret komplets.

German policy presented a double threat to Polish children in that it identified secondary school students as future intellectuals, a group that had to be eliminated in order to enslave the rest of the population; it also targeted children of 12 and older as a source of slave labor. Therefore, although it might sound trivial, the work of obtaining identity cards that Pani Eugenia mentioned was crucial because without them children as young as 12 years of age could be detained in street roundups (*łapanki*) and deported to work camps in Germany.

The "matura," mentioned by Pani Eugenia in the preceding quotation, was and is an exam with written and oral components that all students in their final year of liceum (college-preparatory secondary school) in Poland must pass in order to graduate from secondary school. As such, it constitutes a major rite of passage in the lives of young people. Despite school closures, students continued to prepare for the matura through the secret komplets. Olgierd Z—— told me with great pride about the boys who studied in his komplet, beginning in 1939:

> I was in the fourth class [of gymnazjum], and I took part in a komplet and also passed my matura in the komplet in 1942. So, the matura exam in the komplet [he takes a deep breath]: If you please, on these chairs on which you and I are sitting—which were carried to the neighbor's during the uprising and by some miracle saved, because these are our chairs from before the war—old. On these chairs, on this one where I sit now, I sat then [he pauses to allow this to sink in]; and around the table sat the exam commission who questioned me, and in this way we passed the "big matura." In my own home.

The memory of the matura examination is made tangible, is evoked, by the table and chairs on which Pan Olgierd and I sat. As if calling each of the students who had passed the exam back into the room with us, he continued:

> Four matura students came from this house: in 1941, one matura. During the occupation some—not *Państwo*[10]—acquaintances lived here whose cousin came to stay. He was school aged. He learned and took the matura

[here], Władek Gabszewicz. Later he was killed very tragically. Do you know why? Because the Germans arrested him during his friend's wedding. I don't know if you heard [about it] so, [it happened] here in the Church of Saint Alexander on Plac Trzech Kryży [Place of the Three Crosses]. The wedding was there. [It was] the wedding of one of the Home Army conspirators, an officer. His wife was also in the conspiracy. When all the guests arrived, and the priests, and everything took place, there was the wedding ceremony. Well, the wedding mass was celebrated, and at that moment the Germans surrounded the entire church. They gathered everyone up to the *buda,* a truck, and they took them outside of the city here and shot them all. The bride with her bouquet in her hand and the groom, and also that Władek Gabszewicz. His brother was a pilot and fought under the British, but that's another story. If you please, and so it was like this: he [Władek Gabszewicz] took the first one, because he was the oldest; in 1941 he had his matura. In 1942 I passed my matura, right here as a matter of fact in this house. The oral exam here at home, because the written exam, that we took in one of those so-called vocational schools, there we had our written exam, because we all had to take the written exam together, at one time, and it would be difficult to do that in such a group [at a private home]. But, because that school was an official one we took it undercover. Some class was taking place to cover the fact that we were taking the written matura. Later, in 1943, the son of our acquaintances who lived here, Zbyszek Montkiewicz, passed his exam. And in 1944, my brother, the youngest [passed the matura]. So every year during the occupation, one matura came out of this house. That's how it happened, every year one matura.

In a city that was reduced to rubble in the wake of the General Uprising of 1944, when Germans looted and then destroyed 90 percent of Warsaw, physical continuity with the past is rare indeed. Żoliborz is itself unique in this regard in that, as a newer neighborhood, it did not rank high in terms of cultural and historical value and thus was one of the last to be marked for destruction. Most residents who returned found their homes in ruins and their possessions burned or simply gone, stolen by the Germans or looted by people from outlying areas. As most people took little more than the clothes on their backs when they were forcibly evacuated from the capital after the uprising failed in October 1944, few Warsovians have any mementos, let alone furniture, from their lives before the war. This makes Pan Olgierd's table and chairs all the more remarkable.

The preceding quotation illustrates something about how memory works. The interview from which this excerpt was taken was focused primarily on Olgierd's memories of Żoliborz before the war, but in telling me about a preschool that he attended in the 1920s that was located across the street from his house, the very same house he lived in when I conducted my fieldwork in the mid-1990s, he gave me his educational history. The matura exam is a major rite of passage for young people, and in telling me about the unusual circumstances of his matura, the memory of those other boys who took the exam in that same house came to mind and found its way into his narrative. Often, as is the case here, it was when I was discussing a seemingly unrelated topic with an informant that particularly sad or traumatic memories came up in these interviews. Somehow, memory is triggered by a subject that may not be directly related; as in the case of this interview with Pan Olgierd, though unsolicited by the question I had posed about the prewar character of the neighborhood, once recalled to mind by a turn of the conversation first toward education, then toward the matura, the story of Władek Gabszewicz emerged. Once bidden to memory, it seems as if his story and that of the doomed bridal party had to be told.

Like Olgierd, many people I worked with expressed the view that the standards of wartime education were quite high, in part due to the small class sizes of the komplets and the high quality of the teachers available to teach them. As Pani Eugenia's description of clandestine lessons and Olgierd's experiences in the secret komplets suggest, schoolchildren were drawn into the conspiracy to resist German occupation simply by continuing their education at the secondary level or by studying banned subjects such as Polish literature and history in the lower grades. Sławomira had this to say about attending school during the war:

> So, I returned to school. Well, among other things, school was also a problem because we didn't have any books whatsoever, and, in fact, we were not allowed to carry books to school, because that was something that could be, you know [seen, and thus the pretext for arrest]. There were, however, notebooks. One had to have sort of indifferent notebooks in which there were notes on "the properties of goods" (*towaroznawstwo*), or something like that, but in which we had our homework for Polish, or literature, or something. One had to make sure that this wasn't seen and to have a hiding place at home for them [the notebooks] so that if there was a search it wouldn't be the first thing in sight, so that it wouldn't attract attention, and they [the Germans] while looking for something else would not see it. So, there was also that feeling of threat. Well, . . . it is possible to say that as a result of it being illegal for us to learn, maybe in the end we all learned eagerly, on the principle of opposition.

Olgierd Z——, who was seventeen years old and about to begin his first year of secondary school, echoes Sławomira's sentiments:

> Well, war broke out and school was closed. I remember how I experienced that moment when I found out that the school had been closed—it was this sort of joy, "Ahhh, there won't be any school, isn't it great!!!" Afterward we all reflected that it was not good at all, and that we should learn, and so we started to learn. . . . And it's a good thing, right? So everyone really prepared for lessons, because it was about showing the Germans that Poles could learn and that we were capable of being educated people.

The very real risk of arrest created a sense of threat surrounding what otherwise would have been normal activities, which lent learning an air of importance. The price for teaching and studying forbidden subjects was high for both teachers and students. If discovered, such activities could lead to arrest and deportation to various types of camps for all those involved. As Olgierd B—— pointed out to me, "Many of those komplets were, unfortunately, liquidated. That means the Germans found them out and arrested everybody. A lot of teachers were lost, among them several from Poniatowski Secondary School [in Żoliborz]." Perhaps the best illustration of the risk involved in participating in the komplets is the following account written by Wiesława, one of my informants, for a booklet published for a reunion at the secondary school she attended.

> On October 2, 1942, in our apartment on Polish Army Avenue, a history lesson led by Pani Docent Hanna Pohorska was to take place. The evening of the previous day, I prepared the table by adding the leaves and laid out the maps and the necessary volume of the *Great World History*—the theme of the lecture was an overview of the First World War.
>
> My father worked the night shift and had a pass allowing him to move about the city after the curfew. My younger brother, and two Jewish ladies with a small, maybe year-and-a-half-old child, were also in the apartment. In the middle of the night, amid crashing and screaming, the Gestapo came, surrounded the apartment with weapons drawn to shoot, and then seated themselves comfortably and waited. A few days earlier the Soviets had bombed the city, at which time I had been lightly wounded in the head by a bit of glass. I was still feeling the effects, but above all I had to overcome the understandable panic that took over the Jews, because their behavior could result in the end of us all. I succeeded in assuring them that what was happening touched only me.

As I discovered after the war, in the morning the porter ran to my aunt's, who lived near by and who knew that a secret lesson was to take place at our home. So my aunt took her three-year-old son Andrzej and on the street in front of the entrance to our building she took a walk, played ball and tag. It lasted so long that the little one started to cry from exhaustion. But my aunt persisted and stopped all the girls who could have been students and all ladies, who could have been teachers, telling them not to go to Wiesia because the Gestapo was there. Of course, the first of them, Hala Buszówna and Romka Zdziarska, quickly warned the rest and Pani Docent Pohorska. The porter waited for my father at Invalids' Place to warn him also.

Through many hours I trembled with fear about the fate of my school friends and Pani Docent, but when ten o'clock came and no one arrived, a stone fell from my heart. The search conducted by the Gestapo was of a completely normal character, leaving the apartment in ruins. However, none of them turned their attention to the preparations for the lessons. In the afternoon, two civilians came, asked me a few questions regarding my identity, and led me to a car.

Today I understand that, but for the calmness and quick action of those few people, if not for the discretion of all the women and girls that were stopped on the street, the history lesson would have run a dramatic course. I know of cases in which an entire graduating komplet along with their teachers were caught, in which the pupils finished their graduation exam during their walks in the prison courtyard and during roll call in the camp.

In Pawiak, during the first week of my stay in so-called quarantine, I was called from my cell by Dr. Czupurska on the pretext of checking the cleanliness of my hair, and she asked if I had any important information for "my patrol," and when I had nothing except greetings, she told me to contact her if I needed anything. I sat in the cell for minors at Pawiak until January 17, 1943, when I was deported to Majdanek in a large transport of prisoners and about a thousand people who were detained in a street roundup. Among these was my classmate, who was later released and who took to my father a brooch that was missed by the SS men in Pawiak. It was returned to me after the war. I was at Majdanek until April of 1944, and the next six months in Auschwitz, and seven months in Ravensbrück.

During my long stay in Majdanek I had proof that friends and teachers from my school thought of me—I received packages which were a source of great consolation and hope. They were also a subject of great pride because I was the only one who received them from classmates, which awoke wonder in my fellow inmates. I regularly thought of school and shuddered that I did not have my diploma and that time was running out. I longed for the atmosphere of my school. In one secret letter that they saved, I wrote to Jola Michalska, "Please, kiss for me, greet for me, and remember me with sincere fondness and gratitude to, above all, all my best TEACHERS."

Wiesława was seventeen years old in 1942 when she was arrested by the Germans and incarcerated at Pawiak for her work as a courier in the underground. Her concern for her teacher and her classmates illustrates the danger they were in, for once a member of the komplet had entered the building they would have been determined guilty by association and, in all likelihood, would have shared Wiesława's fate. The very real risk of arrest associated with wartime education created a sense of threat that lent learning an air of importance. Thus, by participating in secret komplets and studying banned subjects, children could feel that they were taking part in something extraordinary. Indeed, learning in secret schools was the first step for many young people in becoming involved in what my informants often referred to as the "conspiracy," a vast network of affiliated organizations whose goal was Nazi resistance.

Wiesława's desire to acknowledge the important role that her teachers played in helping their students through the occupation was not limited to this essay written for an audience of former classmates. On the contrary, it was a recurring theme in our conversations. Pani Eugenia, she said of her former teacher, "taught us life." She described how Eugenia had taught her pupils many useful skills that helped them to adapt to the shortages of the occupation, such as how to make something wearable out of worn-out clothes, how to fix a broken windowpane, how to stretch rations, in short how to live in difficult conditions. Classes with Eugenia, she said, were more than handwork, but survival, life. That Wiesława remembered these practical elements of her wartime education, expressed her gratitude to her teachers in a variety of contexts, and recalled longing for the atmosphere of her school while imprisoned in a series of progressively horrific concentration camps demonstrates the important role that education played in the lives of young people in general during the occupation. Whether they gave secret lessons for komplets, lectured in secret classrooms, or taught children banned subjects under the guise of teaching them to be shopkeepers, Polish teachers preserved the familiar for their students and, in doing so, helped them to re-create a sense of normalcy beyond the walls of the classroom.

Learning was not, however, just a first step toward the underground but was itself a form of resistance against Nazi attempts to erase Polish culture. As Olgierd said, "It was about showing the Germans that Poles could learn and that we were capable of being educated people." Wiesława's recollections of the girls and teachers who continued their studies, even taking their exams in concentration camps, is also revealing. One might well wonder why these girls would place themselves at additional risk for a diploma when their very survival was in doubt; or why, when surrounded by death and suffering, the fact that she had not finished her education was a source of ongoing anxiety for Wiesława. While one could argue that focusing on school subjects served some functional purpose in the environment of the camps by providing an escape from the horrors of daily life (though some have argued that this was not possible in the conditions of the camp, see, for example, Langer 1991) or by offering additional motivation for survival (see, for example, Frankl 1962), it seems to me that it is equally possible that intellectual growth itself was the goal. In striving to become educated people or to aid others in that goal, the people with whom I worked resisted Nazi attempts to de-Polonize the population. It is clear from the passages I have quoted throughout the chapter that opposing the occupation of the mind through learning in secret imbued young people's lives with a sense of the extraordinary. That they remember this education with great pride illustrates the role that learning played in preserving personal dignity, which ultimately aided them in resisting demoralization, an occupation of the spirit brought about by the brutality of the Nazi occupation.

Occupation of the Spirit

Thus far I have discussed German efforts to depopulate and de-Polonize the citizens of Poland by an occupation of place, body, and mind. But in occupying Poland the Nazis set out to create a new kind of human being, *Untermenschen*: subhumans not just in name or according to Nazi constructs of race but in the utter lack of ability to resist domination on any level. This required an occupation of the spirit, one that would alter the ways in which individuals saw themselves and their own opportunities for the future, as well as the ways in which they perceived their fellow human beings.

Of course, the most obvious way to occupy a group of people in a spiritual sense is to undermine their religious institutions and religious leaders. Prior to the outbreak of war on September 1, 1939, an estimated 92 percent of those residents of Poland who listed Polish as their native language (as opposed to the other languages spoken by citizens of Poland, among them Ukrainian, Yiddish, and Hebrew) also listed Roman Catholicism as their religion (*Petit annuaire statistique de Pologne* 1939: 26, cited in Gross 1979: 12). Servicing the needs of these believers were 10,017 Roman Catholic priests and approximately 2,000 men and women who had taken vows in religious orders (Lukas 1986: 14; Roszkowski 1997).

The German occupation of Poland brought with it an unprecedented level of repression of Roman Catholic clergy whom the Germans targeted as members of the Polish intelligentsia. As a result the Germans arrested and imprisoned even clergy of the Episcopal rank, a policy that was only implemented in Poland (Lukas 1986: 13). An estimated 2,400 members of the Catholic clergy, including priests, monks, and nuns, died during the war, 212 of these men and women were from the diocese of Warsaw (Roszkowski 1997; Lukas 1986: 14–15). In the so-called annexed territories of western Poland, the Nazis closed churches, seminaries, and Catholic schools. In the city of Łódz, with a population of 700,000 ethnic Poles, the Germans closed all but four churches (ibid. 15). The Germans also "Germanized" the clergy by replacing Polish priests with Volksdeutsche priests (ibid.). Moreover, the use of the Polish language was forbidden both in mass and confession (ibid.). Clearly, such policies must have had a devastating effect on the ability of individual members of congregations to participate in the religious practices they had observed in their daily lives prior to the war. One commentator described the effect as "reducing religious life to what it was at the time of the catacombs" (*Polish White Book*: 35, cited in Lukas 1986: 16). That having been said, religious practice and the role of religious institutions during the occupation rarely came up in interviews with my mentors. In the pages that follow I will briefly explore at least three explanations as to why this may be the case: differences in Nazi policy toward the Catholic Church in the General Government, the structure of the interviews themselves, and some events of the postwar era that are specific to Żoliborz.

German policy toward the Catholic Church in the General Government was considerably less severe than that in the annexed territories of western Poland. In Warsaw and eastern Poland, the Nazis attempted to control the Polish clergy by co-opting the Roman Catholic Church to the Nazi cause, which was initially represented as a fight against the Bolshevik enemies of Christianity (ibid. 14–15). Although the hierarchy of the Roman Catholic Church (along with the majority of the population in general) was decidedly anti-Bolshevik in attitude, the Roman Catholic Church in Poland was an institution of the Polish people. Poland draws its claims as a state from the year 966, when Mieszko I, the first king of Poland, converted to Christianity. The Roman Catholic Church in Poland also has long-standing historical and cultural ties with Polish opposition movements against various foreign invaders. This history, coupled with the obvious anti-Polish attitude of the

Nazis, which I have detailed throughout the chapter, rendered the attempt to co-opt the Church in Poland, as an institution, largely unsuccessful. In an effort to minimize the Roman Catholic Church's influence in the General Government, the Germans limited the number of masses held, prohibited the singing of patriotic hymns such as "God Who Saved Poland" ("Boże Coś Polskę") and "Tender Mother" ("Serdeczna Matko"), and mandated specific sermons in German (ibid. 15). They did not, however, ban the use of Polish, nor did they attempt to Germanize the clergy or close churches en masse. This difference is key, because it means that, aside from openly pursuing a Catholic education, individuals living in the General Government were better able to continue to attend mass and take part in other religious rituals and practices than their counterparts in western Poland. With so many other aspects of their daily lives disrupted and distorted by the rules of the occupation, religious practice may have remained a refuge of familiarity in which continuity with prewar practices was preserved. This is, of course, in keeping with the nature of religious ritual, which seeks to preserve continuity of belief and practice with a community of believers. In this way Catholic religious practices may have been relatively unaltered by the occupation and thus their impression on memory much lighter.

Meeting a person later in life makes it difficult to know whether their attitude to religion and their religious practices at that particular point in time are representative of the whole of their life. On the subject of religion and spiritual beliefs, then, I took my cues from my informants, which is to say that attitudes toward religion and spiritual practice came up as a topic of discussion in these interviews only when introduced by my informants (with one exception related to incidents that took place in the 1980s and 1990s, which I discuss at length in Tucker 1998). As a result, religious practice during the war was not something that I discussed with the majority of my mentors. This should not be interpreted as meaning that religion was not an important part of their lives. With one exception (Dr. Jan S——, who was raised in the Russian Orthodox Church), all were brought up in the Roman Catholic Church. Many displayed religious symbols such as crucifixes, pictures or replicas of the Madonna of Częstochowa, or other religious icons in their homes. Following Christmas, the doors of the majority of their homes bore the inscription written in white chalk "B+M+K," which I discovered referred to the initials of the Three Kings or Wisemen: Balthazar, Melchior, and Kaspar. The inscription indicates that the owner of the home had hosted a parish priest for *kolenda*, during which time the home is blessed with holy water and prayers and the head of the household (ideally) makes a donation to the Church. Several of my mentors attended mass regularly, some attended retreats (*rekolekcja*) for Catholic intelligentsia during Advent, and some had close relationships with members of the clergy from their local parishes. We discussed these things in the context of their daily lives in the mid-1990s. During the course of my fieldwork, I also attended memorial masses with my mentors and made a trip to the cemetery on the Feast of All Souls. Thus, while things religious came up infrequently in the context of the war, religion was not altogether absent from other conversations we had. On one occasion, after patiently answering my questions about her life, Pani Eugenia turned the tables and asked me about my religious upbringing and, upon discovering my Protestant roots, engaged me in a lengthy conversation about why Protestants have, in her words, put Mary, the Mother of God, "on the shelf." Pani Sławomira and I frequently talked about the subject of religion and the Church in Poland, and upon the birth of my son, she sent me a prayer that she had taught her children. Clearly, then, religion was an important part of the lives of at least some of the people with whom I worked and also, albeit for fewer, an engaging topic of conversation.

How, then, to explain the fact that it rarely came up in our discussions of the war? The most obvious reason, of course, is that I did not ask, so there was not a question that would have directly prompted recollections of this sort. While in retrospect this was an unfortunate omission on my part, it is not an entirely satisfying explanation. After all, the vast majority of the data I have comes from open-ended questions, which is to say I have a great deal of information on several topics about which I did not directly inquire. Also, I did ask questions about people, events, or situations that made a lasting impression on them; about places that serve as triggers for memory; about how they coped with trauma and the memory of trauma. All of these would seem to offer opportunities to discuss things, people, and events of a spiritual or religious nature. Yet, few did.

In searching for possible explanations, I turned my attention to the relationship between the Church and the intelligentsia in the interwar era. Under the partitions of the nineteenth century, the Roman Catholic Church was in a sort of survival mode, trying to maintain its existence vis-à-vis Russification and pressures on the populace to convert to Orthodoxy in the East and Germanization in the West (Bratkowski 1998 317). Once Poland regained its sovereignty following World War I, the Church focused its efforts primarily on attacking changing social norms such as women's sports and sporting outfits, shorter skirts, divorce, family planning, and the like (ibid.). This brought the Church into an oppositional relationship with those Poles who held progressive views, particularly those affiliated with the Polish Socialist Party (PPS), which had a strong following in Żoliborz. As historian Stefan Bratkowski has observed: "The Church fell into a conflict with the leaders of the Polish intelligentsia, in whose eyes the Church was perceived as a bastion of backwardness" (ibid.). In contrast, Polish fascist groups of the 1930s, a relatively small but boisterous part of the political spectrum, pointed to the Church as supportive of their cause (ibid. 318). Bratkowski suggests that in the 1930s the atmosphere that dominated the Church was best embodied in the figure of Maksymilian Kolbe, a Franciscan priest with what Bratkowski describes as "an exceptional talent as a manager and charismatic organizer, a man of ostentatious personal humility, traveling barefoot(!) [*sic*] all over the world. He published widely distributed writings, religious writings, huffing and puffing [*ziejace*] with astonishingly primitive antisemitism" (ibid., translation courtesy of Robert Szudra).

If Maksymilian Kolbe—said to have undergone a personal transformation from anti-Semite to Auschwitz prisoner to Polish Holocaust martyr canonized by Pope John Paul II—embodied the Church of the 1930s, then the Church's role in society and its relationship with the intelligentsia also changed both during and after the war. Thus while in the 1930s many of my informants who were raised in PPS families may have shaken their heads at the Church's conservatism even as they attended mass, their experiences with the Church in more recent years would be qualitatively different as the Church's relationship with the intelligentsia underwent multiple permutations, playing a role as supporter of human rights, providing a sanctuary for the opposition, and ultimately joining the opposition itself prior to 1989.

Another possibility that might explain this silence is that the risk of public expression of religious belief and practice, as well as the repression of the clergy during the occupation, may have been displaced in memory (qualitatively if not quantitatively) by postwar, communist-era events. In Żoliborz, following the war, such repression was not merely an abstract possibility. Father Trószyński, a priest who served in Żoliborz and the neighboring district of Marymont before, during, and after the war, faced such treatment. Pan Olgierd Z—— served at masses celebrated by Father Trószyński and recalled how, even with bombs flying as the priest said mass, he did not move from the altar. He told me about the priest and his work during the war:

> Father Zygmunt Trószyński, who was the chaplain, I mean provost. He was
> born there [in Marymont] [in 1886]. Later he was a chaplain, he was provost
> for many years, and later during the occupation he was very active in helping
> people. During the Uprising [of 1944] a well-known figure was that of Father

Zygmunt Trószyński, who walked through all of Żoliborz with a cross in his hand spreading news while giving communion, offering communion to everyone in the Żoliborz area. [Dressed] in a stole, and he wore a sort of patchwork cassock made of bits [of cloth] that had been sewn together, his hair was gray because he was an older man. An unforgettable figure, a gray-haired chaplain who walked, crisscrossed [the neighborhood], celebrated mass in various neighborhoods of Żoliborz throughout the entire uprising. Later he was one of the first to reappear in Żoliborz [after the liberation in January of 1945], and he quickly brought about the exhumations of those who had been killed and buried in Żoliborz and their reburial at the proper place in the cemetery. So, this was an extraordinary man, extraordinarily kind-hearted, very modest. He lived in a little wooden house, slept on an iron bed, his mattress was made of straw, he covered himself with this little blanket, and heated his house with a tiny iron stove. He went, and for example, if he received a comforter from somebody or if someone brought him a pillow, the very next day it was already gone because he had given it to the poor. He would say, "Ahh, this family has children and nothing to cover them all with," and gave everything away. That's exactly why I thought he deserved at least a small [memorial], and there is such a street that can be found opposite the church. Tiny, that is a tiny street named after Father Zygmunt Trószyński.

Father Trószyński was arrested in 1947 and sentenced to six years in prison, as Pan Olgierd put it, "for being a chaplain and because he was a Pole, and that was our own government." He died in prison in 1949, at the age of 63, nearly a decade younger than Pan Olgierd was when he told me about him. The street opposite the church in Marymont where Father Trószyński served is, in fact, Olgierd's own public tribute to the life of a man whom he considered to be a "great patriot" and humanitarian. Indeed, beginning in the 1980s, Olgierd spent fifteen years convincing city officials to rename the street in memoriam to the priest turned political prisoner and finally a martyr.

Residents of Żoliborz suffered the loss of another beloved activist priest at the hands of Poland's communist government in 1984, when members of the secret police abducted and murdered Father Jerzy Popiełuszko, Solidarity chaplain and parish priest at the Church of Saint Stanisław Kostki. Indeed, it was only when I inquired about a street that had been renamed in honor of Father Popiełuszko that Olgierd told me about his mentor, Father Trószyński. (For a discussion of both the priests and the streets, see Tucker 1998.) For Olgierd, who knew both men personally, questions about the younger reminded him of the older, and the two are inextricably linked in his memory. Olgierd is the only one who mentioned Trószyński by name.

This raises a number of questions, not just about these incidents but also about memory in general. Had the loss of the younger priest eclipsed that of the older, the activism of Popiełuszko, the Solidarity chaplain, displacing the memory of Trószyński, the Home Army chaplain? Does memory work in such a way that events experienced strongly later in life displace similar ones from our youth rather than connecting them? Is the fact that no one else recalled Father Trószyński, or any other priest, by name attributable to the fact that so many other aspects of daily life were impacted negatively, that other events like the ones I've discussed on the preceding pages impressed themselves on memory more strongly? Of course it may very well be that this gap reveals less about memory of the war than about the ethnographer, less about how memory works than about how the questions I asked or omitted shape the representation of these remembered events that I am able to offer.

Occupation of Memory

In the preceding pages I have identified patterns in the types of events and situations recollected by my mentors when asked about the Nazi occupation. In doing so, I have organized their narratives according to different realms of occupation in an effort to illustrate the many ways that war and occupation erode the familiar, destroying normalcy on both an individual and a societal level. Before moving on to a discussion of how the people with whom I worked responded to this loss, I want to take a moment to reflect on the place that recollections of the war occupied in various mentors' memories when I spoke to them in the mid-1990s.

The vast majority of my mentors were born in the interwar era and are members of what is known as the "tragic" or "lost" generation. In Poland it is commonly believed that, after experiencing war and occupation as young people, this generation never experienced anything else as intensely and that war was the most salient experience of their lives. Seen as the defining characteristic of the "tragic generation," this experience of profound loss is also imbued with the power to transform the individual's state of being, leaving him or her not just "tragic," due to losses suffered, but also lost. This assignation went beyond the notion that these young people were scarred emotionally and spiritually by what they had witnessed and suffered, but it also referred to a certain confusion about their place in postwar society.

This would also suggest that nothing else imprinted itself in memory quite so vividly and that memories of the war have eclipsed all others. During the course of my fieldwork, I often had the impression that all conversations with informants ultimately returned to the topic of the war. In formal interviews, for example, my attempts to learn about events during the communist era were, for the most part, thwarted, in some cases by constant digression to topics related to the war, in others by the encapsulation of decades into a few short dismissive phrases. Casual conversations with informants in other contexts also had a tendency to turn to the war without my introducing it as a topic. For example, on most weekdays I watched the evening news with Pani Sławomira and our neighbor Pani Zosia. Reports on Chechnya were regularly featured at that time, and the panorama shots of Grozny in ruins reminded them both of the destruction of Warsaw following the failure of the Uprising of 1944. To illustrate their understanding for what the Chechens were suffering, both also expressed enormous sympathy for the Chechens, relating their own stories of encounters with Soviet soldiers following the liberation of the capital in 1945.

The war often came up as a topic of conversation at many of the name-day celebrations and dinner parties I attended as well. People were always curious about my reasons for being in Poland, and few were willing to accept vague answers about the nature of my research. Sometimes it was enough for a person to hear that I was interviewing people about the war for them to offer their own reminiscences or even to tell me about other people's experiences. After a while everyone I knew personally, and many whom I did not, knew of my research. This means that the war may have come up in conversation simply because people knew it interested me, or perhaps my presence caused some to associate the war with me and I myself came to serve as a sort of trigger for memory. Was my presence the catalyst for much of this conversation, or would people have spoken about the war even had I not been present? Was I there long enough for them to see me as just another neighbor and to forget about my research? At Zosia's name-day party, when the topic turned to Polish-Jewish relations and by extension to the war, someone jokingly warned the others, "Be careful, because you know Pani Erica will go home and write this all down." Everyone laughed, and then someone changed the topic.

Brief chance encounters with strangers on various forms of public transportation were also fraught with references to war. I once offered my seat to an older man on a bus who shook his head as he accepted it, explaining to me that I couldn't possibly know what it meant to have a spine because I was too young to have lived through the war. It was unclear to me whether he was referring to back pain or suggesting that young people like myself have no backbone or both. For some who lived through it, World War II was a basis for relating to or identifying with others who had suffered loss. But for others, like the man on the bus, it was invoked as a way to distinguish and distance one generation from another. In this same way, some of my informants would caution me that some things could not be conveyed to people who had not lived through the war; some things were beyond understanding but had to be experienced.

In the chapters that follow, war experiences are invoked by some informants as a sort of standard by which other people's sacrifices and suffering are to be measured. In others these experiences serve as a conduit for understanding, for bridging differences of time and place. One final example illustrates this latter point. When floods devastated many towns and cities in southern Poland in the summer of 1997, I arrived at Pani Wiesława and Pan Adam's for an interview and had to navigate my way around several large piles of sheets, blankets, and clothing before arriving at a clear space to sit and talk. Wiesława apologized for the chaos and explained that these things were all intended for flood victims and were awaiting pickup by a relief organization. "We know what it is like to lose everything and to have to start life over again," she told me. Later the next evening, I knocked at my neighbor Zosia's door around eight o'clock to say good-bye until my next visit. To my surprise, she answered the door in her nightgown, her hair in curlers. I apologized for disturbing her and reminded her that I was flying back to the United States in the morning. She explained that she had spent the day organizing donations for the flood victims and had gone to bed early. She laughed as she told me that she had even given away the mattress from her own bed and was sleeping on bare boards, but she added it would not be the first time—when she had returned to the apartment in 1945, she hadn't had a bed at all. She said this with such mirth, so pleased with giving up her own bed that I found myself laughing too.

Empathetic responses to the plight of people featured on the news, if not formed from informants' own experiences during the war, were at least explained in that context. This realization confirms the notion that memories of the war eclipse other experiences in the minds of the "lost" generation, while at the same time it undermines the implicit assumption that such an occupation of memory is detrimental to the individual and his or her ability to function in society. Although many of the experiences of later life may have been filtered through those of the war, the joyous generosity with which Zosia, Wiesława, and Adam responded to the flood victims suggests that this way of relating to life did not necessarily diminish later experiences. For them loss was understood as loss, and whether it was brought about by a natural disaster or human-driven catastrophe made little difference because in either case life had to be started anew in the face of destruction and grief. The fact that they were in a position to draw from their experience and their material resources to help others do so was the source of pride and exuberant, even contagious, joy.

4 The Conspiracy

ELT: How did it happen that you took part in the conspiracy? Was that because you were in the scouts or—

Olgierd B—— [interrupting]: Everybody was.

ELT: Everybody was?

Olgierd B——: I simply cannot imagine a young person who wasn't. It is simply unthinkable. All the youth. All of them, it was absolutely an exception to find someone somewhere who wasn't, or maybe, what do I know—maybe someone who was disabled, something like that could happen, but in general all young people were involved. It was not any, any act of great service to be a soldier in the conspiracy. It was simply automatic.

OLGIERD B—— TAKES AN ATYPICALLY unromantic view of resistance with the declaration that it was no great feat to be a soldier in the underground, but he is not alone in the perception that Warsaw's youth participated unanimously in the resistance movement; indeed, it is an impression shared by the majority of people with whom I worked. Jerzy, who graduated from the same high school as Olgierd B——, shared the view. As he put it, "Practically the whole society was conspiring." He could think of only one exception—a friend whose mother was German and thus under pressure to show special allegiance to the Germans, which she was reluctant to do on religious grounds. Although this young man was not able to join the Home Army, he did take part in the conspiracy by writing for an underground newspaper.

With the exception of Irmina B—— and Joanna S——, who were nine and seven years old respectively when the war broke out, and Maria

K——, whose sons took part, all of my informants claimed participation in the underground resistance movement in one way or another. Equal in importance is the fact that their claims of having done so have been recognized on a number of levels. Some received military honors from "London," the Polish government-in-exile, while others were persecuted by the communist-era government of the 1950s precisely because of their participation. All have been recognized by their own community of veterans within Warsaw, and all who were combatants (a designation which includes medics and couriers) have received special identity cards for World War II veterans, entitling them to discounts on telecommunications services and to free rides on Warsaw's public transportation system, courtesy of the post-communist government.

But did everyone participate in the conspiracy as my informants suggest? If secret schooling is excluded, an estimated 24,000–25,000 young people living in the General Government participated in underground youth organizations (Hillebrandt 1973). Gross (1979: 171) points out that this figure may be a bit low, as many young people participated in adult underground organizations, in particular the Home Army. He also suggests that, while these may have been "the best of Polish youth," they were nonetheless "only a fraction of the younger generation." How, then, does one understand this discrepancy? First, participation in underground organizations by the youth of Warsaw was, most likely, disproportionately high when compared to that of youth in other parts of the country, and participation in Żoliborz was unusually high, even for Warsaw. This is not surprising when one considers who lived in Żoliborz prior to the war: the neighborhood was the site of a housing addition for Polish army officers and their families and cooperatives for government employees and teachers, and it was also popular with journalists. Moreover, in 1939 Żoliborz was still a place where a young person could know all of his or her peers. Prior to the war there were three secondary schools in Żoliborz, Poniatowski for boys, and Aleksandra Piłsudska and the Sisters of the Resurrection for girls. Thus, Olgierd and Jerzy may have assumed that, because virtually all of their classmates were involved in the underground in some way, this was true for all of Warsaw. However, while many believed that participation in the underground among youth was nearly unanimous, many held the seemingly contradictory view that it was primarily youth from intelligentsia families, in other words from the elite, who participated. In Żoliborz, however, these two notions were not in contradiction as even Worker's Żoliborz, represented by the housing complex built by WSM (Warsaw Housing Cooperative), was inhabited primarily by residents from the so-called working intelligentsia: teachers, clerks, municipal employees. Again, the perception that the movement was strictly a movement of the elite was predicated on a generalization of the situation in Żoliborz to the city as a whole. Thus, because my informants knew few young people from working-class backgrounds, some assume that working-class people did not participate.

Another cause for the discrepancy between the statistics on youth participation and my informants' convictions that "everybody was doing it" may come from different perceptions of what constituted resistance. For my informants their notions of resistance were shaped by the conditions of the occupation, specifically the German plan to transform eastern Poland into Lebensraum (living space) for Germans and turn Poles into their slaves by means of a policy designed to strip Polish society of its leaders, and then depopulate, de-Polonize, and demoralize the Polish people. While the Germans' level of success in implementing this plan varied over time and in different regions of the country, the mere existence of the policy meant that much of what was previously considered a normal part of everyday life was suddenly rendered illegal and punishable in ways that were out of all proportion to the "crime." This raises the question, if much of everyday life is rendered illegal (things so mundane as listening to the radio, playing the music of Polish composers, going to school, buying white bread and meat), is any act that violates Nazi policy resistance?

To address this question one must first understand how Poles organized their resistance during World War II. With a history of resisting foreign domination going back to the partitions of the eighteenth century, Polish leaders and Polish citizens had many examples of military, social, and economic resistance on which to draw in opposing German occupation. A vast underground network of resistance organizations, Poland's wartime government consisted of two distinct but closely linked parts: the Polish government-in-exile in London and the underground state in Poland. Participation in the latter was known as taking part in the "conspiracy." Defined in its broadest sense, the underground state included all organizations that recognized the government-in-exile (Stola 2003: 88). In re-creating the government-in-exile abroad with functioning social institutions in Poland, the nation's leaders created a system of government that ran parallel to the one imposed on the country by the Nazis. Domestically, this secret state included social service agencies, courts, underground universities and schools, publishers of books, periodicals, and news dailies and weeklies, as well as intelligence and military organizations that developed into an underground army called the Home Army (*Armia Krajowa*) or AK. For this reason, participation in the conspiracy could take the form of a wide array of activities in conjunction with one or more of several governmental organizations.

Some scholars argue that the Polish government-in-exile was primarily a government of war against the Germans, whose ultimate goals were to serve the Polish cause of regaining independence (ibid.). Indeed, according to Polish historian Dariusz Stola (ibid.), the vast majority of those involved in the underground were in the military wing of the underground, the Home Army. Others argue that the primary goal of the Polish underground was not resisting the Nazi occupation but rather preventing social atomization by creating the institutional support under which social solidarity could flourish as a subtle yet effective tool for opposing the destruction of Polish society and culture (Gross 1979: 255–56). In this sense it was first a secret state and only second an anti-German conspiracy (ibid.). This view also has value, especially if one considers the numbers of people who benefited from the services provided by institutions operating as part of the secret state and supported by the government-in-exile. In fact, most estimates of participation in the underground do not include statistics on those who were educated in underground schools and universities. These two conflicting views raise a number of questions about both the nature and purpose of the Polish underground. Were its goals primarily military or social? Were only deliberate political acts directly affiliated with the Polish Home Army or the government-in-exile considered conspiratorial? Or did conspiratorial acts also include any act of opposition to Nazi policy, such as emotional or intellectual resistance? In nineteenth-century Poland there was a similar debate about the form that resistance should take. Should resistance be solely or even primarily a matter of taking up arms? Or should it take the form of "organic work," the purpose of which was to maintain and improve upon the nation's social, cultural, and economic institutions so that Polish identity would be strong enough to endure even while the Germans and Soviets occupied or partitioned the nation (Davies 2004: 169)?

To explore these questions I first discuss some of the literature from anthropology and Holocaust studies about resistance, in order to lay a framework for understanding informants' narratives of their own oppositional activities, their evaluations of various types of opposition, and the way their participation in the underground changed over time. The underground state that existed in Poland during World War II initially sought to strike a balance between, on the one hand, governmental agencies that resisted the de-Polonization through social and cultural institutions that fostered social solidarity and, on the other, military organizations that promoted and prepared for armed revolt. However, I will show how over time the underground subordinated the social service agenda to the goal of liberating Poland from German rule through armed revolt and how romantic notions of sacrificing one's life for the nation proved stronger than the positivist notion of working for the good of it.

Conspiratorial Acts

I began my exploration of conspiratorial acts with someone who Sławomira assured me had been deeply engaged, Stefan W——, a former officer in the Polish Home Army (AK) and someone who had worked with her father.[1] In some sense Stefan was still engaged in the underground when I met him, serving as president of Żywiciel Veterans' Organization, one of Żoliborz's many AK battalions during the war. Stefan gave me this very matter-of-fact description of his career in the conspiracy:

> In 1939 I was called up to the army. I took part in the war against the Germans. I fought on the northern front, and later I took part in the defense of Warsaw. I defended the Grochów neighborhood, Grochowska Street, until the capitulation. After the capitulation I tore the military insignia off [my uniform]. When the Germans captured us, they took me along with the shooters, so I was with the soldiers [rather than the officers].
>
> That was very good, because we weren't guarded so well, and officers were guarded around the clock. So, in the evening I escaped. I returned to Warsaw. That was around the 15th of October. Warsaw had capitulated on the 27th of September, so when I escaped I went to my in-laws outside of Warsaw.
>
> On October 15, 1939, I was asked if I wanted to work in the underground, rather [if I wanted] to fight the Germans. That same day I was sworn in and my activities—I also worked for a living in a firm, a sort of big concern that the Germans took over in December. So as of December I was unemployed. In order to have something to live on, I played at working as a glazier and later, as usual, during times when there are Germans, I engaged in business. I traded, but because I don't have a head for business, none of my interests worked out. So, I started to work in the underground. I trained soldiers. I was the leader of a platoon. I trained soldiers. And I'm not going to tell you about all the different actions I had, because it's not that essential.

Direct engagement with the Germans, however, required not only training but strategic planning, which could only be achieved through the careful collection of information. The Home Army, or AK, as was the case for most if not all branches of the secret state, organized itself into cells, so that as few people as possible knew about the existence of others, their locations, and activities. Pani Krystyna, a member of the AK, volunteered as a courier, carrying messages and documents across the city from operatives in one cell to those in another.

> **ELT:** Did you take part in any underground organizations?
>
> **Krystyna:** While I was going to school, no. Only after I passed the matura. [I became involved] here [through the housing cooperative], through contact with the B——s who lived on the first floor. You know B——, right? And through Danka Jaksa-Bykowska I found my way into the conspiracy, through them I became a courier. . . . I was also connected with, you know, now he is—was the Foreign Minister, Bartoszewski. I've known him since the time of the occupation from the underground. . . . I delivered packages, mail. I did not know what I was carrying or to whom, it was only after the war that I discovered who he was, who those people were with whom I had had contact, right? But, that's what I did until my arrest. Later I participated in things that were a bit different. I was not in it so much. Instead I participated in training for the uprising. Morse telegraph code, and things related to the courier service. I didn't carry messages any more.

Pani Krystyna was ideally suited for her work as a courier through both her gender and youth. German patriarchal ideology defined women as inherently intellectually inferior to men, politically unsophisticated, emotional, and passive; for these reasons women were often perceived as beneath suspicion. Therefore, the Germans were not prepared for opposition from this segment of society (Tec 1986). However, while Polish women may have been perceived by the Germans as less dangerous than men, and thus in less danger themselves, carrying messages for the Home Army was not a risk-free endeavor. This point is well illustrated by Krystyna's arrest and detention at the infamous Gestapo prison, Pawiak.

> **Krystyna:** I wanted to tell you something interesting that just came to my mind about the arrest, when I was at Pawiak arrested as a courier. I remember that I had taken a package to Bartoszewski and also to Pani Maria Kan, a writer, and they smuggled *gryps* to the prison at Pawiak. Do you know what a gryps is?
>
> **ELT:** No.
>
> **Krystyna:** A tiny roll, a letter on a small card, which was possible to smuggle— gryps. A sort of secret letter: tiny, written on tissue paper. In some way everything penetrated Pawiak, because the service at Pawiak was German, but there were also Polish staff, though they were meant to serve the German guards. . . . Among other things, as a courier I took packages to a guard who went to Pawiak, in a German uniform, right? But she was in the service of the

AK (Home Army), in the Polish service, the Polish underground, but she had access as a German guard. Actually through her I laughed at receiving rolls with ham [while incarcerated at Pawiak], it was probably through her. It was possible to somehow give packages, so that's why I'm telling you about the rolls with ham. But I also wanted to tell you about my experiences because I knew her from the conspiracy, and I had been in her apartment. I don't remember [where] now—on Srebna [Street] or something, and I took things to her from the underground, not knowing what I carried and to whom. And the first day I was in Pawiak, in prison, the first person who came into my cell along with a German with a dog was exactly she, and it was terrifying! Neither she nor I could give a sign that we knew who the other was, right? And that was terrifying. But that was a very strong *przeżycie* [intense experience] to have lived through. And our eyes [were] like glass that we knew nothing, but she knew immediately from the first day that I was at Pawiak, but that had no, no connection to my release.

Other informants perceived activities like Stefan's work—training soldiers for covert action—and Krystyna's courier work as conspiratorial, and both clearly fall on the military side of resistance.

However, informants did report other ways of serving the underground. Olgierd's interest in medicine led him to seek employment in a hospital, and this in turn brought about opportunities for resistance. Nazi policy required that all people over the age of 15 work and carry proof of their employment with them at all times. Without such documentation of gainful employment, they faced the risk of deportation to forced labor in Germany, which was typically on farms or in the war industry, or worse still, to concentration camps within Poland. Most young people were only able to find the most menial of jobs. However, the occupation and its accompanying policies had created a shortage of doctors and an abundance of sick and wounded, which made anyone with even rudimentary training in medicine desirable as an employee. As a result, after passing his matura exams and beginning to study medicine through underground classes at the University of Warsaw, Olgierd found employment at the Maltański Hospital located on Senator Street. As Olgierd recalls in the excerpt below, Brothers of the Maltese order had founded the Maltański Hospital during the siege of Warsaw in September of 1939.

The Germans did not make things especially difficult for us at that hospital because it was Maltese and connected with the Italians. It was Italian, but of course nonetheless, it was risky all the same, because the conspiracy was active at that hospital. There were underground cells at the hospital who were trained as cadets, secret exercises, and being there at the hospital in addition to fulfilling my duties as a doctor [in training] . . . I was engaged in the underground. Among other things my role was to go to those who were wounded in various actions fighting the Germans and change their dressings. They had their operations at the hospital, but afterward they were lodged in private apartments so that the Germans would not know, because someone could denounce them, and the Germans would find them [if they recuperated at the hospital]. My role was to go from house to house and dress their wounds. So that's how [my work at the hospital] looked.

Working at the hospital was Olgierd's point of entry into the underground. Through his work there he became involved not only with the care of patients but also with the "conspiracy" to hide the existence of such groups from the Germans.

I remember how after awhile, when I was a little more involved with the work, the director of the hospital suggested that I take night duty. I was terribly afraid, right? As a young student in the second year of medical school, I was afraid of that. But I told myself that I had to get by. So, I was on call at the hospital, because there weren't any doctors. I was on call. That was a big *przeżycie* [intense experience]. So, at a certain moment in the night, when I was on call, the Germans came. They surrounded me, the doctor on duty. They were very surprised that I was so young in my white coat. I spoke a little German, right, I knew how to say that I was the doctor on call and "What's this about?" And [I understood] that they said there were bandits in the hospital. "What bandits?" I asked. Ahh, that they were from the Home Army or—well it wasn't called the Home Army then, but that they were here, hiding in the hospital, that they were hidden, actually terrorists. Well, indeed, when there was an action in Warsaw and there were wounded, they were brought to the Maltański hospital as well. Only in the medical records it was not written that the patient had been shot, rather that they were hurt in a tram accident. [It was described] in that way so as to trick the Germans. Well, at the time I knew that there were a few [wounded] who we hadn't yet been able to transport to private apartments, and they were lying in the hospital. I took the Germans to a ward for old men. There were elderly men who were paralyzed, so in general there was—because they [the old men] wouldn't allow the room to be aired; well, the odor there was awful. Well, they went in and had a look, and I said, "I'm surprised because we only have elderly people here." And then, we went to the second ward where there were women, just as old, and when they saw that they retreated. The young patients were in the middle room that had once been a ballroom, and there were beds, but the Germans had had enough, and so they backed down. Obviously, somehow God helped out, and the Germans left, but for me that was a big *przeżycie.*

Olgierd recounts the happenings of his first night as the doctor on call with little, if any, exaggeration or exaltation of his own role in the events of the night. Indeed, he attributes the success of his deception not to his own cleverness or even to that of the hospital staff, but to God. The narrative still functions as a sort of coming-of-age story, albeit in miniature, in the sense that Olgierd faces his first night as the doctor on call and encounters a trial in the form of the search by the Germans, which he successfully thwarts, thus saving the patients in his care. That Olgierd does so by drawing on his knowledge of the Germans' distaste for disorder and anything that suggested uncleanliness makes it all the more satisfying, for Olgierd emerges as clever but humble.

For many this might have been the end of the story, but Olgierd remembers something more:

> Later, after the Germans had left, when I went to the room, to the boys who I knew were in the conspiracy. I said to them, "Listen," and they said, "We saw, and we heard." And they told me, "Sir, we've got grenades here under our beds, and if the Germans had come, we would have gotten them with the grenades!" Well, so fortunately! Because with those grenades they would have [killed] us all! Right? Immediately, there would have been shooting, and they'd have taken us all. That would have been an awful story. Well, so it was that kind of moment.

The Polish soldiers, those "boys" who were most likely his age mates, were ready to risk their own lives if it meant in doing so they could also kill a few Germans. Far from representing this as heroic, Olgierd recalls hearing of their plan with something akin to horror. Olgierd offers an image of youth dictating a course of action that would end their own lives in a blaze of glory (rather than in torture and anonymity at Pawiak or in a concentration camp, which would have been a probable consequence had they been discovered) while causing the deaths of countless others. Thus, it seems that Olgierd's actions not only saved the patients and staff from the Germans, but from the boys as well.

Olgierd's work at the Maltański Hospital continued until the summer of 1944, when he injured his finger and was unable to properly wash his hands without risking infection. At that point he was given leave from work in writing, a document that he still had in his possession when we met. Olgierd presented his work as conspiratorial insofar as it involved treating underground soldiers wounded in actions against the Germans, covering up the true cause of their injuries, and hiding them until they regained their health. In this way a task that would typically be seen as supporting the population during the time of war is regarded as an oppositional activity because the beneficiaries are involved in the military wing of the underground. As will become clear in the pages that follow, Polish society in general and the underground state in particular viewed working in the health service as conspiratorial. Moreover, members of the health service took an oath of loyalty to the Home Army and were full-fledged members of that organization. During the uprising, all health-care workers were members of the underground, and regardless of whom they served, their work was conspiratorial.

Although the beneficiaries may or may not have been members of the underground, Pani Eugenia's volunteer work during the occupation was quite substantial; however, she undertook it through her role as a teacher.

ELT: During the war did you take part in any underground organizations or in the army?

Eugenia: Proszę Pani, I did not belong to any military organizations, although there were attempts to recruit me, but my director protested. She didn't allow me to be pulled into any work [of that kind] because I was needed at the school to take care of things, to keep an eye on things, to take care of the schedule. She relied on my sense of responsibility and all, but I did belong to the Committee to Aid Teachers, which was organized by the Director of Public Schools because . . . well, a lot of teachers were in Warsaw, but many were from the western lands. They did not have apartments, they did not have clothes, they had nothing. They came from Poznań so encumbered, or from Płock, or from somewhere there by the Warta, because Poland was after all divided. We [Warsaw] were in the so-called General Government; that is what it was called. So, those from the western lands were driven out to the General Government. Teachers were thrown out of that area. So the committee had the aim of helping those teachers primarily, but not only. It tried to get supplies: food, clothing, shoes. It allotted these supplies to schools, and the schools were responsible for distributing the goods. So, I must tell you, immodestly, that I sewed things [for these displaced people]. It also happened that my friend's brother from Szymanowo, where we worked together, her brother was a city administrator who was chairman of the supply division. He was the chair, and because of that I went to him, and he gave us a great deal of flour, sugar, kasha, ration cards for food and clothing. We had a great deal at our disposal to send to schools, and the schools divided these things among themselves. Well, in that way for example, displaced teachers from Poznań, received twice as much as those from Warsaw.

I not only worked there at the office of the committee, but I also ran the chapter at the school, and no one ever protested. Each one was glad because when I received rice or kasha, well, during the war that was an enormous thing. Plus, they received shoes. They got a card and went to a normal shoemaker and could choose. Well, they paid for them, but they were there, and they got them. Indeed, I discovered a big role on that committee. Beginning in 1941, throughout the whole occupation until the end, until the uprising, we worked.

When the Germans closed all Polish secondary schools as well as a number of primary and middle schools throughout the city, many teachers were left without a regular income and thus were in need of the services that the Committee to Aid Teachers provided. Eugenia's volunteer activities reflect her professional loyalties. Her efforts at food procurement also aided the faculty, staff, and students at the school where she taught. From 1941 to 1944 she undertook this task without remuneration. Such a task does not involve engaging the enemy so much as minimizing the impact of Nazi policy on people's lives by providing them with the essentials of survival. In this sense Eugenia's work is much more in line with Gross's assessment of the underground state. Her work embodies the characteristics of resistance without fulfilling expectations for conspiratorial behavior; there are no secret meetings or messages carried to people known by pseudonym; there are no searches. Yet Eugenia took on this work under the auspices of the secret state, and therefore, she was clearly a part of the conspiracy.

Another essential part of the underground state was the secret press, something Jerzy N—— took part in early in the war.

> **Jerzy:** The secret press began to turn up, that means little dailies and brochures. First they were typed, and later they were printed . . . and, kind lady, in Warsaw there were hundreds of these papers. Some were weeklies, and it varied at different times, but in any case there were a few hundred titles.
>
> **Basia:** But not right away, not right away.
>
> **Jerzy:** Not right away, of course. Among other things in that first period of the war, with my friend from school, Jurek Suchocki here on Polish Army Avenue, because his mother was a German, and they had a radio at home.
>
> **Basia:** Because they confiscated radios, so one had to give them up.

Jerzy: Germans were allowed to have radios, but everyone else had to give them up. . . . So, at Jurek's there was a legal radio, and therefore, we illegally listened to London and made note of the news, and later I typed up—

Basia [interrupting]: And it went out to people—

Jerzy: A few dozen copies on the typewriter which were then distributed through the [housing] cooperatives. Pani Suchocka was scared to death, because she was a German, so she in particular would have been an easy target if we'd been caught. I remember how once when Jurek wasn't at home—because it was Jurek who arranged it all, and she said to me [imitating her German accent], "Mr. Jurek,[2] for the love of God, just don't tell anyone where you listened to the radio! Because you know what would happen!" I said, "Of course, nobody will know even if they cut me into pieces." And in that way we went on until May of 1940, and after the fall of France, it wasn't worth doing it because there were so many official [underground] publications that we could put it aside. And also in 1940, actually with Stefan and our mutual friend Zyga Grodewski—

Stefan: Lost, passed on.

Jerzy: So, in any case, the first papers were delivered to his home there on Mickiewicz Street. Stefan lived along the viaduct, so the greater part of the issue was distributed from there to other points. So I remember that I was riding a bicycle, and I had a wad of papers under my sweater, and I rode to Bielany with the wad to Barczyńska Street, and there I handed them over to the next courier. These were our beginnings [in the underground].

I found myself wondering if Jerzy and Jurek's paper may have been equal parts cure for boredom and journalistic endeavor. However, the value of the information they distributed and the way the existence of such papers functioned to create a sense that opposition was possible cannot be underestimated.

Pani Suchocka's reaction to the fact that Jerzy and Jurek listened to the radio suggests the conspiratorial nature of the act. Indeed, many described listening to the radio as an act of resistance. Sławomira described how her father would lock the door to their apartment with a chain on the inside so that the family could gather around the radio that belonged to the German officer quartered in their home to listen to news reports from Allied Europe without fear of being discovered: "In any case, for listening to the radio, there was the death penalty. One had to turn in one's radio. There wasn't a radio to be found in any Polish home. Well, that means radios were hidden somewhere, and some people would listen, but it was incredibly dangerous. At the same time distributing any kind of news, well, those who did that were running a terrible risk."

In 1939 in Warsaw, there were 18 clandestine papers like Jerzy's, and in 1940 this number grew to 84. Like Jerzy and his friend most of these journalists relied on broadcasts from England and France as their source of information (Szarota 1973a: 374; Gross 1979: 254). The number of underground publications, as well as their circulation, increased steadily each year of the occupation, and Bartoszewski has established that a total of 650 different underground papers were published in Warsaw during the war (cited in Gross 1979: 254).[3] Moreover, clandestine publications were not only limited to newspapers but also included journals published by political, social, and military organizations as well as professional groups and educational societies (Bartoszewski 1968: 390). Jan Tomasz Gross (1979: 255–56) points out that underground press and publications not only played a key role in distributing credible information about the state of the war but, in doing so, also undermined the Nazis' claims to legitimacy, acclimated Polish society to illegality, and legitimized the underground.

Despite the inherent risks involved, conspiratorial activities also served to fill a void in the lives of young adults who, like Jerzy, Basia, Stefan, Krystyna, and Olgierd, completed secondary school in the first years of the war. With the possibilities for continuing their formal education greatly limited, the conspiracy offered a sort of alternative education. Moreover, the usual sites of informal learning and entertainment such as libraries, museums, theaters, and concert halls were closed, and cinemas that remained open only played German propaganda films. Works by Polish artists, composers, and writers were banned from public presentation in cafés and other alternative venues. As a result private homes became venues for clandestine lectures, concert recitals, poetry readings, and plays. Jan R——— was one of several informants who recalled attending such events:

> I remember during the war, right away at the very beginning I was pulled into secret colloquiums in these small groups of eight or nine people. Immediately the history of Poland, the future of Poland, and exactly there Próchnik Street. Later, that became very common among the youth, and in this house, in this room such meetings of young people took place: discussions and lectures on various very interesting themes. First, the late Professor Bogdan Sucholdolski directed our attention to Catholic social philosophy of the French school of personalism. It was a philosophy which one could say was the most effective attitude against Marxism-communism. Manifest personalism became translated by my friends from French to Polish and published. . . . Later in 1941 even more interesting lectures took place, and I made contact with a professor who escaped from Russia. He was born in Siberia and escaped

right after the revolution of 1917 from Russia, and he taught in France and Czechoslovakia. Later, he married a Polish woman, and he spoke Polish well. He was named Sergiusz Hesen, and he gave a series of lectures on the topic of what was happening. His primary thesis was that communism was not at all the cure for the mistakes of capitalism. If the world has a complaint with capitalism, that it is unjust, that a lot of people suffer poverty, that they do not have any wealth, then communism doesn't erase that, and may even make some problems deeper. There were nine meetings on the themes of society, politics, economics, and cultural organizations. They took place in this room, and young people came who were very interested and they discussed. There was a movement of those people here.

Krystyna also recalled that intellectual activities outside the classroom took on a new intensity:

And now while talking to you, I'm reminded that the intellectual life in my school was very lively during the occupation. Before the matura we still had our academic circles and clubs, and there was low, middle, and high. We had private meetings. Performances were organized, and we created our own cultural life—it was half play, half serious. For example, we performed *A Midsummer Night's Dream* for our friends. I still remember how they kissed through the hole in the wall. Somehow, it keeps coming back to me now.

Olgierd Z——also recalled the importance of cultural life:

Aha, concerts were also organized in private homes. Those concerts were limited to playing on the fortepiano or the piano, and there was some sort of recitation too. Because no one went to—because there were theaters in Warsaw, but none of the Poles went to the theaters or the cinemas. There was a saying, "Only pigs sit in the cinema." Sometimes there would even be an action [carried out] by Polish saboteurs [*z grup dywersjnych Pola Polskich*]. To ensure that no one would go to the cinemas, they set off teargas in the theater so that people wouldn't go, because [the cinema] was profit for the Germans, of course. So it was about boycotting. There were these cafés that were run by actors; among others there was a well-known actress, Barszewska, and she worked in one called At the Actors on Mazowiecki, I remember. Well, and many, many other actors who worked in cafés recited or played instruments, but that was inside—small chamber concerts. Because it was about culture, about cultural life, about keeping it alive. In Żoliborz it was different in that everyone knew everybody else. In general everyone knew each other. So if there was some sort of roundup, immediately one warned others. They phoned, "Don't go out because there is a roundup here, a roundup there," so that people would stay put. So those days were very gray, right? But because a person was young, everything was interesting, and everything was a great adventure. It was a great adventure.

Such events were avenues for personal development, creative expression, and the exploration of intellectual curiosity. The impact on morale for both participants and audience members, though difficult to measure, cannot be denied. Of course, these productions were an important source of entertainment that brought people together, reaffirming their knowledge that their culture had value and that they, as individuals and as a people, were capable of artistic and intellectual achievement—the existence of which the Nazis sought both to destroy and to deny them. It is unclear whether work in the underground aided young people in preparing for a future in times of peace (see Gross 1979), but it did afford them a path of personal development that was otherwise closed to them due to the circumstances of the occupation.

Childhood Underground

People of all ages participated in the conspiracy. The narratives I have presented thus far reflect the experiences of adults with families and careers of their own and those of young people in their late teens and early twenties. In terms of recruitment, the underground recruited adults on the basis of specific skills that they possessed, as noted by Eugenia and Stefan. In contrast, young adults sought out the underground and tended to join it in one of two ways. Some were approached by friends who were already involved in the underground, on the basis of their trustworthiness, and then trained. Others sought out the underground by joining scouting troops or seeking connections among their friends and family members; this latter route is typical of school-aged children. Regarding their roles in the underground, adult males like Stefan tended to be in military positions, making preparations for combat. Just as Eugenia and Janina K—— worked to help refugees resettle and set up secret classes and schools for children, most adult women involved in the conspiracy took part in activities aimed at helping others survive the occupation. As the narratives of Olgierd Z—— and Krystyna illustrate, young men and women old enough to have completed high school filled supporting roles in the military wing of the underground by working as hospital technicians and couriers.

School-aged children also took part in the conspiracy; however, there were some substantive differences in the ways and reasons that children became involved, as well as in the types of activities in which they took part. In the preceding chapter on the occupation, I have suggested that the teaching and learning of banned subjects and the creation and maintenance of a system of secret secondary and post-secondary schools was a form of resistance against attempts to occupy the mind, to demoralize individuals, and to de-Polonize Polish society. Thus, children's initial forays into the underground came in the form of learning. For some, this was their only participation in the conspiracy; however, for others clandestine education was a point of entrée into other forms of resistance ranging from those aimed at creating social solidarity to training for armed resistance. In this way the activities of children in the underground mirrored the tensions and shifts in the underground state more broadly.

Sławomira's motivations for joining and her path to the underground are typical of those of many children between the ages of 12 and 16: "Of course, all of that [the conditions of the occupation] burdened normal life. It also changed my childhood, first of all because I had to grow up rather quickly. Well, these actions, so-called little sabotage [*mały sabotaż*] began. Little sabotage was, most of all, young boys who drew on the walls of the city 'PW'—a P with an anchor, which meant *Polska Walczy* [Poland Fights]."

Initially, children engaged in "little sabotage" were tearing down posters, throwing stink bombs into movie theaters where German propaganda films were the only featured films, or writing anti-German slogans on the walls. A favorite was "Only pigs sit in the cinema!" [*Tylko świnie siedzą w kinie!*] Many of these activities, however, were not individual acts of opposition but were actually organized by scouting troops. Yet, trivial as they may seem, even activities like these were punishable by death. Perhaps because one could just as easily be executed for tearing down a poster as committing a more significant act of opposition, the resistance activities of scouting organizations expanded in their scope. An older woman I talked with had two sons involved in scouting during the war, both under the age of 18. When I asked her whether she had not been afraid that they would be arrested or killed for taking part in all this, she retorted, "What for? They were just painting graffiti on walls!" Yet her sons' involvement grew beyond writing anti-German slogans to working as couriers for the Home Army, a job that eventually cost one of them his life. Sławomira recalls that her awareness that children her age engaged in resistance activities fomented her desire to be a part of the underground, too:

Indeed, underground military organizations [*organizacja walki podziemniej*] were created incredibly quickly because, actually, already by the end of the month [of September] when Warsaw was defending itself, people were already beginning to understand that they would have to capitulate, and the foundations of [the underground] were established. Well, of course, that being the case, I soon began to bother my parents that I wasn't going to sit at home idle, that I had to join something. You know, that first year came and later school started, and then I started to feel absolutely worthless that—it was an impossible thing that I hadn't already taken part.

When Sławomira recollected her despair in not taking part, I could hear the sadness in her voice. While her reaction may be similar to that of any child hurt at being excluded from activities deemed age inappropriate by her parents, it also reflects the enormous social support and approbation that participation in the resistance brought with it. After all, Sławomira is not merely protesting that she is left out but that she feels worthless for not participating. The realization that both her parents as well as her older sister were involved in the underground exacerbated her sense of being inferior and excluded.

I realized that my father was very deeply engaged in the underground, and Mama too, but in any case one didn't speak of those things exactly. Once, when I asked Father, "Listen, tell me something more," Father told me, "I won't tell you. I won't tell you, because if you don't know, you can't tell. But if you were to know something, you don't even know how much you can withstand. If they caught you, if they were to beat you, if they were to torture you, you don't know that you wouldn't tell, but if you don't know, you can't tell." You know, that was a very concrete lesson. Later, for example, he told me that if there were an arrest and an interrogation, and if I wrote a confession which they ordered me to sign, that you must sign immediately after the last word so that it's not possible [for them] to write anything more. Well, you know this was the type of knowledge—except that the Germans probably didn't follow protocol. Everything had changed, because Father remembered how it had been before during the first war, and here it was the second and everything was different. So, I began to rebel and demanded that I must get involved in some underground organization.

ELT: How old were you then?

Sławomira: I was 14 years old. At my mother's clinic there were a few offices, and it was an excellent point of contact—most of all people came about their teeth. As a result, practically all of the doctors there were engaged in some sort of underground work, except with different groups: the right, the left, the center, but it all went off exceptionally harmoniously. Also, the janitor who cleaned and lived there was a smuggler. So, in general the whole clinic was not kosher. Well, in the neighboring office, next to my mother's, worked her friend, Pani Halina Sadkowska, who had contact with the scouts, and she contacted them for me.

Sławomira was not alone in entering the underground through the Scouts. The majority of children who took part in the conspiracy began their work in the Polish underground through scouting organizations. As Sławomira explains:

So, I had contact with the scouts, and a girl came to me who later became my scout leader. She told me that we were going to start a new troop, and as a result we had to choose a few girls in order to create, first, a troop, then leaders, then the leaders would make their own troops, which would hatch their own leaders, and in this way it would grow. Well, of course, most of my acquaintances were girls whom I'd made friends with at school, so I talked to them, and we became a troop. First the group [of friends] became a troop, then a troop of leaders. That was already a very big thing for me, because I had joined an organization. And also it was well organized. From the beginning, we had the educational task of personal growth, because the point was that, although there was war and it was horrible, one had to develop; we couldn't allow the war to hamper that.

But how did scouting lead to membership in the Home Army and participation in armed insurrection against the German occupant? Sławomira explains in the following passage:

I was 15 years old at the beginning of 1943 when my scouting adventures began. We learned different types of skills. At the same time, we began to train for armed struggle, all of us. Because there was the attitude that at some point the uprising would break out, that the Germans would be repelled, and that would be the final chapter. In the process of preparing, we went through hygienic training in order to be, just in case, something like a medic. So, first we had lectures [in members'] homes, because, of course, we met together a few at a time, and if someone came from the Germans, well, we were simply playing. First a nurse and a doctor came and lectured on various fundamental things. Later we had training in hygiene, at the outpatient clinic at Dzieciątka Jezus Hospital. And think how well organized it was!

New groups were continuously going to the clinic for training. . . . It was wonderful because those groups were always changing, you know; it was very good training because we came into contact with various, authentic patients who were undergoing various surgical procedures which we took part in. We helped, let's say, not as qualified nurses but each time as a person who is becoming familiar and who is learning certain things, right? We saw what it meant, which tools and what they were used for, how one should bandage, how to give an injection, how—well a thousand different things. We were very happy with that . . . it lasted for all of 1943.

At the beginning of 1944, we took the Home Army oath and were sworn in to the Organization of Women's Military Service. This was terribly important for us! [*Szalenie ważne to było!*] I remember that experience. We made the oath to Doctor Joanna. We only knew her pseudonym—later we discovered who it was—and we made the vow in unison. We felt then that we were full-fledged soldiers in the Polish underground. At the same time, we went to school, right? If it's about my civilian life, if I can say that, well somehow it normalized, because my parents were very deeply engaged, especially my father.

While Sławomira trained as a medic, other children in different troops took courses in order to become couriers for the underground; this was the case for Hanna.

> **Hanna:** Now, if it's about Żoliborz, Żoliborz was very organized during the occupation. Because, this was a neighborhood of government clerks, and sons of army officers, and the like, so Żoliborz was very organized and various [underground] units were established here, above all Boy and Girl Scouts. I belonged to a troop. It wasn't just scouting. It was also at the level of the paramedic and courier service. I was with the courier service.
>
> **ELT:** What did that entail?
>
> **Hanna:** That meant telephones, carrying messages. Everything involved with connecting one with another. So, of course, we were trained. I belonged from the time I was 13, after the uprising I was 15. . . . But it was organized and so forth, and among us, shall we say teenagers, well there were a few of us, I belonged to the youngest caste [of scouts], but there were even younger ones . . . there were children, who were maybe ten years old then, and they carried letters, and the like, but that was something too. That was called the Gray Ranks—scouting. "We are marching together we scouts of the gray brotherhood" [*Idziemy szeregami my harcerska szara brać*].[4] That was our slogan. Of course that was all conspiratorial, one couldn't tell others.

However, as the occupation grew in duration, the differences between types of conspiratorial acts blurred, and children became involved in increasingly dangerous activities. This point is well illustrated in the following excerpt from an interview with Olgierd Z——:

> Since we're talking about the komplets, I wanted to tell you about an interesting occurrence that took place in 1943. The group was made up of my younger brother and his colleagues. There were five boys here. If you please, somebody reported that a group of young people were here, and the Germans came, surrounded the entire house and made a search. They searched, but all the boys had vocational school identity cards, as if they attended vocational school, and they said that they were studying and that they were preparing for a class at school and were getting ready to go. Fortunately the professor wasn't here. He was running late and had not yet arrived. They [the Germans] would have left, but one of my brother's friends had hidden in the wardrobe. The Germans opened it and saw what the situation was and took him.
>
> That they took him—that was nothing! My brother was interested in mechanics and he repaired weapons. You know, he was a gunsmith. If someone here needed [a weapon]—because all of us were in the conspiracy from the very beginning in various fields of action. Because my brother was already a handyman and he liked those things, and knew how to do it, so he repaired weapons. A variety of his friends brought weapons here, and he repaired them, because, of course, it was illegal to have weapons then.
>
> So, they [the Germans] took him [the boy who had been hiding in the wardrobe], and [as he was led away], my brother gave him a revolver he had repaired; he slipped it into the boy's pocket. And we thought, "Now they'll arrest us all." My mother was the only one who stayed here [in the house]. The mother of the man upstairs and the other couple stayed. They were older, but all the young people that night, we all went somewhere else to sleep. In case the Germans came, right? So it was a little—because they could have taken our parents. They might have taken Mama if we weren't here. It wasn't very sensible, but you know, under such pressure and all. But the situation was such that, when they left we searched the entire house to see if maybe he had thrown the revolver someplace. It wasn't anywhere to be found.
>
> Proszę Pani, as the Germans led him out through the gate, because it was autumn there was a pile of leaves . . . and he threw the revolver under those leaves because they were soft. So he was clean. Later they cleared him of the charges—some organization worked for his release. In some way they bought him out of jail. The organization bribed [the Germans], because

Germans could be bribed for a certain sum, and so they released him. When he came back, the first question was, "And where is the revolver?" "Well it's here" [in a pile of leaves]. The revolver was here all along, but the Germans hadn't found it.

The boys in this komplet were secondary-school students, and Olgierd's brother at least was sufficiently engaged in the underground to have been entrusted with repairing weapons, a scarce commodity in high demand. As much as their involvement in such activities implies a maturity beyond their years, the boys' actions during the search demonstrate that their judgment is that of adolescents. One boy panics and hides in the wardrobe, bringing himself, if not the whole group, under increased suspicion, while Olgierd's brother gives the boy a gun, which, had it been discovered, would have resulted in the boy's certain death as well as the arrest and imprisonment of all the boys in the komplet and possibly that of the entire household. Presumably Olgierd's brother wanted his friend to be able to defend himself against the Nazis, to have the option of not being taken alive, and should he have chosen death, to have the option of dying a heroic death by taking a few Germans with him. Later, as the search for the revolver suggests, Olgierd's brother reconsidered the wisdom of his gift. The fact that all the young people left the house for the night suggests that they realized or were made to see all the consequences that discovery might have entailed.

While the boys involved in the incident Olgierd described were in their last year or two of secondary school, children of a much younger age also became drawn into resistance activities, as Janina K—— recalled:

I had a pupil who was from Poznań—I don't know if he survived the uprising or not . . . Mirek T——. That was a very polite and nice little boy! One day, he was waiting for me in front of the classroom, the entrance was through the bathroom. [Because] my class was hidden, one had to go through the others to get to it. He took me to the bathroom and said to me, "Please Ma'am, I came by tram and lifted a German pistol with its holster, and I have it in my bag, and I am afraid to have it because the others could see it, and it's not the first time that I lifted something, but later I always throw them in the cellar of a burnt-out house at the corner of Marszałkowska and Wspólna. So please, Ma'am, could you please hide the pistol for me until the end of lessons?" An 11-year-old boy!

He was small and because the first three rows [on the bus] were reserved *fur Deutsche* [for Germans], he stood on the edge, and when some German turned his back, he used a sharp knife to cut it, then he hid [the gun] in his bag. [The German] didn't feel it, right. So, naturally I hid the gun, and naturally after the lessons I quipped, "Well, Mirku, come and walk me to the tram," or something like that so his classmates wouldn't hear it. We went, and he threw the gun, I still know exactly where, into a burnt-out house. The only thing left of it was the basement. I really would like to find out someday what happened to him; maybe he didn't survive, because no one knows.

That Mirek threw the guns into the same building each time so that somebody else could retrieve them later suggests that he was involved in stealing guns from the Germans on behalf of a Polish underground organization. It is equally possible that Mirek was not necessarily stealing arms for the underground but that he and some friends may have been collecting them independently. It is not clear which of these scenarios is closest to the truth, and indeed, had he been caught, the consequences for Mirek would have been the same regardless of whether he was doing so in an official capacity or had taken to stealing guns as a sort of game. Taken as an act that began and ended solely with Mirek, it illustrates the extent to which conspiratorial behavior, and all the risks it involved, had become normalized in the context of resistance and the eagerness of even young children to take a part in the conspiracy. Were it to be an activity undertaken as part of a group effort, it would point to the erosion of preexisting Polish social norms regarding the role of children in combat.

Social Norms Regarding Children in Combat

The narratives of people who experienced the war as children illustrate the allure of the underground for even young children, the scope of children's participation in the conspiracy, and how that participation changed over time. There are at least two policies of the Polish scouting authorities that shed some light on the experiences of children who, like Sławomira and many other, came to the underground through scouting. First, in 1939 it was considered inappropriate for primary-school-aged girls like Sławomira, who was then in the third grade, to participate in underground activities (Zawadzka 1995: 109). There was also, initially, a ban on accepting new members to troops, which made it difficult for someone who was not involved in scouting before the war to join. This effectively limited scouting membership to older children (ibid.). However, once this policy changed and new members were accepted during the war, they were recruited through existing members, as was Sławomira, rather than through the usual sort of open enrollment through neighborhood schools.

The slogan of the Polish Girl Scouts was "To endure, to help, to prepare" (ibid. 123–24). During the occupation, endurance for scouts was more than a matter of mere survival; rather, they were to endure in "the fullest sense of scouts" by developing their intellectual and moral lives through service to others. Thus, weekly meetings covered topics related to social service work, their school lessons, discussions of the difficulties of life in an occupied country, as well as self-education (ibid. 132). Much time was also devoted to the nature of morals (ibid.).

Some Girl Scout troops fulfilled their vow to actively help as early as the siege of Warsaw, in September 1939. In October of 1939, following the fall of Warsaw, troops with older members started working in the conspiracy (ibid. 109). At this point in the occupation, these conspiratorial activities included things one might expect of Girls Scouts in peacetime, such as reading to patients in Warsaw hospitals, writing letters for them, decorating hospital wards for the holidays, and running clothing drives for those in need. Other activities such as writing letters and sending packages to prisoners of war, taking part in the care of the children of prisoners of war and those wounded in the siege, volunteering at soup kitchens and reading rooms (*świetlicy*) that operated as after-school programs for children, and staffing night shifts at three Warsaw hospitals are more reflective of the strain that the conditions of the occupation had put on Warsaw's social services (ibid. 111). Some Girl Scout troops fulfilled their pledge to help through activities that were conspiratorial in the most literal sense, such as finding safe places in civilian homes for wounded Polish soldiers to stay while convalescing, finding them civilian clothes and civilian documents, and thus helping them to avoid arrest (ibid.). By taking part in training programs such as the ones that Sławomira and Hanna described, girls fulfilled the third part of the Girl Scout pledge, "to prepare," which during the war was taken as a call to prepare for service to the civilian population in the event of an uprising.[5]

Involving scouts in conspiratorial activities appears to have been a conscious choice on the part of scouting and underground authorities, one made in response to the fact that children were already finding ways to resist on their own. Indeed, it seems that underground organizations and the scouts deliberately trained children between the ages of 12 and 16 for noncombatant support roles specifically as a means to ensure that they were *not* on the frontlines. As Polish scoutmaster Jan Wuttke wrote in a letter to a colleague in the underground: "If we do not give the most active members of the troops of *Zawisza* something to do, these youngsters are going to start looking for things by themselves and can get recruited by some mindless line commander. . . . Youngsters in soldiers' units and frontline services are a disgraceful business" (quoted in exhibit at Museum of the Warsaw Rising).

On January 16, 1940, the Polish scouting organization created the Gray Ranks (*Szare Szeregi*), an underground scouting organization led by Father Jan Mauersberger along with three laymen and three laywomen (Zawadzka 1995: 102). The Gray Ranks had little trouble contacting scouting troops that had existed before September 1939. Soon, neighborhood scouting troops began working in conjunction with other, adult-staffed underground agencies, including social service agencies such as City Health Center (Miejskie Ośrodki Zdrowa), Polish Red Cross, Main Welfare Council (Rada Główna Opiekuńcza), and the Patrons for the Care of Prisoners (Patronat Opieki nad Więznami), as well as Service for the Victory of Poland (Służba Zwiecięstwa Polski), the last of which became the Union for Armed Struggle (Związek Walki Zbrojnej) (ibid. 104). The Union for Armed Struggle was a military organization that evolved into the Home Army (Armia Krajowa or AK), which took armed resistance as its goal (ibid.). Through their cooperation with these full-fledged underground agencies, children became more deeply involved in the underground, and their contributions to it became increasingly essential to the underground state's operations. As these organizations changed over time, shifting from a focus on aid to the population to endure the occupation to a focus on military resistance, children came closer and closer to battle.

Several studies conducted with children embroiled in more recent conflicts suggest that ideological commitment gives children a framework in which to understand political violence, thus mitigating the effects of psychosocial trauma associated with war (Punamaki 1996: 55, 56). One scholar has suggested that exposure to political violence increases ideological commitment among children and adolescents, increasing their willingness to risk physical harm in support of their beliefs (Punamaki 1996: 66; Punamaki-Gitai 1990: 34; Punamaki 1987). While Punamaki's findings are thought-provoking, ideology is treated as a variable in Punamaki's studies, with little attention given to the specific beliefs underlying it and the means by which they are interwoven into a worldview. For this reason it is impossible to know how it is that a particular ideology functions as a sustaining force for its adherents. Another important factor that lies beyond the purview of these psychological studies is the context in which ideology arises. In the case of political violence, those willing to take action in service of an ideology do so largely because they rightly or wrongly perceive themselves to be threatened by others; thus, the ideology that drives belligerent societies is key in shaping ideological responses to it. While it seems reasonable that an increase in violence would far outweigh any of the beneficial effects of ideology so as to diminish them completely, something different seems to be going on in the narratives I have collected. In the case of Poland during World War II, suffering only increased with time; yet so too did young people's resolve to overcome oppression and to reclaim control over their city. Their desire to free their nation, even at the expense of their own lives, only became stronger as the war dragged on, leading many young people to commit themselves to the military effort to overthrow German rule in Warsaw.

Resistance and Resilience

Attempts to problematize resistance as a concept offer some useful criteria in understanding informants' own perceptions of what constituted conspiratorial acts. Theories about resistance point us toward distinctions concerning which activities ultimately benefit self versus the community, toward differential evaluations of short-term and long-term activities, to judgments about the inherent risk of some activities (or lack thereof), to differences in the beneficiaries of acts motivated by ideology and those motivated by empathy or the suffering of others. These criteria certainly play a role in informants' perceptions of acts as conspiratorial. Yet, informants' ideas about what did and did not constitute resistance also illustrate the limitations of these theories to describe resistance in particular, to grasp the meanings assigned to activities in which real people engaged at a specific moment and place in time. Acts that benefit the individual actor may also serve the community and entail a willingness for self-sacrifice, as Pan Olgierd's work at the Maltański Hospital suggests. Pani Eugenia's work as a teacher and with the Committee to Help Teachers serves as a reminder that self-sacrifice can constitute something other than a willingness to die: it can be a devotion of one's time and energies to the well-being of others—a willingness to live for others. In practice, heroic and ordinary virtues become intertwined: caring for others can demand a will for self-sacrifice if offers of help run foul of the law. The narratives about going to school during the occupation (presented in the previous chapter) are full of phrases that suggest ideological commitment. Olgierd and Sławomira both assert that they were all the more motivated to learn by the Germans' assertion that Poles lacked the intellectual capacity to do so. Yet, while excelling at school might have confounded German attempts to enslave Poles, its immediate benefit was to the students who, in learning to the best of their abilities, developed personally, affirming the worth of their culture and history as well as their own dignity as human beings. Ideological goals become intertwined with those that benefit the self and the community. It is clear from the narratives of teachers like Eugenia and Janina K——that children were the immediate beneficiaries of their efforts in the underground schools, but surely such efforts also served the goal of preserving Polish culture. Scouting organizations also embraced and sought to inculcate in their members characteristics belonging to both ordinary and heroic virtues. As a result, the emphasis in workshops and training for Girl Scouts was to cultivate the self through service to others while at the same time developing individual abilities; and service to others was framed in terms of service to the nation. In this way, Polish scouting organizations cast the development of ordinary virtues and the enactment of these virtues on behalf of specific beneficiaries as furthering the abstract goal of freeing the nation.

Normalcy is essential for children to grow physically, intellectually, emotionally, and spiritually so as to develop as individuals and members of the community. Maintaining or re-creating the familiar amid the conditions of German-occupied Poland required conspiratorial behavior on the part of parents and teachers and a host of other adults who organized schools and scouting troops, found ways to entertain them, and procured food beyond the starvation-level rations allotted them. However, the only space for childhood in any normal sense was underground, and thus children themselves became members of the conspiracy: they went to underground schools and learned forbidden subjects from banned books. Their entertainment could hardly have been other than illegal, and their very existence depended on breaking rules about who could buy and consume certain types and quantities of food. It is this re-creation of the familiar underground that allowed the will to survive to be sustained during the years of the Nazi occupation, and it is the will to survive that surely leads us to rebuild life worlds damaged by the experiences of war.

When a group of people is confronted with an enemy that seeks to alter everyday life in order to facilitate their utter subjugation and exploitation, conventional definitions of resistance do not suffice as tools to explain how people interpret their own behavior. I am not claiming that children who learned enthusiastically or teenagers who put on plays for friends or wrote their own underground newspapers or women who purchased meat from smugglers or their families who consumed it were heroes. Rather, I have asked whether we perceive these acts as resistance in an effort to illustrate that resistance is not some abstract concept but, rather, a response to a particular set of circumstances. Ultimately, resistance is about perceptions of threat, of suffering, of risk, and of what sacrifice entails. In this way it is unique and varying, depending on the goals, or the perceived goals, of the people and policies one seeks to resist. If one sees the destruction of one's culture as foremost of the enemy's goals as many Poles did (rightly or wrongly), then reading the literature, learning the history, performing plays, and listening to the music of one's own country becomes a political act. It becomes an act in which self-interest and community benefit are intertwined in that it is simultaneously an expression of one's own dignity and worth and an act that preserves one's culture.

Self and Community: Concluding Thoughts

In the preceding pages, I have drawn on informants' narratives to illustrate that, in practice, boundaries between self and community—in questions about who benefits from an act of resistance—are not clearly defined. Recent research on the effects of political violence suggests that the type of resistance that grows out of ideological commitment may actually have psychological benefits for the individuals involved (Punamaki-Gitai 1990: 29).

If individuals reap the benefit of resilience from ideological commitment to opposition, then by extension social solidarity is one potential by-product of states' use of random violence in collective punishment (see Gross 1979: 203). Indeed, the cultivation of social solidarity would seem to be a necessary step in re-creating life worlds. Many of my informants mentioned the sense of community that was created in the face of shared threat, something that Pani Sławomira recalled quite fondly:

> Of course, one thing that was wonderful during the occupation was the unity of Polish society, you know. That a person could feel at home despite all the horrible external circumstances, could feel at home and know that it was possible to ask anyone [for information]. If there was, for example, a roundup, then immediately someone would run through the streets yelling, "Roundup! Hide!" And everyone then would clear out. If there was a roundup someplace, everyone would telephone, and they said, "Well, don't go out today, because it's raining," although the sun was shining beautifully, because it was understood that one shouldn't go out because something was happening there, and so on, and so forth.

Examples of this type of solidarity are abundant in my interviews. Because the German occupation of Poland lacked even the facade of legitimacy, those who opposed it could claim a degree of moral authority by exhibiting

commonly held values such as patriotism, loyalty, and compassion. In this
way even small acts of kindness gave those who witnessed them a sense of
shared hardship and a sense of shared values. Olgierd Z—— describes this
quite clearly:

> Well, working at the [Maltański] hospital I had many *przeżycia.* One of these
> that I remember was Christmas Eve day, I haven't forgotten it yet. Christmas
> Eve [*Wigilia*]. It was very picturesque, because [the hospital] was once a
> palace. . . . Now, the garden there is very small, [but] before the war there
> were many little parks there in back of the palace. . . . When it was quiet,
> one could sit in the little park and imagine that one was somewhere in a
> hospital on the front in an old palace, on an estate—field hospitals like one
> used to read about somewhere in mansions or palaces in the woods. Pani, we
> had *Wigilia* there: there was a Christmas tree, everyone sang carols, and we
> shared Christmas wafers [*opłatki*] with all the patients. So, for me as a young,
> beginning doctor, that was a great, great *przeżycie.* That was that.

The sharing of Christmas wafers has been the climax of all the Christmas
Eve celebrations I have taken part in during my stays in Poland. The ritual,
which takes place before the meal, is begun by the head of the household—
or in the case of workplace observances like the one Olgierd describes, the
director—passing out very thin, white wafers (often embossed with a star or
a representation of the Holy Family in a stable) to everyone in attendance.
He or she then wishes all who are present the best for the future. This
entails more than joyfully proclaiming "Merry Christmas!" Often there are
speeches that include apologies for the offenses of the preceding year, as
well as expressions of hopes and concerns. It is a very solemn moment,
followed by each person going to all the other guests in turn to offer their
wishes for the New Year. When each has asked for the other's forgiveness
and wished the other a variety of things for the future, they each take a piece
of the other's wafer and eat it. Each person present thus consumes a piece of
everyone else's wafer and gives and receives wishes to and from all who are
present. This ritual recalls the sacrament of communion in the use of wafers
to symbolize the bread at the Last Supper and the body of Jesus, as well as
in the spirit of community that this religious ritual is intended to evoke.
Olgierd continued with his recollection of that wartime Christmas Eve:

> The curfew was eight o'clock in the evening. So one had to get home before
> eight. I went home by tram, and I remember that at a certain point a drunk
> got on the tram, a sort of tipsy guest, and he said—and it was the drunk [who
> said this], "Ladies and gentlemen, we are riding on the tram, right? And here

is our poor conductor who doesn't have money. Let's all pitch in for him on Christmas Eve." And the change began to pour in. And that is interesting that such a tipsy drunk, who, it seemed to me, was a man from the margins, that he took the initiative and that everyone took part. And I remember the happy face of the conductor who must have been moved by it and who didn't have money, because those earnings that the Germans paid were very low, and he must have had a family, and he was happy because of it.

And when I got off at Plac Wilsona, I remember that, as I walked home, there was this fog already that day, so it was foggy, and so it was difficult to see, and at a certain moment I heard a violin playing "Lullaby for Jesus" ["Lulajże Jezuniu"—a Polish carol]. And here on the corner of Krasiński was the so-called House under the Mother of God, on the corner of Kanieżna and Marymoncki Street, where at this moment is the drycleaners and the shop with the secondhand clothes, here on Mickiewicz across from Feniks. And there stood a man with a little boy, playing carols on a violin. And it was so moving.

The atmosphere Olgierd describes borders on magical: the image of a palace in the woods, the city enveloped in fog. So, too, are the people he describes: the impoverished drunk who takes up a collection for the grateful conductor, the image of the musicians playing carols, scenes that Olgierd remembers for the rest of his life. In this remembrance of a wartime Christmas Eve, Olgierd vividly describes the feeling of connection, of communitas, that he felt with all those he encountered that night. It is a scene that inscribes humanity and solidarity on all therein. But the sense of unity comes from symbols that are, if culturally transcendent, religiously specific, and in that sense the solidarity created is a limited one.

By seeking to develop intellectually and culturally, by serving others, and by remaining decent human beings, in other words by cultivating and practicing ordinary virtues, Poles sought to embody the values denied them by the Nazi occupation and to weave a web of solidarity that would allow them to preserve their culture. Though important aspects of resisting, these were only preludes to the enactment of the heroic ideals on which my informants had been raised. Above all else, these ideals celebrated sacrifice for the nation and for the continued existence of the Polish state and Polish culture. As is apparent in the narratives, the sacrifice sought was not time or energy but life itself.

5 Reflections on Helping Polish Jews

NOT LONG AFTER RETURNING from my fieldwork, I met with a friend and fellow anthropologist whom I had not seen for some time. As we talked about our experiences in the field, I described my informants as people who had taken part in the Polish resistance. At some point in the course of conversation, I mentioned my disappointment and dismay in discovering that one of these people not only had been a member of a fascist organization before the war but also still harbored anti-Semitic views. My friend, who is a Jewish American anthropologist, was shocked and asked how someone who hated Jews could be in the resistance. For my friend resistance to the Nazis meant to help Jews; in her view it was the primary reason for the existence of the underground. I suspect that many Americans share my friend's understanding of anti-Nazi resistance. The reality, of course, is that the main goal of those involved in the Polish resistance was not to save Polish Jews but to prevent the disintegration of Polish society as a whole and ultimately to liberate Poland from Nazi control. Ironically, aiding Jews, which many Americans see as the epitome of Nazi resistance, is something that few of my informants, including those who were active in aiding Polish Jews, described as opposition. In the pages that follow, I explore wartime assistance to Polish Jews through a variety of my informants' narratives about helping Jews. One might ask why we should concern ourselves with their narratives on the subject when relatively few of them were involved in extending aid to Jews. My informants on this topic are representative of the Polish intelligentsia who came of age during the war. It is this segment of society whose recollections of the occupation are most commonly represented in Polish popular representations of the war, be it in film or print. It is precisely this population that we might expect to be the most knowledgeable about postwar scholarship on the plight of their Jewish compatriots during the war. Finally, it is this group's discourse on the topic that we might expect to carry the most influence in Poland in terms of changing misperceptions or reinforcing them. These narratives offer insight into informants' perceptions of who was involved in helping and the amount of help given by Polish society as a whole. More significant, these anecdotes of help, whether it was opportunistic, short-term, or long-term, reveal some of the barriers to offering assistance and the risks involved for those who undertook such efforts. By focusing on how elderly residents of Żoliborz talk about wartime assistance to Polish Jews, I hope to illuminate the processes by which misunderstandings and ignorance about the plight of Polish Jews and those who sought to help them have been perpetuated through discourse.

Although I typically use the term "Polish Jews" or "Jewish Poles" with reference to Jews living in Poland, my informants do not and tend to refer to their Jewish compatriots simply by their individual names or as "Jews" (*Żydzi*). Whether they do so because we are talking about Poland, and to them this seems implied, or because they do not see Jews as Polish is difficult to ascertain. I personally prefer to err on the side of generosity and assume that they feel this is implied unless the informant has given me reason to believe otherwise—but this is something that the reader must decide. In any case, my informants' usage is, for better or worse, standard throughout contemporary Poland. When discussing individuals who according to my informants were assimilated or who had converted to Christianity, I describe them as being of Jewish *descent*. I am aware that some scholars use the term "heritage" in such cases; however, to an anthropologist, heritage suggests a cultural identity with a group, a connection that I lack the necessary data to infer. In contrast, descent simply implies a geneological tie.

Historical Background: Disparate Points of View

Prior to World War II, an estimated 3.5 million Jews lived in Poland. Jewish Poles comprised an estimated 10 percent of the country's population, the largest Jewish population within a single country in Europe. This figure does not include people of Jewish heritage who self-identified as Catholic but were defined by Nazi policy as Jewish. In some urban areas like Warsaw, Jews made up one-third of the city's population. Though not the largest of Poland's prewar minorities (there were 4.5 million Ukrainians living in Poland before the war), Jews were quite possibly the most satisfied minority in the sense that unlike Ukrainians, Byelorussians, and Germans living in

Poland, who identified with other nations and whose loyalties lay outside of Poland, Jews tended to view themselves as Polish citizens (Tec 1986: 14). However, scholars estimate that less than 10 percent of Polish Jews could be described as assimilated (ibid. 37). Others have argued that even those who assimilated were not necessarily integrated into Polish society (Heller 1977, cited in Tec 1986: 37). For Polish Jews the issues of assimilation and integration constituted a major barrier both to survival and to rescue during the German occupation of Poland. Most Polish Jews who survived the war in Poland did so either by passing as ethnic Poles—in other words as Christians—or by going into hiding (see Tec 1986; Engelking 2001). The less assimilated, then the more difficulty an individual would have in passing as an ethnic Pole and the less likely he or she would be to have non-Jewish friends, co-workers, or acquaintances to whom to turn as potential sources of help. Moreover, passing was not for everyone. While Germans were often unable to determine who was or was not an ethnic Pole, many Poles felt they could draw such distinctions on the basis of physical appearance, gestures, linguistic fluency, or the more subtle use of certain phrases that betrayed the speaker as Jewish (Tec 1986; Engelking 2001). This rendered Jewish Poles vulnerable to denunciation by their Polish neighbors (Tec 1986; Engelking 2001). Moreover, unless they simply never reported to the ghetto or never followed Nazi decrees to identify themselves as Jews, an approach taken by a relatively small number of Polish Jews, passing had to be preceded by one of the following acts: leaving the ghetto illegally, escaping from a ghetto that was being liquidated, escaping from a train headed for a concentration or death camp, or escaping from a concentration camp (Tec 1986: 31). In other words, it required no small amount of courage, planning, help, and luck.

Regardless of whether an individual chose to pass or to hide, with few exceptions Jews required the aid of non-Jews in order to survive. These obstacles to survival were further complicated by the punishment set by Nazi policy for helping Jews in Poland. Lest the implied threat of the ghetto or the concentration camps—that those who helped Jews would share their fate—proved insufficient as a deterrent, the Nazis passed a law in Poland that made the threat explicit by stating that anyone caught giving shelter or any other type of aid to Jews would be executed along with all other members of the household. The interpretation of household varied: sometimes the Germans limited it to family members of the individual aiding Jews, and other times they interpreted it more broadly to include anyone living in the same dwelling. This meant that the Germans deemed culpable all members of a house divided into flats or an entire apartment building. This punishment was not implemented in other occupied countries where the penalty for sheltering or otherwise aiding Jews was more typically a fine or the imprisonment of the individual determined to be responsible. As a deterrent in Poland, Germans carried out death sentences for aiding Jews swiftly and publically.[1] Sławomira recalled a house that she passed frequently on her visits to a Warsaw suburb during the war. The vacant house and its garden were lovely but had fallen into disrepair, and she wondered why no one was living there. She finally asked an acquaintance from the area, who sighed and told her that since the Germans had murdered the family inside the home for sheltering Jews, local residents considered the house to be ill-fated. No one wanted to live there.

Many Americans, accustomed to viewing the war through the lens of the Holocaust, also view the conflict as a dyadic relationship, one between Germans and Jews. From such a perspective the country in question is typically only a backdrop, the majority population only supporting actors in the unfolding drama of the plight of European Jews, and accordingly the behavior of supporting actors is evaluated only in terms of the extent to which it helped or hurt Jews. This perspective is a valid one. The problem is that, like any, it is positional and partial and therefore, insofar as it strips the events of the sociocultural context in which they occur, limits our understanding of these same events.

Ethnic Poles' understanding of the war is also dyadic in that they view it as a conflict with Germany, one in which the survival of Polish culture and the existence of Poland as an independent state was at stake (Engelking 2001: 23). From this perspective Jewish Poles shared the same fate as all Poles, something that many ethnic Poles still believe. Those who recognized at the time that Jewish Poles suffered in greater proportion and for the sole reason of being Jewish often saw the fate of Polish Jews as intertwined with that of Poland as a whole. As a result these individuals subordinated the alleviation of Jewish suffering to the cause of liberating Poland from German occupation, a goal that they felt would ultimately benefit all.[2]

For Polish Jews the situation was quite different, constituting a triadic relationship among themselves, the Poles, and the Germans (ibid.). Prior to the war Polish Jews had an asymmetrical relationship with Poles that was characterized by dependency. This situation limited their choices to living within Poland but apart from Poles or assimilating and giving up at least a part of their Jewish identity, such as speaking Yiddish or emigrating (ibid. 24). The war only increased this asymmetry: Poles did not need their Jewish compatriots in order to resist the Germans. Moreover, due to widespread stereotypes about Jewish "passivity" that ignored the history of Jewish participation in the Polish uprisings of the nineteenth century as well as their participation in the campaign of 1939 and in the Polish army abroad, many Poles did not see Jews as capable of contributing to resistance efforts. In contrast, Polish Jews needed their fellow citizens in order to survive: to pass or to go into hiding. During the war discriminatory regulations, public humiliation, and the establishment of the ghetto all worked to create a psychological distance that served to reinforce the preexisting social distance (Engelking-Boni 2003). German brutality created Polish solidarity, but it was not an all-encompassing social solidarity, and it often did not include Polish Jews. As Carole Nagengast (1994: 122) has demonstrated, violence has a tendency to polarize society by "creating punishable categories of people, forging and maintaining boundaries among them, and building the consensus around those categories that specifies and enforces behavioral norms and legitimates and de-legitimates specific groups." Barbara Engelking-Boni (2003: 52) argues that Poles in the underground were willing to risk their lives for a variety of conspiratorial activities but not for sheltering Jews. She concludes that Poles did not define Polish Jews as part of that community that resistance was meant to benefit (ibid).[3]

One can read a range of attitudes toward helping Polish Jews and more generally to the place of Polish Jews in the broader community of Poles in the narratives I present. Some accounts assert that Poles gave much help to Jews but are vague on the details, locating the help with anonymous others or commonly in the community as a whole. Others consist of informants' personal accounts of their own efforts to help, typically on a small scale, or their desire to assist and how risks thwarted or dampened their efforts. Overtly or subtly, all speak to the issue of moral accountability and the responsibility that this entailed.

Accounts of Help

Nearly everyone I spoke with while conducting my fieldwork mentioned knowing someone who had helped Jews. However, when I questioned further, this was often an instance that had been widely publicized or a vague sort of reference to a friend of a friend, whose name they no longer recalled, or a contact that never panned out. In other cases, the people who had helped were known to my informants but had been acquaintances of their parents and long since dead. In the following pages I will review and discuss narratives about helping others—primarily, though not exclusively, Polish Jews. These narratives vary from widely circulated stories of help that "everybody knew about" to specific acts of individuals that reflect varying degrees of involvement with and commitment to the individuals they sought to aid.

"Everybody Knew about It": Secondhand Accounts

In Poland it is widely believed that a substantial number of Poles aided Polish Jews during the war. In 1987 Polish scholar Teresa Prekerowa challenged the notion that a large portion of the Polish population had aided the Jews during World War II. Prekerowa estimated that out of an adult population of 15 million, between 160,000 and 360,000 Poles had aided Jews in some way or another. Moreover, she found that about 1 to 2.5 percent of the Polish population had been involved in providing Jews with safe shelter (Prekerowa 1987). Prekerowa's work shows that the vast majority of Poles were not involved in helping Jews. More recent studies suggest that Poland's record was typical for all of Nazi-occupied Europe; in other words only 1.5 to 2 percent of the population of any German-occupied country in Europe became involved with providing shelter to its Jewish neighbors (Gushee 1994: 10).

My informants do not necessarily generalize willingness to help to the whole of the country, nor even to the whole of the capital, but most do see Żoliborz as a neighborhood that was particularly exemplary in this respect, as Olgierd B——indicates in the following passage:

> Well, during the war, Żoliborz passed the test in my opinion. It was a wonderful neighborhood, where it was extremely rare, only sporadically were there incidents of betrayal like the so-called *szmalcownictwo*. I don't know if you know that word. A *szmalcownik* was a person who blackmailed Jews, and if he got some money or some other valuable things, he either turned them in or he didn't. And if he got nothing he turned them in. So this was a repulsive species of human that appeared. Probably everywhere, in every country in catastrophic times, it happens that there are heroes and there are also rogues. So, you know, [this was] simply a low form of man.
>
> In Żoliborz, there were very few of these, very rarely did one come across them, even though Żoliborz was full of—the entire youth was in the [underground] army, the neighborhood was full of Jews in hiding, and so for the szmalcowniks there were, indeed, people to turn in here. All the same, there was very little of that. Those enormous blocks [of apartments] were full of Jews. Everybody knew it, and nobody denounced anybody. For example, that gigantic apartment building on Wilson Place, where there are over 200 apartments, there were a lot of Jews living there. There were no arrests. So, in this sense Żoliborz turned out to be simply a wonderful neighborhood. I would say there is something to praise there, right?[4]

Szmalcownicy, literally "greasy-palmers" or blackmailers, constituted a particularly severe problem in Poland. Holocaust scholar Israel Gutman has charged that it was only in Poland that blackmailing and denouncing Jews, as well as the people who helped them, became a profession (Gutman 2003: 117). What is notable about Olgierd B——'s comments is the observation that in contrast to other neighborhoods there were few denunciations in Żoliborz. His point may be interpreted in a number of ways. Olgierd made his comments in response to a question about aid to Polish Jews, and he therefore raises questions about what is perceived as assistance. Assuming that he is not elevating the doing of no harm to an act of help or of opposition, what was Olgierd claiming for Żoliborz? The assertion that Żoliborz was a place where Polish Jews could hide in the open might be taken as a measure of the neighborhood residents' acceptance of Jewish Poles. Such conclusions are probable, given that the neighborhood was a stronghold of the Polish Socialist Party, which embraced and advanced an inclusive definition of Polishness. Olgierd is also suggesting that Żoliborzians were less willing to collaborate with the Germans, a safe assumption given that many residents had ties to the Polish army and were active in the underground. Thus, in his assertion that Żoliborzians were more loyal to their neighbors and their country, Olgierd suggests that in Żoliborz aid to Jews during the war was a measure not of the neighborhood's opposition but of their humanity.

One of the most frequently told stories about Żoliborz residents helping Polish Jews invariably came up when informants described the geography of the neighborhood. Between Żoliborz and Muranów, the Warsaw neighborhood where the Germans created the ghetto, were barracks for the homeless. Several informants told me that Jews who escaped from the ghetto sought and received refuge from the people who lived there. In recounting this, many emphasized that, although the residents of the barracks were the poorest of the poor, they never betrayed a single Jew.

> **ELT:** I've heard that during the occupation a lot of Jews were hidden here in Żoliborz.
>
> **Joanna:** Yes. Yes, they escaped from the ghetto and hid here in Żoliborz, and you know, it is a very interesting thing. You know where Stołeczna Street is? Between Stołeczna and Polish Army Avenue, there were barracks—housing for the poorest, slums. People there stole, they drank vodka, they did various unbelievable things, but when someone escaped and the Germans looked [for them], if they made it to those barracks, to the slums, they [the slum-

dwellers] didn't turn them in. Yes. They helped an enormous number of people: people from the Home Army, Jews escaped there.

My informants frequently invoked this story as an example of how *everyone* in Żoliborz conspired to rescue Jews. Many others mentioned the presence of Jewish families who lived in Żoliborz throughout the war passing as Catholic Poles to strangers while "everybody" knew that they were Jewish. I heard this story so many times that I began to wonder if everyone was telling me about the same family or if there were multiple families of Polish Jews in Żoliborz who trusted their neighbors enough to hide in plain view. These stories were vague in the sense that no one seemed to know the names of the families or what had happened to them. There were also few references to places, which struck me as odd, given the proliferation of geographic details in the narratives. What bothered me most was that no one seemed to have known the Jewish family or families personally, a fact that also seemed to contradict my informants' conviction that everyone in Żoliborz knew everybody else. I began to suspect that I had entered the realm of urban legend, of retrospective wishful thinking, until Bogumiła (who was too young to actually remember much of the war) and her lifelong neighbor Irmina had the following exchange during an interview:

> **Irmina:** There was always our schoolfriend who everyone knew was of Jewish descent, but we were not allowed to speak of it, to bring it up. They were really wonderfully educated, that family was able, you know, in those conditions—
>
> **Bogumiła [interrupting]:** They were here, not in the ghetto?
>
> **Irmina:** No, here.
>
> **Bogumiła:** And everyone knew?
>
> **Irmina:** Of course everyone knew!
>
> **Bogumiła:** And nobody turned them in?
>
> **Irmina:** No. Well, you know, after all, Pani Kamerwach also taught us.
>
> **Bogumiła:** Really? For the whole war? But I thought she hid somewhere in Świdrze.
>
> **Irmina:** Not for all of it, not for the entire war. Right before the end she lived on Kieleczyźnie where the train station was and [taught] where my aunt also taught. Of course, that was a secret school. Then she hid at the Murawskis' on an estate where many people were hiding. But they hid and even then, however, they taught in those secret komplets, and they taught Polish and everything possible. . . . People were very brave during the war, truthfully.

Here was something more specific: Irmina gives names and information about how she knew this family and offers details about place. Perhaps equally noteworthy though is the fact that the family was clearly integrated into the community. This was an assimilated family with preestablished, strong ties in the neighborhood. Turning them in would have been turning in their own. That my informants assert that many Polish Jews living in Żoliborz during the war neither went into hiding nor had to pass but went on with their lives, successfully avoiding denunciation and arrest can be taken as an assertion that Żoliborz was a safe and comfortable place and that Polish Jews had nothing to fear from their neighbors. It is, in short, a claim about their own decency.

Some informants recounted specific incidents of their friend's or neighbor's willingness to help Jews. Though secondhand, these accounts were about rescuers known to the teller and thus more credible. Olgierd Z——, for example, told me the following story in the course of describing his neighborhood before the war: "In the other half of the double house, where the [public] library is now, lived Pani Skrzydełska. Her husband died and her children, her son and daughter, were in the uprising. At the same time she hid a Jewish man. He was in a hiding place in the wall of her basement, and later, after the war, she married that man. When the Germans occupied Żoliborz [after the Uprising of 1944], they hid here in the ruins until the liberation."

What can we make of informants' claims about Żoliborz? Historian Gunnar Paulsson notes that Żoliborz's Warsaw Housing Cooperative, run by the PPS, provided many hiding places for Jews, citing documents in which Żegota activists described the apartment complex as "swarming" with Jews (Paulsson 2002: 168, 266n6). "Antek" Zuckerman noted that as a neighborhood of laborers and working intelligentsia, "naturally it was more comfortable for a Jew to hide there than in other parts of the city" (ibid. 266n7). Marek Edelman, one of the leaders of the Warsaw Ghetto Uprising and a participant in the Warsaw Uprising of 1944, also remembered Żoliborz as a neighborhood that was better than the rest with regard to how ethnic Poles behaved toward Polish Jews (Assuntio and Goldkorn 1999). Taken together, such accounts suggest that these stories about Polish Jews who hid in the open in Żoliborz are rooted in reality.

Personal Accounts

In discussing informants' personal accounts of aid given to others, I have divided the narratives into three categories according to the type of assistance offered: small acts, short-term, and long-term help. In my conversations about the war, many people talked about taking part in small acts of help. Olgierd Z——'s job mixing medicines at the Pharmacy under the Star in the Little Ghetto entitled him to a pass that allowed him to enter and leave the Warsaw Ghetto in order to go to work. Olgierd used this as an opportunity to help people he encountered there. He recalled:

> We immediately began to actively help the Jews who were there. We carried correspondence, letters [to and from the ghetto] because they weren't allowed to write anything, and even if they had been everything was censored. We also carried packages if someone asked for something. And, of course, we did it for free, none of us thought of compensation, because it was just the normal humane thing to do. . . . We had some possibilities [to help], but at the same time they were limited possibilities. Of course, one had to watch out because if the Germans saw that something was helpful they took it away, so one had to be very, very careful. But fortunately, somehow I was never searched, never. I had a bag that was not very large, and I always had letters, and I could bring things. For such a young man as me, that was an enormous thing to live through, watching those people dying in agony on the streets. And there was nothing to be done, right? Except with what I had in the pharmacy.

Carrying letters may seem like a trivial activity in the face of Nazi brutality in the ghetto, but the information and moral support they conveyed should not be discounted (see Oliner and Oliner 1988: 57). Letters carried out communicated the reality of life in the ghetto to the other side, while those smuggled in brought information, hope, perhaps even possibilities of rescue.

Most of the narratives about small acts of help were offered in the context of answering questions that had nothing to do with either resistance or helping others. For example, when I asked Pani Janina K—— about how often and under what circumstances she thought about the war, she recalled how the Nazis treated prisoners of war. As her husband, an officer in the Polish army, was being held at an *Oflag* in Romania, this was a matter of great personal interest to her. While I was actually trying to get at the issue of what events, places, or people served as triggers of memory, Janina K—— understood the question as pertaining to those occurrences that came to mind most frequently. One of the incidents she recounted is the following story about her efforts to help Russian prisoners of war:

> At a certain point, the Germans established a temporary camp for Russian prisoners of war [near the hospital]. It was a field of the size, well, let us say

the size of four of these rooms, such that in the beginning there was grass, and other than the fence there was no other building. And there were, well, I don't know how many, but around a hundred or maybe more of those soldiers, Russian soldiers. Under the naked sky, without food. When one walked by, there was only one groan, "Lady, bread, bread." And a German walked around the perimeter with a rifle. Sometimes the prisoners asked, "Give me a smoke." So, I took a packet of some kind of cigarettes, and as I was walking by I threw half a loaf of bread, and then I went farther, and I threw the packet of cigarettes.

You know, [the way they were treated] that gave the impression that they were animals, because even an animal, like a cow tied out [to graze] or something, there's water or something, no? [With irony] Those were well-treated prisoners of war.

Clearly Janina's goals in relating the story were not to present herself as altruistic or self-sacrificing but, rather, to draw attention to how Germans treated their prisoners of war, a matter of great personal interest. Dehumanization of the sort Janina K—— described was, of course, the central modus operandi of the Nazis, one that served a variety of functions within Nazi-occupied Poland. In addition to being a powerful way to repress resistance, many studies have demonstrated that this dehumanizing brutality made the work of genocide possible for those who were charged with actually carrying it out (Browning 1993; Lifton 1986; Sereny 1983). Such violence also polarized communities that were already distanced from each other, thus serving to enforce certain behavioral norms within occupied Poland. In other words, by dehumanizing Jews or Russian prisoners of war, the Nazis created a barrier to helping them that was, in part, maintained by the very fear fomented by witnessing their imprisonment. Janina recognized this dehumanization when she said, "that gave the impression that they were animals." Violence of this sort creates social distance between the victims and the witnesses to their suffering (Foucault 1977; E. Martin 1987; Scarry 1987). While the cruel conditions created a boundary between Janina and the Russian prisoners, it was not an absolute barrier, as her efforts to help them illustrate. However, like Olgierd working in the Little Ghetto, the lack of material resources and the fear created by violence limited Janina's willingness to help and, more to the point, her ability to do so.

What both Janina and Olgierd's accounts have in common is that assistance is offered in response to a specific situation in which a need for help is clearly present. These acts of help are sometimes premeditated but often opportunistic: those offering aid see the need for help and an opportunity to fulfill it and seize the moment. Because of their opportunistic nature these acts tend to be small in both scope and outcome, in the sense that an act such as carrying correspondence or tossing bread and cigarettes over a wall is not going to save an individual's life in and of itself. However, such help can give the recipients the sense that others recognize their suffering and are reacting with a measure of compassion.

Some opportunistic acts can have wider repercussions. My neighbor Pani Zofia arrived at the apartment of her friends, a young couple with an infant, just as the Gestapo came to arrest the couple for their activities in the underground. The Gestapo were busy with the couple and took little notice of Zofia, who calmly picked up the couple's infant child as if he were her own and walked out of the apartment and out of the building. Unable to return home with the child for fear of being followed and arrested herself, she hid with the child for several days until she was able to locate relatives to care for the baby. The Gestapo took the couple to Pawiak and executed them, while their child, carried away by Zofia, survived.

Other accounts of help include incidents of short-term help, usually in the form of shelter. For example, Sławomira's parents were friends with the Borman family, who were of Jewish heritage. She recalled her parents urging the Bormans not to report to the ghetto and their attempts to persuade them to allow her parents to find a hiding place for them on the so-called Aryan side. She explained that Mrs. Borman's mother was afraid to leave the ghetto, and so the entire family stayed and perished together. In the following passage Sławomira recalls an incident that illustrates the risks of offering even short-term shelter:

> We were in an apartment not very far [from the Little Ghetto]. It was on Ogrodowa Street. I remember one evening, which was very upsetting. A close friend of my mother's, Pani Ala Purzańska, was very engaged in helping Jews. Her place, her apartment, was a sort of halfway place for all those rescued from the ghetto, and not infrequently there were a mass of people there. Once there, she found them some place where they could hide. My parents couldn't keep them at our place because my father was deep in the conspiracy, and it wasn't possible to take on yet an additional danger. In spite of this, there was a situation when she [Pani Purzańska] had too many people, and so she asked [my parents] if they could keep this lady. I don't remember her surname; I know that they called her "Złota Inka," Golden Inka. She was a poet, and she was to stay with us for a few days. So, she was brought to us. She stayed for three or four days and everything was fine.
>
> All right. One evening we were sitting around the table after supper, it is already past the police hour [curfew], the gates [to the apartment building]

are locked. We sit with the lady, who, after all, is very nice, and very cultured, and of a very Semitic appearance. It was enough for someone to glance at her and they would have no doubts as to who she was. If you please, a car comes. At that time of day, it could only be Germans. It stops at the gate. After a moment–[we hear] banging at the gate. Listen, we—I must tell you, that we didn't even get up from the table because, because already there was no—

ELT [interrupting]: It was too late!

Sławomira: It was too late. And there was nothing to do. At the same time, the tension that took over at that moment, well, you understand, it was colossal. We hear the doorman open the gate. They come in like always so terribly, with their dreadfully loud voices, and we hear how they climb the stairs. They stop at our landing, we lived on the second floor, and they stop on the landing after ours. They go higher for a moment. Then they come down again, they stop— and we are all sitting, you know? They went down and outdoors, and they went to the office, and they took someone from the office. They did not come for us.

But, you know, that was awful, and it was awful that when they went to the office, we all understood that someone there was unfortunate, because they arrested him, because he was going to suffer and was going to be tortured, was going to be beaten, was going to suffer terribly, and despite all that it was a relief. That was horrible! It was a relief because it is a fact that if they had come to us, it would be the death penalty for all of us, because for hiding Jews it was an immediate death sentence for the whole family. You know, that was an experience [*przeżycie*] that was very strong. Afterward, two days later or so they were able to find another place outside of Warsaw, and she was moved there and what happened to her, I do not know. However, that Pani Ala Purzańska, who did so much good, after the uprising she was imprisoned at Ravensbrück and there she died in the camp.

An interesting point in this incident is who and what is perceived to be most at risk. If the Gestapo enter and find the poet, Sławomira has no doubts that they will all be killed. However, this is not the reason given for the family not hiding Polish Jews more frequently. Sławomira explained, "My parents couldn't keep them at our place because my father was deep in the conspiracy, and it wasn't possible to take on yet an additional danger." She elaborated on this at a later date, saying that, due to her father's work in the underground, they could not have any compromising papers in the apartment, nothing that would draw attention or raise suspicions were the Gestapo to make a search.

In their research with Holocaust rescuers, psychologists Samuel Oliner and Pearl Oliner (1988: 126) discovered a range of attitudes toward the risk entailed in helping others: some rescuers saw helping Jews as inviting certain death; others saw it as no more dangerous than other acts of resistance. Notably, Nechama Tec (1986), in her interviews with Jewish survivors and Polish rescuers, discovered that while the death penalty inflicted by the Nazis for the entire household was a significant deterrent, most rescuers also stated that they feared denunciation by their neighbors. Did the arrest of the man in the office cause Sławomira's parents to suspect that someone among their neighbors was a collaborator? Such a suspicion would certainly be an impediment to offering further aid.

Sławomira's parents were not opposed to taking risks, a fact demonstrated by their deep engagement in the underground. Indeed, with their parents' blessing, both Sławomira and her sister Basia trained for work as medics, which ultimately placed them on the barricades in the General Uprising of 1944. In restricting the amount of help the family offered Polish Jews, Sławomira's parents were following a rule set by the underground that urged those involved in helping Jews to refrain from engaging in other underground activities. The rationale was that if the Germans discovered that the family was hiding Jews, the Germans might also learn of Sławomira's parents' underground activities. Such a discovery would jeopardize other members of the underground, as well as the cause of Polish independence. Therefore Sławomira's parents chose to shield the resistance movement rather than individual Polish Jews. In this way they gave precedence to goals that they perceived as benefiting the community as a whole over the life of an individual.

While the underground authorities encouraged everyone to follow this security measure, it was one that many involved in helping Jews found difficult to follow. As Irena Sandler, one of the founding members of Żegota, an underground organization established in Warsaw at the end of 1942 for the sole purpose of rescuing Jews, recalled, "It was often impossible to apply that principle of security" (Bartoszewski 1970: 84).

The underground state's relationship to Jews was ambivalent at best. The minister of civil resistance, for example, issued a directive to the general public through the underground press, making it a capital crime to collaborate with the Germans in the persecution of Jews (Oliner and Oliner 1988: 94). At the same time the Home Army was reluctant to give arms to the Jews in the ghetto because they viewed the fact that Jews were boarding transports bound for Treblinka without protest as evidence of a lack of will for resistance.[5] It was only after Jews within the ghetto attacked German troops from January 18 to January 22, 1943, that the Home Army made more significant contributions to providing the Jewish Fighting

Organization with arms (Lukas 1986: 174). In response to encouragement from Home Army leader General Bór-Komorowski, a Żoliborz unit of Gray Rank Scouts (*Szare Szeregi*) took part in the Warsaw Ghetto Uprising by attacking an SS guardhouse (Oliner and Oliner 1988: 94). Though the Home Army and the People's Army both aided surviving Jews in their escape from the ghetto through the sewers in the last days of the Ghetto Uprising, many Home Army units subsequently refused to allow Jews to join their ranks (cf. Assuntio and Goldkorn 1999).

Yet, Żegota was unique in all of occupied Europe in that it was the only state-sponsored organization devoted solely to saving Jews. The organization's goal was to aid Polish Jews by finding them safe hiding places with ethnic Polish families and supplying food, forged identity papers, and medical care (Oliner and Oliner 1988: 28–29; for Żegota members' narratives, see Bartoszewski and Lewin 1970). Though no accurate statistics exist on how many people Żegota members saved, members' estimates range from several thousand to 25,000 (Pawlikowski 2003: 110). Żegota placed particular emphasis on its efforts to save Jewish children by finding places for them in orphanages, convents, and the private homes of Żegota activists or sometimes of individuals associated with other opposition groups (ibid.). Hanna described to me how her home in Żoliborz served as a way station for a number of Jewish children due to her mother's activism with Żegota. Some would stay for a few days, others for weeks and months until safer places could be found.

> **ELT:** How many were there?
> **Hanna:** Oh, quite a few! They came after the Ghetto Uprising.
> **ELT:** Was it one family that was here the whole time?
> **Hanna:** Different ones, different ones.

Because Hanna's mother felt that the less she and Hanna knew about the people who stayed in the home the safer they would all be, Hanna's knowledge on the subject even as an adult was limited. While those who hid fewer people for a longer period of time often maintained contact with the people they had helped long after the war ended, Hanna knew little about the people who used her home as a way station to more permanent hiding places.

> **Hanna:** I do not know the real names, only one . . . because it was all secret, and after all, the less a person knew the better because then he couldn't tell anyone. There was Olesia, she was very clever, and she was with—God! I don't remember the name. The one who was killed, who went with the children to the gas. You know who I'm talking about.

ELT: Korczak? Janusz Korczak?[6]

Hanna: Korczak, yes, yes. She was [sent] by Korczak, and I remember when I went to school Mother said, "Yes, that is Olesia and that lady is her mother." Though, she only would visit, and she could not go anywhere else to make it look that she was taken from an orphanage and so on. And later . . . when she visited from America, she wanted to give us her surname, but Mother told her, "No, I don't want to know any of the names, I do not want anything, to draw any . . . [profit], that's final." But I tell you, all of us here were very engaged [in helping Jews].

A few children remained with Hanna and her mother through the General Uprising and the liberation, when, as she put it, their fates parted and most emigrated to America, England, or Israel.

Pani Janina R—— is one of two people I interviewed who took part in providing a long-term hiding place for Jews.[7] She was also active in the underground throughout the occupation, working at a health center that provided social aid to families in material and emotional need. She was also a member of Baszta, a division of the Home Army, and later, following the uprising, she joined a relief organization (RGO). In the following excerpt from our interview, she describes the home where she lived with her mother and her younger sister, Wanda, during the war:

Well, there was a lot to do in the conspiracy, because we lived in Żoliborz. Our house was a separate villa at number six Feliński Street. And it was like this: Mama belonged to her underground groups, I belonged to mine, and my younger sister, Wanda, was in school but she also was in the conspiracy, and in addition beginning in 1944 we had a Jewish boy whom we hid and an officer's wife (he was in an oflag), and she also hid with us. Also we had a parachuter from England [from Chichociemne], who was also in the conspiracy, and he lived with us under the pseudonym Lewandowski. In the basement there was a [Home Army] munitions magazine. We lived close to Poniatowski Secondary School, and there was a German hospital there, which was very, very close by, and near our home there was a checkpoint with barbed wire and a [German] guard always stood there. The Germans simply thought that if young people came here, they were simply coming to play because we always turned up the volume on the record player, and they thought we young people were having a great time. Meanwhile, military college lectures were taking place for boys. So, there was a munitions magazine, Lewandowski was here, two Jews were here, and here each had their own conspiracy and all of it right under the Germans' noses! And that is where the conspiracy stayed for the entire occupation.

In the following pages I present excerpts from my meetings with Pani Janina in which she described how it was that her family became involved in helping Jews, some of the difficulties involved, and her family's relationships to the Jews who stayed in their home. Given the enormous risks involved and the need for secrecy, I was particularly curious about how Janina's family became involved in hiding Jews. I learned that, like most rescuers, Janina's mother was asked to help by an acquaintance on behalf of the people she and her daughters eventually aided (Tec 1986; Oliner and Oliner 1988).

Janina: One of my mother's acquaintances from Żoliborz brought to us the T—— family, that was a family of jewelers from Łódz—mother, father, and Piotr—and asked that we keep them with us for a few days, because where she had been hiding them somebody was coming to them continuously and blackmailing them. They paid, but that is dangerous, because they blackmail and blackmail, and afterward who knows if they'll betray, and after all how much can one pay? So, because of this she decided to move them to her family's home in Praga (a Warsaw neighborhood on the east side of the Vistula River), but she didn't want to do so directly, but instead first to our house, and later from our house further on. Mama agreed to this hesitantly because, after all, we had the conspiracy at our house: the military training, and Lewandowski, the old parachuter who couldn't [go anywhere else]. It wasn't possible to pack in a Jewish family because it would threaten him too, and in general all of us, right? But we said all right, we would do it for the time being, and Lewandowski said that he was so convinced that nothing could go wrong in this house that he agreed. He said, "There are already so many things that one more family for a short time . . ." because it was only supposed to be very briefly, a few days. In fact, they stayed a bit longer than a few days. They begged Mother to allow them to stay. Unfortunately, the conspiracy did not give its consent because it endangered the ammunitions magazine here. There was also Lewandowski, the parachuter. Everyone was involved in the conspiracy here, it was not possible. Mama told them (Mr. and Mrs. T——) that she was very sorry, but that unfortunately she couldn't agree to their staying because—well she couldn't agree to it.

ELT: That means the conspiracy didn't allow—?

Janina: That means the commander, yes.

ELT: An AK [Home Army] commander?

Janina: AK, yes, that it wasn't possible because it endangered this and endangered that. Everyone here was endangered.

The various ways in which different members of the household or those connected with it assessed risk is significant. Given that she consulted with a Home Army commander to gain permission for the family to stay, it seems that Janina's mother hesitated to continue to offer the family shelter from a belief that others would object. Lewandowski, himself in hiding at the home, saw the risk as no greater than anything else they were all involved in and agreed to their staying. The Home Army commander for the neighborhood refused to grant permission on the grounds that it would endanger Home Army members, who visited the house for training, as well as the arms for the uprising that were stockpiled in the basement.

After Janina's mother told the T——s that they could not stay permanently in her home, the woman who had brought them to Janina's family went forward with the original plan to move them elsewhere. The following passage illustrates some of the measures taken by Poles who aided Jews to avoid discovery. At the same time it demonstrates how easily such efforts could be undermined by betrayal, fear, and violence.

> So, that lady took the mother and father and left Piotr because she said that she didn't want to move the whole family at once, because that would be dangerous. She moved them there [to her sister's home in Praga], and she was supposed to take Piotr two or three days later. During that time, someone saw that the family had landed in Praga and gave word to the Gestapo, or maybe the Gestapo found out, I don't know. The Gestapo came, and she hid the couple in the basement, and maybe everything would have been all right if it hadn't been for the little girl, her daughter, who, when she saw them beating her mother, cried out, "Don't beat Mama! Don't beat Mama! I'll show you where she hid those people."
>
> When the Gestapo discovered them in the basement they took them, except that they—Piotr told us this later, later because he never said anything about it [at the time]—they had a lot of jewelry and dollars or something with them, so they [the Gestapo] didn't even take them. We tried to find out through the conspiracy "where are Piotr's parents?" Not in Pruszków, or in Pawiak, not in some prison somewhere else either. It is most likely that the Gestapo took everything and just murdered them. Now, Piotr stayed with us. It was exceptional that the Gestapo did not take that lady and her child, and that is the best proof that they seized all the cash, because normally each person who hid [Jews] was taken, and so on [executed, imprisoned], and here—obviously, they understood the situation and left the lady in peace and took Piotr's mother and father.

It is not entirely clear what happened to Piotr's parents; however, the circumstances suggest that some opportunistic Gestapo agents robbed them and, in order to keep the goods for themselves, did not turn them in but murdered them in some remote place where they were never found or identified. The Gestapo agents neither arrested nor executed the woman and her daughter in Praga probably because they feared that the woman and her daughter might have revealed to their commanding officers that they had robbed the T——s. The fact that the Gestapo did not arrest the would-be rescuers would be sufficient to put them under suspicion by the underground.

> And that lady who moved Piotr's parents to her sister's flew to us and said, "*Boże ranny* [by the wounds of God]! I won't take Piotrek because at home I am already being blackmailed, and by some miracle my sister was saved. Do what you want with that Piotrek because I don't know what to do with him." My mother told her quite calmly that she had already arranged another place for him with somebody else, but she wouldn't say where. Not true. It was just so that she would be convinced that Piotrek wasn't at our house. Because if that woman were beaten, she would have told that Piotrek was with us. And that is why Piotr stayed with us.

If the Home Army or anyone else had any further objections to the boy staying in Janina's home, she did not mention it, though it seems that few people if any outside of the household knew he was there. As for Piotrek's reaction to all this, Janina recalled:

> Never did Piotrek ask what happened to his parents. Never. It was only after the war that he was told that they were not living. Piotruś stayed in these short pants that he had outgrown and a little blazer, and in that blazer he had—maybe it's a little funny—his mother's thimble, a silver thimble with little holes. And the whole time he carried that thimble. When they left Warsaw he took the thimble, and when they lived in the village he played with it, holding it all the time, and he would say, "Mamo, Mamo." And one day, Mama was putting wood into the fire, and she put her hand out and that thimble flew [into the fire], and Piotr put his hand into the flames to pull out the thimble.
>
> The first Christmas after the war he gave Mama the thimble as a present. So Mama kept it. And that is how the thimble was saved. When I went to Israel for the first time I took it with me as the one thing he had from his mother. That thimble. I looked at him and said, "Look you gave this to my Mama, and look, this is something to remember your mother by." Because Piotr was very attached to his mother.

The Jewish wife of an officer in the Polish army, Irena P—, whom the family called Teodozja or Todzia during the war, also came to Janina's house through an acquaintance of Janina's mother. In this case, the acquaintance was herself Jewish and hiding in the open, as Janina explains in the following passage:

> Pani Professor Litwin, an acquaintance, brought her. It's a well-known name. She was a professor of international law from Łódz. A very well-known person. He [her husband] was in the oflag along with Todzia's husband, and he returned to his wife, but she was already in Warsaw during the occupation. A Jewess who in general did not hide. She worked in a German firm as a very important director. She did not hide at all, but it never entered anyone's head that she was Jewish. She and Todzia met each other through their husbands, and I don't know how it was that Mama met her, and she (Professor Litwin) brought Todzia. Todzia had her hair colored light blonde, and she believed that she did not look at all Jewish, but we knew perfectly well that she was.

Although Janina seems to think that Irena might be overconfident in her ability to pass as an ethnic Pole, Janina contrasted Irena's appearance to Piotrek's, whose dark hair, brown eyes, and olive complexion were thought of as typically Semitic features and therefore a liability. This made it impossible for the boy to pass and far too risky for him to leave the house.[8]

> In general Todzia didn't leave the house either. But because it was quite hard for us, right? Mama made a few pennies baking cakes and pastries and selling them. In 1939 Father went to the front and did not return again. Father was killed at Starobielsk, demolished by the Russians, and we were left, Mama and the two of us, with the house and that was it. So, we made and baked cakes, Mama made pastries, and Todzia made wooden shoes that were laced with string and I sold them. And that's what we lived on. So, she sat at home. Her first outing was after the uprising!

Piotr and Todzia moved relatively freely in the house when there were no guests, remaining out of sight on the second floor when there were people known to the family on the first floor, and only retreating to a hiding place if someone unknown to the family came to the house. As Janina recalls:

> Piotrek had been told that, if a car pulled up to the house, he was to immediately run up to the attic to this hiding place because normally he ran around the house upstairs as there was the military training downstairs. So

he sat upstairs. Just like all those Jewish children, they were well behaved, they knew what was a threat, and in general didn't go out [of the house]. So it was just that when I was at home, or my sister was there, one had to sit, and tell, and read. He read well on his own, but one had to entertain him a bit. All the time he dreamed of being a pilot, of flying, and I didn't know much about flying but, well, I told him what I could.

Janina did recall what she described as a "tragic moment" that was particularly threatening to the household. About ten days before Easter of 1944, the Gestapo arrested Lewandowski, the paratrooper from the resistance group Cichociemne, in a vast roundup that took place in Żoliborz where he frequently went to visit relatives.

> But he had *kennkarte* [the German word for identity papers] under the name Lewandowski [stating] that he lived at Feliński number six. Well, so [it was] terrifying because if the Germans caught him, they would come to us. And here we were and the two in hiding—that was the worst! A courier came from the conspiracy and brought us this tiny note communicating that Lewandowski, who was at that moment at Pawiak, confessed that he had never lived at Feliński number six, that his identity papers were false, and that he did not know our family at all.
>
> Well, so we got that news. They [people from the underground] came, they told us to leave the house immediately because in spite of everything they [the Gestapo] could come, to search and check. I moved out, my sister moved out. I took Todzia. But Mama said that she couldn't leave to go anywhere with Piotrek. Piotr looked—well, also one couldn't endanger others because, this is what Piotr looked like [handing me a photo]. So Mama said that she would stay here. She said, "Maybe the Gestapo won't come." We got word through our Blue Police, we had our own police too, who collaborated with us here in Żoliborz and Marymont, that our house was under observation but that for the time being it did not look as if the Gestapo would come.
>
> It [Lewandowski's arrest] happened close to Easter, and here there was already tension that the Russians were approaching [Poland's eastern border], so they [the Germans] must have thought that whatever was going on in that villa [of ours] wasn't worth the trouble. Well, actually maybe they thought that here, three steps away from the house, stood a guard, and so maybe nothing could possibly be happening here. Maybe that's what they thought, and maybe not. Sometimes they were very wise, and sometimes very naïve. Well, so Mama sat at home with Piotr except that before the uprising, when it was already clear that the moment for it to begin was at hand, my sister and I returned home.

On August 1, 1944, just hours before the citywide uprising began, the Gestapo executed the paratrooper from Cichociemne that the family knew as Lewandowski. Todzia stayed with the family through the uprising until the liberation, when she was reunited with her husband. Piotr stayed with the family until some months after the liberation, when relatives located him and together they emigrated to Israel.

Talking about Helping Jews

Holocaust rescuers like Janina and her family and Hanna's mother, who voluntarily and at great personal risk sought to help Jews by providing shelter, food, and medical care with no expectation of compensation, embody our every ideal of anti-Nazi resistance. We see them as self-sacrificing, dedicated to the people they help, committed to defeating Hitler's plans for a final solution. Their activities not only benefited the individuals they helped but also the broader Polish Jewish community, ensuring its survival in the face of overwhelming destruction and loss. However, while going to school, joining the scouts, and training as medics were all examples of activities that my informants deemed conspiratorial, helping Jews was not. Neither helpers nor nonhelpers described acts of assistance as resistance.

There are several reasons that may explain why this is the case. Because my informants often undertook aid to Jews independently rather than under the auspices of Żegota, it is possible that they viewed their acts as benefiting solely the individuals they helped rather than the wider community and thus did not perceive them as oppositional. Another explanation for why helping Jews was not considered resistance, even retrospectively, may lie in how my informants became involved in both resistance and offering assistance. My informants *sought out* opportunities to join the underground; in fact it was something they longed to do. Typically, activities they defined as resistance were undertaken intentionally and with premeditation. In contrast, the majority of instances of helping others were responses to specific requests for help or spontaneous responses to the needs of others, as in the case of Zofia rescuing the child. Moreover, while Janina and Hanna took part in helping the people sheltered in their homes, it was their mothers who initially took the responsibility for doing so, by either offering aid or agreeing and declining requests for help. The people I interviewed who were active in aiding others did not describe these activities as oppositional or conspiratorial but as something one did because the particular situation they found themselves in required it. Above all, they saw their activities as the decent and humane thing to do. This accounts for the absence of ideological expression in the narratives. They did it *for* the individuals they sought to help, not as an act of defiance *against* the Germans, and in doing so made no connections to the implications of their actions to the community of Polish Jews or the wider community of Poles, defined inclusively.

Finally, leaders of the Home Army, who viewed helping Jews as interfering with the true focus of their resistance—the restoration of an independent Poland—often thwarted efforts to help Polish Jews. In the case of Sławomira's family, the constraints on hiding Jews appear to be self-imposed out of concern for the underground, while in Janina's case it is external, coming from the neighborhood's commander: the T——family must move on. These incidents illustrate that, despite the existence of Żegota, for the secret Polish state helping Polish Jews was neither a primary objective nor fully embraced as a way to resist the occupation. When the message from local leaders was that helping Jews could endanger the goal of liberating Poland from the Nazis, it is not surprising that those who engaged in helping others did not see their own efforts in terms of resistance.

Vague or precise, substantiated or urban legend, the significance of these narratives lies in the telling. All the accounts reveal something about the war, attitudes toward Polish Jews, and people's attitudes about these things decades later. Secondhand accounts about Polish Jews hiding in the open, for example, obscure the many obstacles that Polish Jews faced in passing as ethnic Poles and the fact that for many this was not an option, due to their appearance, body language, speech patterns, level of fluency, or lack of connections or familiarity with ethnic Poles. Such stories inadvertently reinforce stereotypes about Jewish passivity by implying that because some Polish Jews passed successfully anyone brave enough to try or lucky enough to get to Żoliborz could succeed at it. Similarly, claims that "everybody knew about it" imply that anyone could have denounced those hiding in the open but that nobody did. Though the stories may not be entirely without merit, these narratives allow ethnic Poles to feel that they took part in helping Polish Jews through their complicity in the open secret of their neighbors' Jewish identity or heritage. This locates help diffusely throughout the community as a whole but equates doing no harm to actual help, obscuring the need of the majority of Polish Jews for real and active assistance. In this way these stories perpetuate misunderstandings of the wartime experiences of Polish Jews, which only furthers contemporary divisions between these communities.

Secondary accounts of specific individuals helping others are equally problematic. They cannot capture the circumstances in which ethnic Poles offered help, the difficulties they overcame in doing so, or the dangers they faced as a result. While such stories acknowledge the risks involved, they neutralize the moral implications by locating danger solely with the Germans, rather than in blackmailers, indifference, or human vulnerability to fear and torture. As a result such narratives impede our understanding of all those involved: the situation of Polish Jews, the circumstances and personal qualities of those who offered them help and of those who felt themselves unable to act on behalf of others.

As narratives the most compelling and revealing stories are personal accounts of action taken on behalf of others. Thwarted, limited, or successful, these accounts reveal the qualitative and quantitative differences in suffering that rendered Polish Jews dependent on their fellow citizens for survival. These narratives effectively capture the range of difficulties and the fears and concerns experienced by those engaged in aiding Jewish Poles. Only 2 percent of the population of any German-occupied country gave long-term shelter to Jews. Thus the stories of rescuers like Janina help us understand a small group of remarkable people. I would suggest that, to understand the context in which the Holocaust took place, we need to know more about people of goodwill who did not act in major ways on behalf of their Jewish neighbors. Perhaps the question to ask in such research is not whether an informant helped or not but whether there was someone, stranger or friend, whom they wanted to help or now wished they had helped, or someone they tried to help unsuccessfully and what prevented them from doing so. These are difficult things to talk about. So it is notable that it is only those informants with whom I spent the most time, Sławomira and Olgierd Z——, who offered such stories. Though they cannot be categorized as rescue stories, they do reveal how Polish society struggled with limitations, fears, and conflicting claims of moral responsibility. Such narratives may help us to move beyond the assumption that Poles' lack of action is evidence of anti-Semitism or indifference and through careful and critical research to return to them a measure of humanity lost in such prejudgments.

6 Remembering the Warsaw Uprising

> **Sławomira:** You may think this is strange, but really, the uprising was the most wonderful time of my life. . . . In August the uprising, which we'd all been waiting for impatiently, broke out. That was something that we dreamt about, for which we waited. This was the absolute goal about which we dreamt and in which we believed: that after this uprising there would be Poland again and absolutely independent just like before.

THE UPRISING THAT SŁAWOMIRA recalled with such fondness is the Warsaw Uprising of 1944, which is sometimes referred to as the "General Uprising" in English-language literature, in order to distinguish it from the Warsaw Ghetto Uprising of 1943. Poland's political and military leaders as well as members of the underground and residents of Warsaw pinned their hopes for freedom on this attempt to free the city from German control through armed insurrection. The Germans brutally crushed these expectations, leaving some to question how things could have gone so very wrong and how to draw meaning from defeat. For these reasons it came as quite a surprise to me when Sławomira described the event as the most wonderful time of her life. How could she remember as the most wonderful time of her life a battle that left her wounded, her father dead, her mother in a state of profound grief, her family and friends scattered, her home and everything in it destroyed, and her city in ruins? This chapter and those that follow are the culmination of my efforts to understand how, for many older Warsovians, memories of the terror and anguish of the German occupation are intertwined with memories of a beautiful youth spent fighting for the return of Polish independence.

Historical Background

On August 1, 1944, the Polish underground, under the command of General Tadeusz Bór-Komorowski, leader of the Armia Krajowa (Home Army), launched the Warsaw Uprising under orders from the Polish government-in-exile in London. The leaders only intended the uprising, known by the code name "Tempest" (*Burza*), to last for the few days that the leaders thought it would take for the Red Army, already nearing Warsaw from the east, to cross the Vistula River and come to the aid of the Polish forces. In fact, despite the extreme disparity in the number of forces, as well as the quality and quantity of arms, Polish forces engaged the German army for 63 days of intense urban warfare. By the time the Home Army signed the act of capitulation on October 2, 1944, some 20,700 Polish military personnel, medics, and couriers were dead, and 5,000 were missing in action (Roszkowski 1997: 138). In addition 180,000 civilians died during the Warsaw Uprising as a result of mass executions, bombardments of residential areas, and fires (ibid.). The Germans forced those Warsovians who remained in the capital until the end to leave the city for civilian detention camps. In a breach of the act of capitulation, the Germans sent over 100,000 Warsovians to the Reich as slave labor, and more than 10,000 were sent to concentration camps such as Auschwitz, Mauthausen, and Ravensbrück (Davies 2004: 439).

In retaliation for the uprising, Hitler ordered the destruction of Warsaw. Starting in the Old Town and those parts of the city with greater historical, cultural, and economic value, a special unit of German troops set about systematically burning out, then dynamiting city landmarks, industrial plants, buildings, and homes. They demolished an estimated 80 percent of the city: 92 percent of the left bank (the location of government buildings, the University of Warsaw, and the Old Town) and 56 percent of the right bank, Praga (Borecka and Sempoliński 1985: 296; Davies 2004: 439–40).

The primary goal of the uprising was to liberate Warsaw, and by extension the nation, from German occupation. With Polish leaders in control of the capital when the Red Army arrived from the east, the Polish government-in-exile felt it would be in a better position in negotiations regarding Poland's postwar borders and the form of its future government (Roszkowski 1997: 135). Thus, the uprising was an attempt not only to free the city of German occupation but also to ensure the nation's independence. However, in launching the uprising, Warsaw Home Army leaders made at least three flawed assumptions. First, they assumed that theirs would be one of many armed actions launched simultaneously in major cities throughout the country against German forces (Davies 2004: 46). These plans did not come to fruition.[1] Second, operating on the assumption that violence was the language best understood by the German occupiers, the leaders of the underground saw the uprising as a show of force that would somehow protect the civilian population and the city itself from retribution as the Germans retreated westward (Lukas 1986: 185; Roszkowski 1997: 132).[2] Finally, the leaders believed that the Red Army, already nearing Warsaw in late July, would aid the Home Army in defeating the Germans, their common enemy. Warsaw residents and underground officials in Warsaw had reason to expect Soviet support. In July 1944 Moscow Radio and the Soviet-sponsored broadcasting station Kościuszko broadcast several calls to arms, urging Warsovians to rise up against the German occupants and to free the city (Lukas 1986: 186–87). Having long prepared for such an event, the members of the underground interpreted such broadcasts as a sign of Soviet support for their movement. Moreover, the Polish government-in-exile and the citizenry of Warsaw believed that, through this massive civilian assault on German troops, the Polish nation would prove once and for all Poland's loyalty to the Soviets as an ally in the war (Karski and Friszke 1997). These expectations proved to be fatally naïve. Not only did the Red Army fail to cross the Vistula River, but the Soviets also prohibited British and American forces from airlifting much-needed arms, food, and medical supplies to the city for most of the battle. In Moscow Stalin refused to acknowledge the uprising until August 13, when he attacked it in the press as an action of opportunists, adventurers, and extreme reactionaries. His future plans for Poland included room for only those aligned with the Polish Committee of National Liberation (PKWN). Indeed, Soviet forces did not cross the river to liberate the city until January 1945, long after the civilian population had been deported and the city all but completely destroyed.

Rather than focusing on military maneuvers or the ideologies of various actors in the uprising, I explore the memory of enacting heroic ideals in a city populated by nearly a million people by probing informants' memories of the Warsaw Uprising of 1944 and examining the ways in which Warsovians who witnessed and participated in the event understand it some 50 years later. In doing so, I present narratives of the uprising from people in a variety of positions who recall their experiences from the perspectives of war in three different neighborhoods: Old Town, Śródmieście, and Żoliborz. This is in no way meant to be an exhaustive account of the citywide battle or indeed of the totality of any one neighborhood's experience.[3] As Jerzy warned me, Warsovians' experiences of the uprising were varied, depending on their location within the city:

Are you interested specifically in the uprising in Żoliborz, or in the uprising in Warsaw in general? Because, you see, I'll tell you wherein lies the problem. In each neighborhood the uprising looked a little different. I actually had to appear at my military post in Śródmieście, and throughout the entire uprising, for the entire two months I was in Śródmieście. At the same time, in Żoliborz things were different, and in Praga, different still. So the uprising was not everywhere all the same. It wasn't like we all went out to war and everyone succeeded. For example in Praga, the uprising lasted—well, people say different things—but from three to six days. After six days it was already over because the Germans had such a big advantage that the uprising, shall we say, had to go back underground. Later Praga was cleaned by the Germans in such a way that the people who remained were driven through all of Warsaw on foot to Wola in terrible conditions and lived through such terrible experiences that entire books have been written on the theme of the war crimes the Germans committed. And not only Germans, because in Warsaw it so happened that on the German side Ukrainians, and deserters from the Soviet Union, and Lithuanians were also fighting alongside different formations of Germans. It wasn't just the army because, in addition to the army, there were police units, which were specially schooled for battle in crowds, shall we say, for riots, which is what our uprising looked like in their eyes. . . . So that's why it varied. But in any case some things are common to all neighborhoods, but simultaneously if it is about the details, well, it was varied.

Jerzy's reminder about the variations in the duration of the fighting and in the types of troops and tactics employed by the Germans in different neighborhoods raises a key issue about the representativeness of these narratives. All were participating in or affected by a single insurrection, launched on the same day, at roughly the same time, and under a central command.[4] However, the uprising unfolded differently, depending not only on the speaker's geographic locale but also on his or her position as a soldier in combat, as health-care worker, courier, civilian, or some combination of these roles.

Rather than weaving individual narratives together to portray the historical event at the macrolevel, my goal is to give the reader a sense of how the war played out on each teller's own skin—to use an idiom employed by several of my informants. In order to do so, I have ordered the narratives both chronologically, with regard to their recurrence (as opposed to their retelling), and thematically. In focusing on individual memories of these events, I explore several key themes that are apparent in informants' accounts—among them the destruction of place, deprivations, tensions between insurgents and residents, and horror and death.

Memories of Urban Warfare

> **Jerzy:** You cannot compare it to a normal war in which, shall we say, people go to battle. That war took place in a city of a million people, and the people who lived there were the soldiers. Those soldiers were a few tens of thousands. Poles and Germans. In the uprising, the Germans used both crowds of Ukrainians and Soviet prisoners of war. So, the [German] army was really varied, but in any case there weren't more than 10,000 of them. And this was a city of more than a million people. Proszę Pani, it all—well, first of all, it all came down on our civilians [*odbijał się*]. So there is no equivalent because normally armies fight with each other, and here it was actually a battle with a city, with the inhabitants of a city.

I begin with another reminder from Jerzy that urban warfare is not like a "normal" war fought between two armies but a war fought against a city, in which its citizenry are the soldiers.[5] I will explore the impact of urban warfare on Warsaw residents and the tensions that existed between civilians and Polish soldiers, but I begin with an examination of the disconnect between many of my informants' expectations for the uprising and the reality of urban warfare on the ground. Many of my informants who were in the Home Army spoke of the uprising as something bordering on the sacred in its potential to unite the community and resurrect the nation; this is in sharp contrast with the realities they encountered in their efforts to enact the heroic ideals on which they had been raised (Engelking 2001: 25). What happens to memory and its retelling when what is expected is so drastically different from what transpires? How do narrative accounts of the uprising allow narrators to create coherence out of lived experience, while grappling and coming to terms with the impossibility of doing so (Ochs and Capps 1996: 29)?

Launching the Uprising: Heroic Ideals in Practice

In July of 1944, it was obvious that the Germans were beginning to pull out of Warsaw. A massive evacuation of German civilians was undertaken; German-run institutions began to close throughout the city as the German employees who served as administrators and clerks fled (Dunin-Wąsowicz 1984: 194).[6] Many Warsovians took this evacuation panic as a signal that the end of the German occupation was rapidly approaching (ibid.). Jerzy remembered convoys carrying soldiers and military equipment as well as columns of tanks rolling through the capital, retreating from the Red Army, which was moving westward toward Warsaw:

The leadership of the Home Army [*Armia Krajowa*] decided to sound the alarm to prepare. That was the 27th or the 28th of July. So, the arms for the unit that I belonged to were in Żoliborz in a friend's apartment, [packed] in several suitcases. Weapons, supplies, even helmets, and so on. So when the signal for preparation was given, we had to transport it all to Śródmieście where we had our central collection point. My friend telephoned me and called me to his place along with a third friend, and we packed everything up, and we fearfully began to carry it to the tram stop. We made it to Plac Wilsona and we stood at the tram stop, but the trams weren't running because on the other side of the street tanks were coming, and so the trams were not running at all. All along Mickiewicz Street, just as you walked on your way here, were wagons from a [German] transport. Well, we must have looked suspicious because within moments the tram stop was empty. People realized that something here wasn't [right], that we were suspicious. Well, indeed that suitcase was so heavy that two had to carry it, and it is rare that luggage is carried that way! A person starts to feel, well, you know, terrible! Because there were a bunch of Germans at Plac Wilsona, and we were armed but armed with pistols, the kind you carry in a holster, and it was July, so one couldn't hide a machine gun, and the machine guns were in the suitcases, of course.

Well, if you please, one of my colleagues succeeded in persuading a carriage driver to take us. Why he agreed I do not know because, after all, he could see that we were carrying neither buns nor clothes in that suitcase. But he decided to take us, and we got into the carriage. My friends sat on the seat in the back, and I sat on the bench opposite them, and in the middle was the suitcase. Next to me, packed in newspapers, were those helmets, which was stupid because one could see without even looking that it wasn't usual, but we began to pull away from Plac Invalidów, and we had hardly left when I looked on the other side, and I felt as if the carriage was tipping over—not out of fear but because something had happened. I looked and a *Feltfabel* was standing on the running board of the carriage. *Feltfabel*, that's a German sergeant, [he was in his] military gear. We all thought, "My God! There'll be shooting in a moment!" Well, he just wanted us to take him to the column of tanks because he had lost his wagon. Well, he stood there on that step, and we sat there with that damn suitcase, and we rode with that German along the whole length of Mickiewicz Street. Either he did not notice, or he did not want to notice. It was already hard to tell because at that time the Germans sometimes preferred not to intervene when they knew that it might be dangerous for them. And in this way we rode to the viaduct on Krajewski Street, and there we said that we had to turn because we didn't want to go by way of the viaduct because there would be no chance of escape. Because of the hills on either side, there would have been no way.

He continued, describing how at every turn of their relatively short journey downtown they encountered Germans: "So, the uprising hadn't even started, and I had already had a few unpleasant encounters. Well, we got all settled in, and it turned out that it was not yet time; they called us out of that concentration [meeting point]. So, there was some decision made that things were not quite ready, and we went back home."

Jerzy focused his narrative on preparations for the uprising and the dangers he and his companions faced, but it is also about his disappointed expectations. Jerzy and his friends went to their "concentration" believing that the uprising would start the next day. Rather than receiving a signal to start, as expected, they were given orders to stand down and go home. Jerzy's description of running a gauntlet of Germans only to be sent back home highlights the disjuncture between the young men's expectations and reality.

The discrepancy between expectations for the uprising and what actually transpired is also apparent in narratives about the beginning of the uprising. On July 31 at six in the evening, the leadership of the Home Army issued an order to launch the uprising the next day at five o'clock in the afternoon. However, as Stefan explains, the uprising started unexpectedly early in Żoliborz:

> During the uprising, I began in that building where there is the plaque [commemorating the beginning of the uprising]. The Germans surprised us there earlier [before five o'clock], and because of that we had to begin to defend ourselves. It took around 80 to 100 soldiers and women, who were medics and couriers, and we armed ourselves there. We took up arms [early] relying on the uprising to start at five p.m. because that was the so-called W17 hour. But they surprised us at 1:30, and so we had to defend ourselves against the overwhelming power of the Germans. Underarmed, in the first hour, twenty soldiers died. Eleven were heavily wounded, and how many were lightly wounded we do not know because everyone fled, because they were all children: boys and girls from neighboring houses. So, the lightly wounded were taken to houses and hidden. Later, right, was the uprising. There was some heavy fighting in Żoliborz.

It is notable that Stefan, who was in his mid-twenties when the uprising took place, emphasized that the soldiers fled because *they were all children*. It is easy to lose sight of the fact in more heroic retellings that many of these soldiers were teenagers, unaccustomed to combat and with only rudimentary training. These children were familiar with the structural and literal violence of everyday life under German occupation, but that was very different from the violence of battle. Janina R—— also described to me the premature outbreak of fighting in Żoliborz and the confusion that ensued as a result:

> When the uprising broke out on August 1, my sister immediately reported to her group. At that time I was on Królewska Street. I briefed the boys from my group, Baszta, and I wanted to go to Żoliborz because it was somewhere around one or two o'clock. I wanted to go home to change my clothes because I was wearing a lightweight summer dress, and then I wanted to join our group in Mokotów because that's where we were supposed to be. At that time I walked to the Gdańsk Station, where the viaduct is, and the station was already surrounded because the uprising started early in Żoliborz. It started early because some boys were transporting arms, and a patrol of airmen stopped them, and it ended in shooting, so it had already become dangerous. They [the Germans] finally, certainly, they saw that this was an uprising that we were preparing for.
>
> So, I walked with my hands in the air [toward Żoliborz], except that not everyone had the courage to cross because I met people I knew who said they were afraid to enter [the neighborhood]. I went anyway. So I walked in that summer dress. It had white flowers, I remember. Well, maybe the Germans didn't pay too much attention to me; I was with such a big group. I flew home; there was General Zajączek Street and then our house just next to the Gdańsk Station. I flew home to change my clothes.

Though Janina made it home without further incident, once there she recalled being unsure of how to proceed: "In general there was so much shooting that I didn't know where I was supposed to go; it was already impossible to go to Mokotów because—for example, they were shooting, and a girl who had been shot was lying on the viaduct. So I stayed at home and waited to see what would happen next. I went out later, but it was dangerous: the Germans were gone, and I didn't see the Poles—our boys either, because in that first attack they really got a beating, and they retreated to Kampinos, except that here and there the remaining groups were hiding." Like Stefan, Janina recalls the chaos of the opening moments, as well as the fear of battle that sent some groups into hiding.

Though less focused on chaos, Olgierd Z—— recalled having similar difficulties getting to his post in Śródmieście:

So, the uprising in Żoliborz broke out a little too early. It was entirely accidental, because while carrying arms, a German patrol came by and shooting broke out. So, the uprising began early here. I was at home then, and my post was in Śródmieście, but I did not make it because I couldn't cross the viaduct at the Gdańsk Station because the viaduct was already controlled by the Germans, and they were stopping [those who wanted to cross]. Despite this, I reported immediately for work here as a sworn-in soldier of the Home Army. I reported to a medical unit that had been organized here on Mickiewicz in the so-called Glass House, by the pharmacy.

On the second floor lived Pani Doctor Szalewska, who ran a physical therapy firm, and that is where the medical unit was located. I remember that Pani Doctor Cywińska-Łyskawińska, who had the pseudonym Doctor Stella, was very glad. She was recruiting to fill posts at certain units because people from Śródmieście who were assigned to work at Żoliborz couldn't get in [to the neighborhood]. So it was necessary to fill those posts. So, it happened that the fact that I couldn't make it to Śródmieście was very good, because I was needed here.

Jerzy N—— was also stationed in Śródmieście but managed to make it to his post before the viaduct was closed. However, his unit encountered other problems:

It was only on the first of August, in the morning, that we learned that the uprising would be launched at five in the afternoon. Well, and then for the second time we all gathered at that same location, and things got sad because, proszę Pani, it turned out that—we had been counting on additional arms from the AK magazine, and we received five automatic pistols, but the rest were regular pistols, a few grenades, and so, you see, that wasn't much to start with.

I was with this special unit, which was armed; each of us had some kind of weapon, mostly pistols though, but in the other companies of our battalion, the situation was even worse. The battalion was called Gustaw and had three companies. The captain of Gustaw decided to divide the special unit into three parts and to send each company a sort of assault group. There were six of us in each group, and we were in a unit that could start something, right? But there was still a problem for the group which was supposed to go to the company called Genowefa. The battalion was called Gustaw, and the companies went by women's names, so there was Genowefa, Grażyna, and Gertruda. It so happened that there was nobody in that place where we had all gathered who knew where Genowefa's meeting point was. So, it was only at the last minute that we learned that we had to go quite a little way because it was some two kilometers, probably, from there through the city, and it was already five o'clock, and they were shooting, and there were crowds of people—because people were returning from work, and here our six people actually went through Śródmieście again with that suitcase of weapons and two cans of pickles in which we had stashed the grenades. So, we moved to that company with our own weapons and the weapons for that unit, too, which again were in that damned suitcase.

Eugenia's experiences as a civilian have little in common with those of Home Army members:

When the uprising broke out on the first [of August], I was at home. I was at home, and in fact, I had the laundry, because the laundress was supposed to come to help with the bed linens—I had half a year's worth of bed linens soaking, and the laundress didn't come. So, I had to finish it myself and carry it to the attic. I went to the attic, and exactly at that moment the shooting began. Yes, yes, in the Old Town the shooting began at five o'clock. Our priest, who wanted to get to Żoliborz, came to me because he lived there but was in Old Town, so he came to me to see how I was doing. He liked me a lot, and we had become good friends. But he left and he made it, the Germans let him into Żoliborz, and he made it there in one piece, but later they didn't let anyone in.

Well, the air was thick with bullets. I knew that they were preparing for the uprising; we knew everything: what was about to happen, what was going on, right? So, I lived with Mama, and somehow we were always going to the shelter. It was called a shelter, but it was simply the basement; it wasn't any real shelter. That was in the Old Town next to the Saint Dominican's Church across from Długa Street. You know where that is, right?

Though Eugenia paints a picture of chaos, it is of a domestic nature: the uprising prevents the laundress from coming to help and brings her unexpected guests. In her telling, even the shooting began promptly at five. "We knew everything," Eugenia recalled.

For the most part these narratives all reflect the chaos of the opening hours of the uprising. In Stefan's narrative, it is as if the first unexpectedly early encounter with violent death broke the enchantment of the heroic ideals to which the soldiers were all enthralled, and for a time at least they are revealed for the children they in fact were: children who run home or to the forests to hide. Janina recalled, "There was so much shooting I didn't know what to do"; even when the shooting subsided, the fact that the streets were empty, that neither German nor Polish troops could be found, seemed ominous, leaving her to wonder what to do next. Determined to serve, Olgierd goes in search of a hospital and finds one where his services are desperately needed, while Jerzy's assault unit discovers that they have very little with which to attack the enemy and no idea where the Genowefa company, whose weapons are in their possession, is stationed. Though the young Home Army members who became my informants greatly anticipated the first day of the uprising as a moment of freedom and retribution, their narratives illustrate that they remembered August 1, 1944, as a day characterized by chaos, fear, and violent death. In her accounts of the stream of family and friends who came to her, fleeing the mass executions of other neighborhoods, Eugenia reminds us that urban warfare impacts not just the soldiers involved but all in its wake.

Three Cities

Miron Białoszewski (1977: 137), a Polish poet and playwright whose *Memoir of the Warsaw Uprising* is considered to be one of the greatest literary works of the "lost generation," describes Warsaw during the uprising as three cities: "The first was the one right on the surface. The city of passages through halls and courtyards. The second was the city of the shelters. With a system of underground passageways. And beneath that underground city was this underground city. With traffic. Rules. Signs." Aboveground, Polish insurgents and German troops dominated the streets, taking over buildings for military posts. Although civilians certainly entered this space to get food and water, to travel from shelter to shelter, and to go about some semblance of daily life, most of their lives were lived underground, in makeshift shelters in the cities' basements. Finally, there was the third Warsaw, an underground roadway that allowed Polish forces and sometimes civilians to travel the city unseen: the sewers. In the pages that follow I draw on informants' narratives to illuminate these three levels of Warsaw and the experiences of the people who inhabited them.

The City on the Surface

Aboveground, Polish partisans and German troops dominated Warsaw. As Janina, Jerzy, and Olgierd's narratives suggest, it was the scene of battles and, as such, an area that civilians entered only sporadically in search of

food or water, to take part in building barricades or fighting fires, to help
the wounded or bury the dead, or to escape from the ruins of one shelter
to safe haven in another. For a soldier's perspective of the battle beyond
the opening day, I offer the following excerpts from my interviews with
Jerzy. An avid photographer all his life, Jerzy paused throughout his
narrative to show me photos that he had taken during the uprising. He
often contrasted his own photos to those from an album that depicted
Warsaw before 1939 and in the early spring of 1945, when the city was in
ruins. By making constant references to these photographs, Jerzy gave me
a sort of before-and-after tour of the neighborhood where he had spent
the majority of the uprising.

> So, proszę Pani, my unit was here at Stasica Palace. And we held that area, and
> first we pushed the Germans out. Next to us was that police station, next to
> Holy Cross, and we reached Nowy Świat, and then later the Germans pushed
> us back to Mazowiecki Street. So, throughout the whole war [*sic*], they only
> took that piece from us, and we held this entire terrain.
>
> So, you see what it was like. The street was pretty because this is what it
> looked like before the war [he hands me a photograph]. . . . Later it was all
> destroyed: here is the Stasica Palace and the university across the street; the
> police station was on the corner of Traugutt, and here was the house where
> Chopin lived. Well, all of it was either burned or simply ruined.

In this passage, it is specific buildings and institutions within Warsaw that
figure prominently as the victims of warfare. Jerzy continued, showing me
a picture of the first captain of the Genowefa company:

> He was killed on the fifth of August, and here again I'm sorry to tell you how.
> Here on Krakowski Przedmieście there were these barricades made from
> overturned wagons and various kinds of junk that were piled up to block the
> entrance from Holy Cross Street. And, proszę Pani, here a little further was
> an unfinished barricade, and on August 5 the Germans came through there,
> and they took down that first barricade, and they headed for the second, and
> they pushed people in front of the tanks as shields and commanded them to
> take down that barricade.

In other words, the Germans used civilians, whom they caught out on the
streets, as "human shields" and forced them to do the work of dismantling
the Polish fighters' barricades.

You know, we didn't know what to do! A person literally got goose bumps and one's hair stood on end because, well, first of all, how was it possible to fight a war that way, right? And secondly, what to do, right? After all, it's not possible to just shoot people. So, our colleagues climbed higher, and then they had the Germans within their range—they weren't mixing with the people, just hiding in their tanks, and so from there [higher up] it was possible to shoot at them [the Germans]. And at a certain moment this machine gun starts to fire on their position, and so then we ran to the entrance where all along the street rubble was piled up to the second story of the building, and from that rubble we threw grenades at the Germans. And that Lieutenant Marabut, our leader, he was standing there at that place, and unfortunately he was hit by machine gun fire and died. And this is a picture of his funeral. Because until August 25 it was still possible to organize a coffin, and we even found flowers, and here are my friends carrying his coffin. He was buried on a street that has a stupid name because it's called *Dowcip* [Joke].

Jerzy's description of the way the Germans treated Polish civilians is in marked contrast to his unit's efforts to avoid putting civilians in the crossfire. This suggests that civilians killed in battle were not written off as mere "collateral damage," the cost of doing business for the Polish partisans, and suggests that the Polish soldiers felt responsible for the civilian populace, which will become key in considering tensions between these groups that developed later in the uprising.

Medics also spent time on the surface, in battle, before transporting the wounded in their care to hospitals typically located in basements. In this sense they traveled between the Warsaw on the surface and the undergound world of shelters. Olgierd's experience of the uprising comes from the perspective of an urban field hospital where he served as a medic. His recollections are not focused on the battles themselves so much as on the resulting injuries and deaths, as well as the task of caring for the wounded.

I was with a medical unit, and that post was on the second floor and was directed by Stefan Świątecki. As a medical student I was his assistant, and in terms of expertise I was ready to do so-called minor operations. So, I started work here right away. A patrol of medics was established; these were medics who were sworn in [to the Home Army], of course. There were a few scouts, and among others I wanted to mention by name somebody who really was an example of outstanding courage and who at once approached our task with enormous enthusiasm and that is Danka Jaksa-Bykowska. . . . In addition there were maybe ten other people who were also medics. Our task was aid actions and caring for the wounded here in Lower Żoliborz and Marymont. So, this area right here was our place of work. We went from house to house because the wounded were kept in private homes and apartments, primarily in cellars, but one had to go to them to change their bandages and also to Marymont. Marymont was wooden then. There weren't those tall apartment blocks like there are now. Those were small wooden houses, and it was really difficult to cross Potocka Street, which divided Marymont from Żoliborz, because there were tanks there, and it was necessary to maneuver in such a way so as to run across Potocka when the tanks were driving away. Those German tanks and panzers were patrolling the area. But, in spite of that, we went to Marymont all the same, and there were wounded in the basements there too, soldiers from the uprising.

Olgierd first locates himself in the uprising professionally, then geographically, describing the precise area where he worked and the difficulties he and the other medics faced there. Those who worked on medical patrols were in a particularly vulnerable position because it was their task to evacuate the wounded from wherever they had fallen and transport them to hospitals. This often entailed walking unarmed into the battle with a stretcher. Olgierd went on to explain that the field hospital where he worked was originally located at the Convent of the Sisters of the Resurrection (there were not any permanent hospitals located in Żoliborz at the time); however, when the convent found itself on the frontlines in the middle of August, it had to relocate. This involved evacuating the wounded to Plac Wilsona:

> Well, unfortunately, here in Lower Żoliborz we created this overflow unit for the wounded from the hospital on Plac Wilsona. In these villas here in Lower Żoliborz, we set up rooms for the critically wounded. Well, unfortunately, later a very powerful bomb hit, and everything was destroyed. Lots of wounded, new wounded, and so the hospital was moved to the Glass House through [tunnels in] the cellar. [It took] a few hours to carry the wounded. They were operated on there. Those were macabre scenes: the wounded were lying on coal covered with a white sheet, and because there were no lights, by candle light their leg or an arm was amputated, or they did some other operations.
> So the leader of Żywiciel's health unit decided that the hospital would be relocated on Krachowiecki Street. That is near Słowacki Street, in the Teacher's Co-op, it was a big building. That co-op is still there. It was partially burned, and later after the war it was rebuilt, and at this moment people live

there normally. The hospital was located underground, that means in the cellar. The operating room was underneath the present-day milk bar [i.e., cafeteria]. Deep inside there is this air raid shelter, and that is where our operating room was located. In the rest of the cellar, there were wounded who were there to have their bandages changed, and the nurses cared for them, and the doctors.

That entire terrain there was the hospital. In that hospital—it was night when there was that powerful air raid on Lower Żoliborz. Then at night all those wounded were transported from Wilson Place across those gardens, where there is now a housing division, between Mickiewicz and Krachowiecki because then that was all open terrain. There was a valley, and I remember that we transported the wounded through the valley to the hospital. We stayed there at Krachowiecki Street until the end of the uprising, until the moment of capitulation.

Olgierd expresses horror at the enormity of the casualties, at the wounded being wounded again in subsequent attacks, and in the "macabre" conditions in which he and his colleagues cared for them.

The City of Shelters

In contrast, the city of shelters was primarily a world of civilians. Eugenia's narratives of the first weeks of the uprising provide an insider's glimpse of daily life in the shelters of Old Town:

So, next to us [to our building] was the Dominican church, and people gathered there for morning mass. There was also an army unit at the Dominican church. There was some military formation stationed there, and they established a hospital, but it was very modest. On the ground floor there was a modest refectory, and there was a hospital for the wounded. Well, on the sixth of August, the Feast of the Transfiguration of the Lord, I went to the church in the morning, and they started firebombing the Old Town from the church side. Yes. So, people were taking shelter in the sacristy in the corridor. We left the church and hid there. Well, they didn't succeed in finishing the mass, so I went home. It was literally next door. It was only the park that separated us. I returned to my apartment building, and already they were organizing help there. We stood on the steps, and we passed buckets of water. Fortunately, it was the smaller incendiary bombs. So, we put out the fire, but, of course, there was damage, right? The apartment was soaked, everything was wet. The ceiling—there really wasn't a ceiling, just pieces of it remained.

So, it was only the sixth of August, and already my apartment was flooded [with people]. I went to the basement so tired, and a friend of mine from the Committee to Aid Teachers came to me with a proposition. She wanted to hide at my place. [Laughing] "Enough of this," she said, "I've come to you to die, because there isn't any place else." Later my brother and sister-in-law, and their housekeeper, and some of their neighbors turned up. My brother and his wife lived in Wola. It was very dangerous in Wola during the uprising, because those Ukrainians,[7] or that German army, or the Ukrainians who were collaborating with the Germans, they were shooting people in the basements. They simply went where people were hiding in the basements and shot them. My sister-in-law was in a serious state: she was pregnant, and they escaped from Wola and brought with them their housekeeper and some neighbors and came to my smoldering apartment. I was utterly exhausted. From morning I had run here and there, putting out the fire. But, well, I had to take care of them. And that's how it was through the whole uprising. Well, one had to. There was no place to go in Wola then.

The German assault on Wola that Eugenia mentions began on August 4. The following day German forces murdered a reported 10,000 in mass executions (Lukas 1986: 199).[8] News of the massacres spread quickly throughout Warsaw, brought by Wola residents who had managed to escape.[9]

Eugenia recalled life in the shelters:

Because there was no apartment, really, we sat in the basement, in the corridors of the basement. As long as water was flowing in the pipes, it was all right, but when those bombs hit the pipes and it started to flood the basement, it was tragic because we sat in the water. So, my brother, with the other men who were there—residents and some newcomers—they took down doors and found some tables, and they put the doors on the tables. So we walked on the doors, and that's how we lived in that water for a couple of weeks. Later still, my brother set up an iron stove, a small one with two rings and a pipe, and so we had a stove on which to cook something to eat. It was full of children there, not just from our residents but also newcomers. I had some supplies that had not been ruined, and I cooked dinners, but each of us had a given time to use the kitchen, and we could only cook when the Germans had their dinner. When the Germans had dinner between two and three, then there weren't any flights. We could cook because, after all, there would be smoke, and one couldn't cook otherwise. So, I had to cook really quickly, and here one had to walk through that water or jump from door to door.

I'll add that my poor sister-in-law, who was with child, and my poor mother were very peaceful. Luckily I brought an armchair, the last comfortable one, and Mama sat in that chair. She was very calm, she didn't make any scenes. Absolutely none, except that she had diarrhea from the stress. She had problems with that. My sister-in-law behaved calmly, only she must have worried because my brother was constantly out somewhere putting out fires. He went to those who were organizing help, and so he walked on the rooftops putting out fires and digging graves for those who were killed so, you know, he was working very hard, and at any moment a person could get it in the head because of those bombs. So, we took everything we could to the basement, and then we walled off the entrance so that when we returned we could find it. Because the first one who came along and saw what was hidden would take it. So, that's how we lived from the first of August to the second of September. I cooked what I could and went to the wounded because there was a hospital for soldiers at the Dominicans. So I went there. My cousin was recovering there after all. Well, and a person had to move around, had to somehow live normally, and to share what they had, already that was very little.

Eugenia's memories of the uprising spent in the basement of her ruined apartment building are for the most part concerned with hanging onto aspects of everyday life in increasingly difficult circumstances. Her recollections capture a certain element of black humor, of resourcefulness, as well as an appreciation of the difficulties that the situation presented for her elderly mother and her sister-in-law. Her recognition that the conditions of the uprising were particularly burdensome for the elderly, for those in frail health, and one might add, for small children reminds me of a conversation I had with Olgierd. He described the war in general, and the uprising in particular, as a great adventure for him as a young man but also acknowledged that, while he would not change a single moment of it, it would be something quite different to live through it as a septuagenarian. Indeed, memoirs of the Warsaw Uprising tend to reflect either a political-military perspective or that of a young person, typically one engaged in the Home Army or the People's Army. Relatively few have been written from the perspective of those who experienced it in mid- or late life as civilians. Indeed, there are few scholarly studies on the subject of the civilian experience of the uprising. Historians tend to agree that, at least initially, the civilian population supported the Polish fighters enthusiastically (Hanson 1982; Dunin-Wąsowicz 1984; Lukas 1986). This may be attributed in part to the expectation that the uprising would only last a few days or to the assumption that Polish forces would be successful in liberating the city. One can also attribute the support to the fact that the majority of civilians had at least one family member, friend, or co-worker who was involved as a soldier, health-care worker, or courier (Hanson 1982). Eugenia, for example, was aware that the majority of her students were in the Home Army or scouting. In this way civilians viewed the Polish forces as an extension of themselves, as their representatives, while they perceived the Germans as the enemies not just of the partisans but also of the residents of Warsaw and of the city as a whole. For the opening weeks of the battle, then, the Polish soldiers had civilian support. However, as Jerzy notes, the citizenry was fighting, but it was also the citizenry that suffered and not just those who had taken up arms.

The relationship between Polish forces and civilians seems to have varied from neighborhood to neighborhood, as did the ways in which the German troops treated civilians. As the uprising continued, members of the nonfighting populace were no longer enthusiastic supporters but simply terrified. Żoliborz residents welcomed the uprising, as did the vast majority of Warsovians. However, when the AK forces retreated after the disastrous events of August 1, those civilians who were aware of the retreat felt the soldiers had abandoned them to the wrath of the Germans (Hanson 1982: 187; Podlewski 1957: 38–39, 44). In his memoir Białoszewski (1977) wrote of Polish partisans in Old Town asking for volunteers to work at building barricades, digging graves, and transporting the wounded. In contrast, upon arriving in Śródmieście, he learned that "there were drafts of civilian labor. Not exactly roundups, but, in case of need, passersby were stopped and half commanded half requested to do such and such. And since it was for two or three hours, everyone went gladly. Generally, people didn't refuse such tasks. Although it's not safe to speak of everyone. At that time practically everything was done. But since there were an awful lot of people, probably more than 200,000, no one asked me to do anything. And so I went about on my own" (ibid. 166). One soldier is reported to have written that by early September military personnel in Żoliborz had resorted to threats as a matter of course to "get people to work" (Szymczak 1948: 145, cited in Hanson 1982: 187, 306). In other respects the neighborhood was well organized, providing food, child care, clothing, water, and health care to the civilian population (Hanson 1982: 188–90). This contrast suggests a tension between civilians and Polish combatants in that part of the city. Writing of Old Town, where he spent the first month of the uprising, Białoszewski (1977: 75) notes, "In general, relations with the partisans were good. Although I remember one painful scene on Freta Street in front of the Dominicans. Some women were cursing out some partisans who happened to be passing by. Because of what they had done."

In one of the few books dedicated solely to the topic, historian Joanna Hanson (1982) suggests that during the uprising Warsaw civilians tended to fall into three categories. The first supported the uprising both in their attitude toward the Polish forces and in their actions of joining in the fighting or volunteering for social-welfare work. Hanson describes this first group as "those who remained active throughout the battle and did not allow themselves to succumb to the strains and stresses of insurgent life" (ibid. 256). The second group, so-called shelter dwellers, spent the majority of the uprising in the cellars taking shelter from the fighting. Hanson comments, "Many of them were suffering from shock or were ill, most had lost all they possessed and others simply did not have the stamina to withstand the demands of insurgent life" (ibid. 257). The underground authorities considered this group to be self-centered, too frightened to be worried about more than their own immediate survival, vulnerable to propaganda from the Polish communist party, and therefore a potential source of dissent (ibid.). Finally, in the last category Hanson groups together those who were hostile to the uprising and those who saw the chaos of battle as an opportunity to gain from the suffering of others, in other words "dogs of war."

For a variety of reasons, I find this analysis problematic. First, I do not see a basis for combining "dogs of war" with those who opposed the uprising. Those who profited from the war were unlikely to be hostile to more fighting. Moreover, one can imagine a variety of reasons why an individual might have opposed the uprising: he or she might have subscribed to a worldview that emphasized nonviolence or had an assessment of the likelihood of Soviet help that was less optimistic than that of the Home Army leadership. In addition, one might have viewed the endeavor as counterproductive by recalling the disastrous consequences of the 1830 and 1863 insurrections. As Hanson's own data from Żoliborz suggest, people might have been willing to help with humanitarian aid work, such as caring for the wounded, the displaced, and the like, but unwilling to join the fighting. Another possibility is that people were afraid or otherwise unwilling to engage in types of work perceived as being dangerous, such as building barricades, digging graves, or transporting the wounded. However, the main problem with this taxonomy of civilian types is that it assesses civilian behavior from a patriotic-nationalistic standpoint, assuming that civilians should have been supportive of the uprising. Thus, those who fought or worked as medics are esteemed, and those who engaged in relief work are assumed to be supportive of the uprising when in fact they might have been motivated solely by concern for their fellow citizens. Finally, Hanson disparages those who were afraid, who opted to stay in shelters, as not up to "the demands of insurgent life."

Hanson's analysis does, however, reflect how participants in the uprising seemed to categorize civilian behavior. For example, Pani Basia recalled several incidents that make clear the varied reactions of civilians to the fighting and the Polish fighters.

> There was another beautiful adventure, but it wasn't mine. A bomb fell on Old Town, on the diagonal. You know, the house was standing, but the bomb fell through the first floor to the basement, or maybe it didn't make it to the basement, I don't know. In any case, we heard cries, and we medics grabbed our bags and flew there to save people. Well, we are running through the corridors, which were terribly overcrowded because people took shelter there. In general, they didn't go out, they just sat in those basements. We run a bit further, and we hear this strange, weird sound, and every strange sound was intriguing, right? It wasn't clear what it was, so we get closer, we go in. Well, there was a broken wall and standing next to it was a barrel—like for water or for pickles. At the barrel stood two guys and another stood in it, and so we look and we ask, "What's going on here?" And he says, "There's marmalade in the barrel." Marmalade, they had seen that there was marmalade in the barrel, and they had found, I don't know, a bucket or something and were dipping it out of the barrel. Well, it was cool, but, you know, people react differently. One could only burst out laughing, because here we were, debris grinding in our teeth, ashes and dust everywhere, somewhere people are buried, and here these two guys are busying themselves with the marmalade! Instead of helping!

Basia also recalled some encounters with civilians that revealed a gap between their experiences and those of the young people caught up in the fighting.

> So, listen, if there were horrible, terrible things, nightmarish problems with wounded who were beyond help, there was also a certain amount of laughter. Like when we were going to Old Town on Dąbrowski Street, and at a certain moment someone found a gramophone and records. Well, we had to play the records, right? There was a terrace, it was calmer, we weren't on call, and so, all right, we danced. All right, and suddenly from somewhere, from some cellar or something, appeared a distinguished older gentleman who looked at us and said, "How can you behave in such a way, when heroes are lying [dead] beside us?" And indeed there were corpses lying there covered, and one of

our friends looked calmly at the man and he said, "Really, it's just by chance that we are not the heroes that are lying there, so please let us dance." So the man cleared off because it dawned on him that really it was true: it was a question of chance. After all, it [the dancing] didn't last long, a brief moment. So, that's how it was.

The older gentleman in this story had not ceased to support the uprising, indeed he was incensed by the seeming lack of respect and reverence that the young people displayed for its fallen soldiers. He did not recognize that the young people (or at least Basia and the young man who spoke) did not regard their fallen comrades as more heroic or holier than themselves, just as less lucky.

In an interview given to *Gazeta Wyborcza* on the fifty-ninth anniversary of the uprising, Wiesław Chrzanowski, like Pan Jerzy a member of Gustaw, recalled that when he was wounded and lying in the hospital, he saw civilians trying to raise a white flag of surrender long before the actual capitulation (Kurski 2002: 2). Białoszewski (1977: 75) mentions similar incidents: "In another place (but this is only hearsay) some partisans cursed some women. Because when the Germans announced that people could come out with white cloths or handkerchiefs and surrender on the Żoliborz viaduct several women set out. Information about this incident varies. At any rate there was probably more than one such surrender. Or rather attempt. One it seems was lucky (for those women with the white handkerchiefs). Another time, it seems, the Germans shot at them. And maybe it was then that the women retreated in horror. To the nearest house. The partisans slammed the door in their faces, disgusted. Then, it seems, they cursed them but let them in at last. But some of the women were offended in turn. And went to another house."

The Third Warsaw: The Network of Sewers

The city's sewers comprised Białoszewski's "third Warsaw," the most restricted layer of the city. At first used primarily by couriers for safe passage through the city, this system of subterranean roads became the route used by Polish forces to move from one part of the city to another and eventually to retreat from areas that they could no longer hold. Entry into the sewers required a special pass. As Białoszewski, a civilian, recalls in his memoir, "We thought about the real sewer mains. To Śródmieście. But there were probably crowds waiting to get in. And to get in you had to have passes. And there were crowds waiting for those passes" (ibid. 101).

Because the Germans considered the Polish forces to be bandits, and therefore subject to immediate execution rather than capture, soldiers, medics, and couriers in neighborhoods that fell to the Germans had two options: to conceal their identities and join the civilian population as it was marched out of the city or to escape through the city's labyrinth of sewers to neighborhoods controlled by the Home Army. Basia took the latter route when she and her company escaped from the Old Town on the night of September 1, 1944.

> It looked like this: it is round at the top and on the bottom has a narrow path, and it's even at the bottom, so you walk on the even [path], but everything else is disgusting, slimy, truly repulsive. For example, when I went into the sewer, I had that terrible feeling of suffocation or stench but only for a moment; later a person stops thinking about it and stops feeling. It's like being in a very stuffy room; first you hold your breath, and later you adapt. Well, so one walked as slowly as possible, and later a regular courier from one side led the way. In general the column held on one to another single file, or held on by the belt, or held onto a rope which ran from the beginning to the end of the column, because it would be insanely easy to get lost. There were no lights; it was not possible to burn anything, and sometimes in a second there where the courier was—the courier would know where it was safe to turn on a flashlight—though certainly not at the manhole because the Germans opened the manholes, and they sat there, and they either shot or they didn't shoot, it was a question of luck, like always. Well, we were told not to raise our heads as we were walking. In the dark we couldn't crane our necks because in the dark you could see a white face. Well, and so that's how we squished, squished through that sludge for many, many, many hours, and when we left we were almost one of the last units to leave Old Town. The only units that remained were so-called cover patrols; that meant those who were supposed to give some semblance of a defense [*pozorować obronę*]. After all, we were loaded up [like donkeys], we had to bring the ammunition, weapons, medical supplies, so each medic had as much as she could carry, as much as she had the strength for, right? You know, [one's] strength multiplies in those situations and klip klam one stops, the column comes to a standstill because something happened, so they [the Germans] poison us or don't poison us, they shoot or don't shoot, right? Although one doesn't—at least I didn't— think about that so much.

Basia was one of the last of an estimated 1,500 Polish soldiers to leave Old Town that night. Along with them came an estimated 500 civilians, all clamoring to escape the neighborhood before the Germans entered to occupy the area the next day (Bór-Komorowski 1951: 286–89). Basia recalled:

> Well, and at last we got to the manhole on Warecka Street. You know where Warecka is, you've been there. Well, on Warecka, slowly people began to come out. So, some could still get out by their own strength. We were relatively unburdened by wounded because the wounded had made the trip earlier. Transporting the wounded through the sewers was more difficult, right? Much worse, but because we were one of the last groups out, we had fewer wounded. If there were wounded with us, they were lightly wounded. Although, for example, Dr. Morwa, he was our battalion's doctor, he went with one boy, only he went a bit earlier, and he practically carried him on his back. And he [Dr. Morwa] was a tall gentleman. Think of how he was doubled over with that weight, it must have seemed that his back would break. And, also, a person had this desire to sit down, "Well, I'll sit. It's all the same to me." But they couldn't sit down. They couldn't, the column had to keep moving forward. And the boys from Śródmieście were standing at the manholes, and they helped and pulled us out. Well, a few were transported in such a way that they were pushed, and so they dropped a rope so that they could pull them out. And so we climbed out around five or six a.m.; it was already light.

Though Polish units travelled relatively short distances through the sewers, it often took hours to navigate them in the dark. Indeed, the journey that Basia describes from Old Town to Śródmieście was only about a mile long but took several hours (ibid.). Many became disoriented by the deprivation of sight and surface sounds, which wreaked havoc on their sense of the passage of time. Soldiers' disorientation was only exacerbated when they left the sewers for the comparatively normal looking world of Śródmieście. As Basia noted, "We climbed out on Warecka Street, and suddenly houses are standing, panes are in the windows, it was hard to wrap one's mind around it. It was simply that they hadn't bombed here in that way." The experience of the sewers, described as a descent into the depths that sometimes led to salvation but just as frequently to utter disorientation or to the sense of not caring whether one took another step or not, has become a metaphor, perhaps the defining one, of the lost generation.

But what had Basia's unit escaped from? Basia recalled the place they left behind in this way:

> We had left that great ruin, because in Old Town there were no houses that were standing. Just fragments of walls, stumps, falling apart here, smashed

there, and bricks, piles of bricks reached two or three stories high. Because the most important thing that they [the Germans] depended on was the east-west crossing. Well, Old Town especially was in their way, and later they began to deal with the next neighborhoods. But the first impression was incredible because in no way did it remind one of a city. Somehow there were outlines of the streets but everything was covered with glass, and in fact it just wasn't very clear. There were paths beaten through [the debris]. It was also necessary to be careful because there were still snipers, and very often in the course of an hour you had [posted on a wall] an arrow and "warning: sniper." In other words, you had to go a different way or jump out of the way because they were shooting, and they shot well, because when they shot there was no discussion, just a corpse. Well, sometimes heavily wounded.

Several hours earlier, Miron Białoszewski had made his journey along the same route. He and two friends were able to gain passes because another friend, a Home Army member, had suggested that they volunteer to carry a severely wounded soldier. Białoszewski (1977: 143) recalled the exit from the sewer and the contrast between Old Town and Śródmieście in this way: "I only remember myself. It was quiet. For the most part. The barricades. Narrow Warecka Street. I walked. We walked. Exhausted. Emotionally drained. . . . The gate. Warecka. The square. Szpitalna. Familiar. So familiar. Indeed. We walked quickly and freely. A corner. Chmielna. Everything is standing.We make a turn. Into Marszalkowska. The only thing is that it's dark. Barricades. That atmosphere. But otherwise it's normal. Houses. Night. Peace. Midnight. Summer. Warm. Everything is there." They left behind the ruins of Old Town, the civilians, and the wounded. Basia recalled:

> So it [the experience of the uprising] was full of different things. But there were also kind people, people who would share everything. Later it was unbelievably terrible when we left Old Town. There were those who swore at us like sailors [*którzy klinęli nas w żywy kamień*], but there were others who understood that it was what it was and nothing could change things, right? That there was nothing to do but evacuate. A terrible number of those people died horribly. Those who were healthy, well, somehow they walked it. Well, because they were ordered to leave. They [Germans] simply couldn't have shot them all and, also, the German army [the Wehrmacht] didn't want to do that [shoot civilians] very badly. I mean, when they were ordered to they did, but they mostly used SS units for that. In any case an awful lot [of people were killed].

Białoszewski wrote, "Everyone felt guilty about those left behind. Not so much about the civilians. Obviously, the young men posed a special problem. But the partisans? The seriously wounded? Much worse. Because they wore uniforms. And were there en masse. And were helpless. What would happen to them? We deceived ourselves that . . . yes, somehow, anyway. . . . And then it turned out. What. How. Horrible. Others have described it already. I shan't repeat it. Only to say that what happened in Wola happened again" (ibid.).

Eugenia, one of the many civilians left behind by the retreating Polish forces, was in Old Town on September 2 when the Germans arrived.

> Well, but on the second of September they gave the signal to leave, that the whole neighborhood was going to be destroyed, and so we had to leave. We left on the second of September and, indeed, they bombed the church and our roof too. In that church a few hundred people were killed because they weren't only on the main floor—I mean in the church—but also underground and it was blocked, and six hundred people died. They suffocated. . . . They had somehow created [a shelter] there, and when it collapsed later those who could make it out made it out, and those who were trapped below, people couldn't get to them. And we left. And here [in Żoliborz] on the banks [of the Vistula] is—I don't know if you know where Traugutt's cross is? Traugutt was killed at the Cytadel, and there is a hill there, and we stopped on the hill, and there the Ukrainians searched us—or the Germans, they took our watches, or whatever we had of value. . . . So they looted us, and later they chased us forward in rows at gunpoint from Traugutt Park along the train tracks to Wola. It was only once we got to Wola that we walked on the roads.
>
> There were corpses lying in the streets. Among us there were people who could not go on, and they simply killed them. Older people they just . . . They led us to Wola and then to the West Station. There it was terribly difficult because people had baggage with them. So it was hard walking to that West Station. There was a point where they took all those who—they knew what the fighters looked like—so they pulled them out of line. On the way to the West Station, they took the young people, and there in the church at Wola they shot them.
>
> My mother came last. I was afraid that they would kill her because she absolutely did not have the strength to walk because it is a terribly long way. How many kilometers is it! We walked through all of Warsaw to the West Station. And, proszę Pani, . . . I walked, and I was just afraid that they—I pulled her along so she would make it somehow. And I had two suitcases,

my own, a little overnight bag, and my sister-in-law's, who couldn't carry anything because she was pregnant, and my brother had my mother's coat, and something else, the blanket in a linen bag. Mama didn't carry anything except a little pot, but in the end even that was too heavy for her. She was in misery. She was so tired because she constantly had that horrible diarrhea. And when we got to the station they packed us into wagons and to Pruszków, to a camp there.

The lost generation's experiences may be epitomized by the horror of the partisan's journey through the darkness and stench of Warsaw's sewers, but the suffering of those left behind in the ruins is equally emblematic of the catastrophic consequences of urban warfare.

Narratives of Deprivation

Many of my informants' narratives about the uprising are not about specific events but rather about the conditions in which they lived, worked, and fought. All of my informants recalled encounters with hunger, exposure, and thirst during the uprising, and the details of these deprivations find their way into their retellings. When compared to narratives of battles and their aftermath, accounts of deprivation may initially seem trivial; however, when one's home is destroyed, finding safe shelter becomes an overwhelming concern, just as food becomes the subject of much thought when one is hungry. For example, Pani Basia took time out from a description of a battle inside the Church of the Holy Cross on Krakowskie Przedmieście to tell me about jam:

> **Basia:** So, we were on the side where the priests' quarters are located. Now it looks a bit different. There used to be a tiny little courtyard there, and on the other side sat the Germans. There from the top on the galleries they were running back and forth. Once we, once they [were in control], depending on the situation, and in the priests' house—the priests were not there anymore; however their fruit compotes and preserves were. Mmm . . .
>
> **ELT:** They were tasty?
>
> **Basia:** Very, very much so. . . . Sometimes there was something [to eat] still, but as for cooking it was really bad. Those priestly preserves and those priestly compotes, they were wonderful. Well, and we defended ourselves there for a relatively long time. The Germans were a systematic people, so when they finished with one house they went on to the next.

In recollecting and describing to me the layout of the church grounds and how it related to the battle, Pani Basia could not help but recall the food that the priests had left behind. Though it is clearly not the main point of the story, the experience of hunger assuaged by the priests' preserves is as strong as that of the shooting, if not more so.

As the uprising continued, much of Warsaw was without running water. While this had enormous consequences for hospitals in particular, Janina K—— remembered becoming acutely aware of its indirect consequences when the hospital staff encountered Germans during the negotiations that led to the capitulation: "Three German officers, who were very elegant with clean boots and white gloves on their hands and—just imagine how we looked after not bathing for nearly two months, practically without a change of clothes, because there was neither the time nor the means." The humiliation of meeting the meticulously clean German officers when she had not had the water to bathe for weeks was something she had never forgotten. The contrast between the immaculately dressed Germans and the unwashed Poles was something that others commented on as well.

The following passage from one of my conversations with Basia illustrates a range of deprivations faced by her unit. The events she described took place just after her unit had emerged from the sewers on Warecka Street.

> Well, it was around five in the morning, and they ordered us to go to some quarters. There were just bare floors, and we laid down on that floor like sardines. We were terribly tired. Well, let's say we napped. It wasn't sleeping, but in any case a rest and among the others two of my friends—because they were lying—well, they were lying next to me, one on each side. So, it was better for me because I was warmer. Well, all the same we were frozen. After all, we were terribly hungry, not even feeling that hunger. Because during the last days in Old Town, there wasn't even talk of cooking in fact. However, there were sugar cubes, and in fact everyone carried dirty sugar cubes in their pockets, and if one was very hungry one sucked on the sugar, and it was a wonderful help. One prospered, right? And when we had slept for a few moments, I suddenly woke up, and I heard this strange ringing. We had one coat [to cover themselves with], and I was in the middle so I was more covered than they, and it was one of my friend's teeth ringing. Well, I pulled the coat over him to let him warm up, and we slept on. After a half an hour or 45 minutes I heard that someone on the other side was ringing, so I pulled the coat to the other side. Well, and that's how we slept until six or seven when they woke us and let us go. Some of the people had family in Śródmieście, right, or friends or acquaintances.

Well, we were given time off for a few hours, in order to wash and get tidied up somehow because, after all, it was stinking and hideous. Well, and one of my friends told me that when they left—[they were] terribly dirty in fact—one of the officers with a nurse took a photograph, and they were clean and tan—all as it should be, and that young lady said [to my friends], "Ugh! How you stink!" And that friend of mine flew into a fury and said, "And if you had waded through that shit, would you smell good?" She was embarrassed most of all, right?

Basia chuckled when she recounted the above incidents for me and told me about finding a German coat, which she called a "monkey" and which she recalled with great affection because it solved the problem of staying warm until she had to give it up before leaving Warsaw. However, while she was able to find humor in suffering from coldness brought on by hunger in the warm days of August and September; not all experiences were so easily transformed in retrospect.

Well, at our barricade[10] . . . there, at the very end of the street, lived two sisters, and one of them gave birth to a child—a little boy as I recall—two weeks before the uprising. And they sat there the whole time, without moving [from the house]. One of their husbands was no one knew where, and the second didn't know where her husband was either—in some other neighborhood. Well, and they were there with us, but that little one—she [the mother] lost her milk, and the little one was terribly hungry. So, we were standing on our heads trying to find milk, so it was that sort of story.

"It was that sort of story," meaning that it was the sort of situation for which there was no remedy, a phrase that indicates that the child was not saved "by some miracle" or by anything else. Janina K—— also told me a story of that sort, one that took place at the hospital the night that Żoliborz fell to the Germans: "There was a maternity ward. At night 14 children had been born. There was nothing we could do but baptize those children with water, because no one knew if they would live to the next day without their mothers' milk, because their mothers were hungry, and there was nothing to feed them, and because there was no milk either." Narratives of deprivation illustrate that the lack of food, shelter, and water shaped both the experience and the memory of the uprising. As illustrated most dramatically by these accounts of malnourished mothers and starving infants, it is precisely this lack of the essentials of daily life that contributed to the suffering and also to the deaths of many Warsovians.

Narratives of Destruction

For those unfamiliar with Warsaw, the way my informants painstakingly list the details of street names, buildings, and their associations with cultural and historical figures might seem like distractions from "what happened," in effect, from the point of the narrative. I would suggest, however, that such details are precisely the point. These events may have been experienced as "time out of time," but not in place out of place. On the contrary, they are firmly embedded in the cityscape. Such details can be understood, in part, as chronicling material loss. Thus Jerzy in his photographic tour through central Warsaw emphasized the material losses in order to show the effects of violence on the buildings where people fought, killed, sought refuge, and died.[11] In this way his narrative is not just a chronicle of a battle and his place in it but also an account of the destruction of the city. In the same way, then, that his battalion's leader falls victim to the Germans, so, too, does the Stasica Palace, the University of Warsaw, and Chopin's house. Through his photographic tour of the neighborhood, Jerzy also drew a distinction between past and present. For my informants the past inhabits the contemporary landscape. Thus, past and present are intertwined. In this way, through narrative, Jerzy created a demarcation between those who experienced the war and those who did not.[12] The part of Warsaw that Jerzy described in the preceding quotations was reconstructed in the 1950s to look as it had before the war. As a result to me the photographs of what Krakowskie Przedmieście looked like in 1939 were more familiar than either those taken by Jerzy during the battle or those taken of the city in ruins in 1945. On my first visit to Warsaw in 1989, I had to remind myself constantly that this part of the city was a reconstruction and, in the literal sense, one of the newest parts of the city. At that time I saw the destruction of Warsaw as a story of rebirth, but for Jerzy and other informants the verisimilitude of the reconstruction did not erase the violence enacted in the cityscape. Rather, it created a need to communicate to others who had not witnessed its destruction the violence that, for them, still remained inscribed on its walls.

In contrast to Jerzy's narrative of destruction in Old Town and Śródmieście, Olgierd's account is situated in Żoliborz, a neighborhood that was not razed to the ground. Many of the locales he described are still intact. Olgierd was also very specific in locating the various sites of the field hospital in contemporary Żoliborz. He cited not just street names but also specific buildings, emphasizing their continued existence and contemporary uses, drawing connections between the past and the present as he did so. He pointed out that the hospital was located below the milk bar, that the space now taken up by a large housing complex had then been a community garden. In relating the pasts of these places, he infused the present-day landscape with meaning. In many narratives of the uprising, such details serve to present Warsaw, its history and culture, not just as the place on which violence was inscribed but, also, as a victim of the battle.

Miron Białoszewski (1977: 51) also devoted a great deal of attention to the destruction of Warsaw in his *Memoir of the Warsaw Uprising*, in which he described in detail the locations and architectural features of many of Warsaw's landmarks. He commented, "Perhaps I am speaking too much about these monuments. But they were important. Because they perished with us." Not only did Warsaw and its monuments perish with the Warsovians, but it is through the cityscape and its *lieux de mémoires,* places where the past seeps into the present, that the past is remembered and recalled to the present (Nora 1989).

Narratives of Death

My informants pay a great deal of attention to memories of death and the dying in their narratives of the uprising; in fact, it is impossible to filter out such references from their accounts of any given day in battle, at a hospital, or in a shelter. This is the case for civilians and military personnel alike. However, in the following narratives, informants do more than recount a death and its circumstances as one more event in a longer story. They describe being overwhelmed by the dead, by a specific death, or by the possibility of dying. In the pages that follow I discuss three different types of death narratives. The first group is perhaps best described as accounts of the narrator's near-death experiences. The second focuses on encounters with the anonymous dead associated with mass death in battles, bombings, and executions. The final group is comprised of informants' recollections of the deaths of individuals, people who were intimates of the teller in some cases and strangers in others, known almost exclusively in their dying moments, their names, last words, and the circumstances of their dying still remembered decades later.

The first type of death narrative I will discuss is one in which the teller describes a situation in which he or she has a close encounter with death. Although I discussed similar narratives in the chapter on the invasion of Poland, I return to them again as they are prominent and occur in far greater abundance in informants' recollections of the uprising. Olgierd Z——, for example, recalled three such moments:

So, to return again to those moments of the uprising in Żoliborz itself, I wanted to return to certain moments when I was saved, I would say, by a miracle. There was a moment during the attack on the Gdańsk Station [located in Warsaw] when literally all around me there were a great number of dead and heavily wounded, and I was saved. I was just lightly scratched. Next, after that attack, when I was working on Tucholska Street, here in Lower Żoliborz, I was organizing the hospital rooms—beds—for the wounded from the hospital, and at that moment the first of those shells, so-called wardrobes or cows, hit. And in the neighboring room where I had been, one nurse was killed on the spot, another's arm was torn off, and another's leg. So, I was miraculously saved, in fact.

Later, I remember another moment when there was the funeral for Klara, [that is] Danka Jaksa-Bykowska. A gentleman came to me and said, "Please sir, give me the shovel, I'll help you. You are tired." I stepped aside and kneeled at the side [of the grave]. A moment later a bullet hit that man in the head. At that spot where I had stood. So, also some miracle.

Hanna S—— also recalled three incidents in which she was miraculously saved from death.

I was saved three times by a miracle. First there was that bomb. Second, when I left the house with Mama and I said goodbye to her, and my friend—this was on the other side of the street—at that moment a shell hit, and Mama opened the door, because if it hadn't been for the door, everything would have fallen on us; I don't remember a thing. It's characteristic that when a bomb falls one doesn't hear it. Those nearby do, but I only heard a noise and as it hit stuff started to fall. I saw that suddenly it was dark, a red circle. I can't breathe and the smell of sulfur, because it was as if someone was sprinkling ashes. So, I escaped. It was burning here and there, but I didn't see anything. I don't know how I found myself in the garden, I don't know. I have absolutely no idea. I only know that I didn't hear a thing. Mama grabbed me by the leg. Mama fell and caught me by the leg, and Auntie had been in the bathroom, and she came out and was putting on her wristwatch when she saw us, so she didn't hear either. I knew that you didn't hear when it [a bomb] fell.

When we were walking to our meeting place on the last day through the rubble—because the sidewalk was blocked and so we went between [the piles of rubble]—and we went from one to the other, and between us I look, and there is a shell. Well, and it would have been the end for us if we had been hit. Well, these are those types of reminiscences, you know, because in general I do not reminisce.

These accounts differ from those presented in the chapter about the invasion in a number of ways. The most obvious pertains to the level of detail with which they are recounted. Additionally, informants' close-call narratives about the invasion typically contain multiple points of intervention by individuals who act deliberately so as to contribute to the narrators' survival, sparing him or her from execution, arrest, or deportation. In these narratives from the early days of the war, the miracle is not based on circumstance alone but also on the presence of a helpful person who is in the right place at the right time. In contrast, in these narratives of close brushes with death during the uprising, the narrators in most cases are saved not by the kindness or leniency of others but rather by being physically removed from harm's way at the last moment. These stories follow a pattern: had she not left the room, had she been standing here and not there, she would have been killed. Thus, survival is attributed to the seemingly trivial circumstances that caused them not to be in the path of a sniper's bullet, or a bomb blast, or so on. In such accounts informants emphasize both the pervasiveness of death and their awe at escaping it.

Pani Basia also recalled an incident that took place during the opening days of the uprising that is similar to those recounted by Olgierd and Hanna. Basia was taking a break from tending to the wounded and was sitting in a window, taking in the fresh air and watching the street below, something that in retrospect she saw as a terribly stupid thing to have done. Her break ended, and she went back to the wounded, who were in the adjacent room, and another woman took her place at the window. No sooner had Basia left the room to rejoin the patients, when shots were fired into the window, killing the woman who sat in the place Basia had occupied just moments before. Basia did not ascribe the fact that she lived while the other woman died to an act of God. People may tell you that they were saved by a miracle or fate, she warned me, but that is just nonsense. She insisted that it was nothing of the sort; it was just timing; it was just an accident that I lived and she died!

The following passage excerpted from an interview with Janina R—— is in many ways similar to the preceding accounts in which Olgierd, Hanna, and Basia describe a close escape from death. It is the frame rather than the content of Janina's account that differs. Janina R—— recalled efforts to evacuate the patients from another hospital originally located on Śmiała Street (also in Żoliborz) to the hospital in the fort in Żeromski Park:

> A friend and I carried a boy, and as we carried him he said [to me], "Dora [Janina's pseudonym], I'm not going to live anyway, I'm not going to live anyway, so why are you taking me? I'll stay here in the hospital." He was

wounded in the leg. I said, "What are you talking about? Your leg has almost healed, nothing is going to happen." And he had with him a bottle of water or juice and I told him, "Hold on to that because who knows what the situation will be there with water." We were carrying him out of there through a window—in general humans have a lot of strength. I cannot imagine where I got the strength [to do that] from. We were carrying him out, and the first shell that fell killed him. That was so frightening because a moment before he was alive, and he talked to me, and he said, "Nothing will become of me." And I watched how he was killed.

I went back to that hole of a basement and told Raczek/Ludwik, that doctor, "Ludwik, I'm not going back out! I am so scared that my hair is standing on end." He said to me, "Don't bother about it. Here," and he poured me some valerian, or some sort of sedative. "Don't think about it, here take this."

When they brought the general's daughter, Ludwik said [to me]—because she was a very good friend of his—"Together you and I will carry her." And we were carrying that *baba*—we didn't say *baba* [slang for "woman"] then, that's something we say now—we were carrying her, and she was alive. She moaned and groaned, and at that moment a shell hit. First one, then another, the planes were shelling us. They killed her, and the doctor was heavily wounded. His entire back and buttocks and his arm covered with shrapnel. So, given the circumstances, I dumped the woman's corpse and put him on the stretcher, but I didn't have anyone to help me so, I grabbed a civilian who was running [from the area], and I said, "Come here, help me carry the doctor." Because we were behind the villas going from Śmiała Street to the fort. And to that he said he couldn't because he had heart problems, and when I heard that nonsense that someone had a heart problem and that doctor—it's terrible to say it maybe, but he was blubbering so and behaving scandalously—and when he went to the boys during his rounds he always said, "Who are you? Soldiers are supposed to be quiet!" And here he behaved like the worst sissy. Well, so I grabbed that civilian, and I told him to go. We were carrying the doctor, and every time a shell hit he dropped the stretcher. It's hard for you to imagine, because it's hard for those who haven't experienced it [*przeżyli*, the verb *przeżyć* has connotations of something one lives through and experiences strongly] themselves to imagine. I mean heroics weren't driving me, only fear. I just wanted to get out of there! So, another shell hit, and that guy threw down the stretcher. I thought I would go crazy! The doctor had a gun because he was an officer. I took that pistol, and I said, "Listen, if you abandon that stretcher one more time, I'll shoot you!" He must have realized that over here there were bullets, here bombs, the doctor lying [on the stretcher], and me: mad, dirty, with my hair standing on end; and maybe he felt that I really would shoot him. In any case, whenever he had the intention of putting down the stretcher, I kicked him in the behind, and yelled, "No, keep going!" We went down Śmiała Street to the school for the military families that's still there. And Ludwik says, "Dora, why not [stop] here at the school under the roof here." And we were so close to the fort, and the fort is well built. It's huge and walled, I was rushing there. I said, "No! No, let's go to the fort." And he said, "No, we'll stop here under the roof." We'd hardly passed the school when a plane took a nosedive and dropped a bomb that blew everything apart, and we made it to the hospital. There, Dr. S—— took care of him right away; he operated. I got an order to return to the hospital, and in light of the fact that there had been so many incidents of the medics or those patients we carried being wounded, we were told to wait until evening [to finish the evacuation] because the Germans always quieted down in the evening.

Janina's account of transporting the patients from the basement, out a window, and to the hospital in the fort continues in this vein: each time she makes it alive and unscathed to the safety of the fort only to have to turn back again to bring another patient to safety. Terror is the dominant motif in her narrative. Janina was quite frank about feeling terrified by the death of first one patient, then another. The fear that she might be hit and killed at any moment is palpable in the frantic pace of her narrative. In general, the people whom Janina remembered are not motivated by the desire to be heroes but by fear, duty, and compassion for others.

Virtually everyone who took part in the uprising had close brushes with death on a daily basis, yet not all people highlight their own survival in these narratives. Basia, for example, is adamant in her rejection of the notion that she was chosen to survive by virtue of a miracle, preferring to see the incident as one of many in which blind chance played a role. Similarly, Janina R——'s account of transporting patients to the hospital in the park is full of moments like those described above by Hanna and Olgierd, in which those around her suddenly die or are severely wounded. Yet Janina recalls the horror and absurdity of their deaths, rather than the wonder of her own survival. It was the horror of seeing a life extinguished so quickly that was preserved in her memory. Framed not as an affirmation of her own existence, Janina's account is steeped in the experience of death, the horror of which nearly overwhelms her. In the following passage, Olgierd Z—— described a similar experience with death on a large scale in the aftermath of two consecutive and unsuccessful attempts to attack German forces at the Gdańsk Station.

So, unfortunately, neither the first nor the second attack succeeded. Many soldiers were killed. There were a lot of wounded, and we transported those wounded to a hospital which was then located at Wilson Place, exactly there where the Wisła Cinema is presently. That was the hospital. So, the wounded waited for triage on stretchers, which were carried there. I remember that picture, how there was stretcher after stretcher along the whole length of the building. One day—because the German planes were flying low, and there was no antiaircraft artillery so they saw that this was a hospital—so one day, purposefully, [during] one of their actions, they intentionally fired on the hospital and on the terrain of Lower Żoliborz. So, there was a massacre here because the health service didn't have any weapons, and all that was left [up until that point] was completely destroyed. That means not entirely, but in any case the majority was very—there were many, many more wounded, there were wounded who were wounded again . . .

Like Janina R——, Olgierd described the feeling of being immersed in death and destruction. Robert Jay Lifton (1967: 479–81), a pioneer in researching the experience of survivorship from a psychological perspective, deemed such experiences the "death imprint," which he describes as "a jarring awareness of the fact of death" that comes from being immersed in death on a mass scale. In his work with survivors of Hiroshima and the Nazi concentration camps, Lifton noted that it was not only the pervasiveness of death that was conveyed but also its grotesqueness, absurdity, indecency— all of which are captured in many of the narratives I have presented thus far (ibid. 480).

In the preceding death narratives the focus is on the informants' experiences of death and the dying. The dead mentioned in these accounts are either anonymous or at least not the focal point of the narrative. The third type of death narrative, however, is one in which informants gave accounts of the deaths of specific, named individuals. Such memorial narratives appear in my interviews in great number and, indeed, are not exclusive to this period of the war. Sometimes, as in the following example from an interview with Olgierd Z——, the focus is not so much on how the individual died as how she lived.

There were a few scouts—among others I wanted to name somebody who really was an example of outstanding courage and who at once approached our task with enormous enthusiasm—and that is Danka Jaksa-Bykowska. She was the daughter of Professor Jaksa-Bykowski, who was arrested by the Germans before the uprising, during the occupation, and she was saved by a miracle because she wasn't at home then, because at the same time they simply arrested her entire family. And they were all killed. Her family was shot by the Germans. And she was saved, and in fact she was at that post. She had the pseudonym Klara.

This is not the first time an informant has made a point of singling out Danka Jaksa-Bykowska, or Klara, for special comment. Though she did not tell me the story of the arrest of the family, Krystyna Z——also made a point of mentioning that she began her work as a courier through Danka, who was her neighbor. Perhaps Danka Jaksa-Bykowska was an extraordinary person; certainly she lost more in one moment than most of the people with whom I worked lost throughout the five years of the occupation, rendering her a tragic figure. What Olgierd did not say here is that Danka herself was later fatally wounded, which makes this brief mention of her work as a medic and the tragic story of her family itself a testament, a witness to her existence. In this way, this brief mention of Danka and her family by name is a sort of memorial narrative commemorating her work and her life.[13]

It is likely that Olgierd knew Danka prior to the war, from primary school and through mutual friends. However, not all memorial narratives give testament to the deaths of people well-known to those who memorialize them, a point illustrated by the following narrative from Janina K——: "One day we received news—that means some one came and told us, 'On Czarniecki Street there are three wounded. Send a patrol.' We had five girls who went out to collect the wounded. 'Send a patrol because the wounded are lying there.' Night time, naturally. So, they run, and they bring two uprising boys and one boy who was a gendarme. It happened that they didn't have their identity cards or something, and the Germans [*sic*] shot them." I strongly suspect that Janina misspoke here because at this point in the fighting, the Germans would not have bothered to check the papers of the Polish fighters; they would have simply shot them on sight. As becomes apparent later in the story, Janina probably meant to say that the boys were shot by other Polish Home Army members.

> And the one, who I remember to this day was named Pietruszka, you know it simply means parsley. He says to me, "Why did they kill me? For what did they kill me? I have a mother, an old lady. Please, lady, get word to my mother somehow. Take my identity card." And he gave me his identity card, and he gave me some gloves that he had. Maybe they were his—well, I don't know— his fiancée's or something. I had those until the uprising [ended]. Later I gave them to the Red Cross so they could find her. They tried to reach her. That

was not a very pleasant impression how he died. A person looks on as a young boy dies, well, and really one doesn't know why. Through some foolishness, because one had to have with one an ID or a password, or something. One could move about if one had a password. That means one would say the name of a city, and they would have to answer with some phrase, but without knowing the password, it wasn't wise to do that [to go out]. It was simply our AK gendarmes [who shot him].

This account of not-so-friendly fire illustrates that, like narratives of the anonymous dead, memorial narratives also capture the senselessness and indecency of death in war. Moreover, just as Olgierd answered a call to bear witness to Danka Jaksa-Bykowska's life and death through his narrative recounted to me, so did Janina K—— feel obliged to fulfill Pietruszka's dying wish and to ensure that his death as well as the senselessness of it is remembered, too.

Death at the hands of the Germans was something the Polish populace had come to expect, and though treated as tragic, they did not view it as uncommon. Occurrences of death brought about by fellow Poles, however, tended to be remembered with a good deal more bitterness. Jerzy had a great deal of admiration for his friend and cell leader "Koń," a pseudonym that means "horse." From his description of Koń, it was clear that Jerzy admired the man's physical strength, courage, and panache. For example, Jerzy recalled that in the end it was Koń who carried the "damned suitcase" by himself to Genowefa company's meeting place. Jerzy also told me a story about Koń that was far more hyperbolic: the Gestapo arrested Koń for his underground activities and sent him to Auschwitz, from whence he managed to escape in an SS man's uniform and an SS commandant's car. Koń then returned to work in the underground. The Gestapo arrested him a second time, but again he escaped, this time by blowing up a room full of Germans with what I assume must have been a hand grenade. At some point during the uprising, though, Koń was accused of treason, tried in abstentia by an underground court, found guilty, then executed by a member of the underground, who was carrying out the clandestine court's death sentence. Koń's death may strike the reader as being as incredible as his escapes; however, underground courts created by the Polish government-in-exile for the adjudication of political offenses heard cases not only of treason, but also of blackmail and banditry, and could hand down sentences that ranged from reprimands to judgments of infamy that carried with them the death penalty (Gross 1979: 166). Jerzy believed the accusation to be "entirely untrue" both at the time of the incident and five decades after its occurrence when he told this story to me. Jerzy spoke to me about the deaths of many of his friends, a topic that I noticed came up over parting cups of tea and only after I had put away my tape recorder. While all of these memorial narratives were tinged with sadness and regret, and one or two with a sense of self-reproach, the story of Koń's death was the one that was most noticeably characterized by bitterness and anger for a friend misjudged.

Death narratives such as these can be read as laments for the dead en masse or sentiments of mourning for an individual. They can be read as testaments to suffering and loss, told so as to become known and so that, in becoming part of public discourse, they can be reclaimed (Das 1985: 5). They also serve as memorials that recall the dead, validating the existence of those who have died as well as those who have lived to tell their tales (Nordstrom 1997: 79–80).

Taken as a collective these three types of death narratives present a complex picture of the uprising, one in which the heroic is balanced, if not overwhelmed, by encounters with death on a personal, individual, and mass level. Robert Jay Lifton has argued that every experience of survival contains an element of guilt about those who did not survive. Many survivors cope with this guilt by formulating the experience in such a way as to find meaning in the reason for their survival and thus meaning for their continued existence. Clearly, this plays a role in the attribution of survival to something miraculous. Lifton also observed that survivors often feel that their encounter with death is the most important and powerful experience of their lives, one that overshadows all others. However, just as my informants frame their death narratives differently, some highlighting their own survival, others highlighting the deaths of individuals or mass death, so too is the encounter with death formulated and understood in a diversity of ways. Thus, some informants find meaning in the awe inspired by their own survival, while others see similar incidents of near escapes from death as only making clearer the horror, absurdity, and arbitrariness of death in wartime.

Although many of my informants may have experienced the uprising as sacred time, they also experienced the consequences of 64 days of urban warfare in the landscape of their city and their social worlds. This accounts for the careful attention they paid to noting places of destruction and to remembering the dead. In these narratives informants commemorate all that they lost. At the same time my informants' narratives of the uprising are permeated with references to the deprivations they suffered in terms of food, water, and shelter and to accounts of being overwhelmed by the pervasiveness of violent death. Some also acknowledge the fear they felt in battle and the tensions that existed between civilians and soldiers. All these narratives present a compelling contrast to their expectations that the uprising would be something glorious. Though powerful, these memories do not seem to influence informants' evaluation of the uprising itself, which remains overwhelmingly positive despite the losses incurred during battle and those that followed the capitulation. For my informants, at least, defeat and the degradations it entailed has done little to tarnish their efforts to restore Polish independence. Perhaps this is because they viewed the uprising, as Engelking suggests, as sacred time, as the enactment of their heroic vision of carrying on a legacy of fighting for Polish independence. Five decades later, they remain confident that their cause was just. That their efforts to free Poland were not only unsuccessful but later punished by Poland's postwar government is something that they consider tragic. However, it in no way diminishes their sense that it was what the situation demanded. Nor does it alter their conviction that the uprising was in some ways the time of their lives.

7 Aftermath—*Exodus and Return*

THE HOME ARMY LEADERSHIP as a whole capitulated on October 2, and the civilian population was given until October 9 to leave the city. Stefan summarized the situation in this way:

> The uprising capitulated under orders [from] the AK [Home Army] authorities on September 30th. We were taken captive. The Germans took us captive. At the beginning we counted on the Russians to help us because they were standing at the Vistula. They just stood there, and it stopped at that. So, we were taken captive. . . . Żywiciel, the cryptonym of our leader [Mieczysław Niedzielski], in the last days of September, Żywiciel was inducted into the Eighth Infantry Division of the AK so that they would capture us rather than shooting us, because we were the Polish army. Because initially, the Germans, when they caught someone they shot him. So we were taken captive. My wife was too . . . and we were captives in different places. My wife was at a camp for women, an Oberlangen, and I was wounded and lying in a Lazarus ward in a hospital at Camp 11 until the camp was liberated. The camp was liberated by Russians, and then I returned to Warsaw.
>
> The units here in Żoliborz numbered 2,500 people: women and men. Losses rose to around 1,000. After the war there were—because not everybody [who survived] returned—around 1,300 to 1,400. At this time, there are only just 630 of us still living.

This chapter is an examination of informants' narratives of three key events that took place in the immediate aftermath of the uprising: the capitulation to the Germans on October 2, 1944, the expulsion of the insurgents and the civilian population from Warsaw, and their journeys back to Warsaw following the city's liberation by Soviet troops on January 17, 1945. I explore how my informants coped with the destruction of the familiar, how they managed to rebuild normalcy (by which I mean everyday life), and the role of memory, place, and reconstruction in their efforts to do so.

The Fall of Warsaw

> **Olgierd Z——:** Żoliborz capitulated on the 30th of September. September 30th, that's the day of Żoliborz's capitulation, and from that time, I mean after the war, each year we gather at the Church of Stanisław Kostki in Żoliborz, and there is a mass, a requiem mass is celebrated for the dead soldiers from the uprising in Żoliborz. In this way the anniversary of the capitulation is very heavy, very difficult.
>
> We experienced it intensely [*przeżywali*]. Everyone cried. Everyone cried whether they were old or young, right? Everyone, all of them cried because that moment of capitulation was very, very difficult. At first, we were threatened with execution by firing squad, the entire hospital personnel, but a Wehrmacht unit came, and the commander of the hospital came to an agreement with them somehow. Those Germans were not SS men but Wehrmacht, and it was easier to reach an agreement. They evacuated all the wounded. They agreed to evacuate everyone to Tworek and not to shoot, but in the beginning we were all to be—the wounded too—shot in the courtyard there on Krachowiecki Street. That was the original [*pierwotnie*] [he laughs] intention of the Germans.[1]

Żoliborz was one of the last neighborhoods in the capital to fall. This began on September 28, and on the 30th General Bór-Komorowski gave orders for a cease-fire. Olgierd notes the precariousness of the Polish forces' position vis-à-vis the Germans, and the situation for civilians was no better. As is clear from the following accounts, the city was in utter chaos, and the situation was dangerous for all concerned. Olgierd B——, a soldier with the Home Army, recalled the moment that his leader acknowledged that the battle was over:

> At a certain moment the Żoliborz units were under an enormously powerful German attack: artillery shelling, bombardments, guns, everything you could want, and then all of it withdrew here to Żoliborz Dziennikarski. In other words here, where we are now, more or less. Then it was like this, our commanders told us, "Those who want to and are able to can throw away

your uniforms and try to save yourselves." Some did not succeed because they were recognized by the Germans. Some did succeed. I succeeded.

I left the city; that means I had to and was sent to a camp in Pruszków. It was a camp for Warsovians because everyone from Warsaw was removed [from the city]. . . . There was a complete evacuation of the population of Warsaw. It was an empty city, a world phenomenon. At a certain point we— the population of Żoliborz was driven out in these columns—we had to cross the street, so I fell back and pretended that I was an older person. I don't remember now, I set out . . . we were taken in cattle cars to Pruszków where there was a camp for the populace. The camp was huge. With the help of some friends who were medics, I succeeded in escaping from that camp.

As important as it was for Home Army personnel, be they soldiers, medics, or couriers, to rid themselves of their uniforms, it was equally important to ensure that nothing they were wearing was German-army issue. During the uprising many Polish partisans made use of clothing captured or left behind by German troops. Basia recalled, "One had to be terribly careful not to have anything that was German issue, because if they saw that you had a belt, or—well, it would be difficult to explain. In Warsaw they simply killed those people, right? I don't know, I didn't have anything. I had a jacket that was German issue, but it was not typical; I had to leave behind my *panterka* [a German shirt made of artificial silk] and my beloved "monkey" [a very warm German army coat]."

Like Basia and Olgierd, Hanna also remembered the importance of removing all traces of Home Army membership. She also emphasizes the threat of the Ukrainians and Vlasovs, whose atrocities in Wola and Ochota were already infamous throughout Warsaw: "Now one could not make it through this street, because these Germans sat there, or some Vlasovs. . . . So I had to go through the trenches along the barricades. This was the only way we could move about because they were killing people. . . . On the 30th I made it home, and in the evening they came, after dark. And they kept us here. Well, of course, I had already removed everything, all signs of AK membership."

What Hanna told me next reveals a great deal about the conditions during the last days of the uprising:

One has to remember that here in our apartment were refugees from Gdańsk who spoke perfect German. Two ladies and two young men. When the German soldiers came here, we were in the cellar. The staircase had been torn apart by a bomb. They came. So Mama said to one of the ladies from

Gdańsk, "Pani Hilda, please go to them," and in German one of the men from Gdańsk said that as long as he was here nothing would happen. Well, but the Germans started to get impatient, and they went to the kitchen; they came to us with some underwear and so on that they wanted young girls—us. So, one even . . . pointed at me, and Mama said to me, "I'll go." And he put the revolver to Mother's breast [to say] that I was to come with him. And at that moment that German with Hilda came and ordered him to put his gun away, and he returned to Pani Hilda and said, "As long as I am here." But he fell asleep or something because they started again! Well, somehow, fortunately they did not rape us. Well, in the morning we were ordered to leave, but there were skirmishes . . . and Żoliborz fell in the evening.

Exodus: Civilian Perspectives

After the capitulation the Germans forced the residents still remaining in the city to walk to train stations. They were put into cattle cars and taken to civilian detention camps, and the city was emptied of the vast majority of its inhabitants. This chapter of Warsaw's history has become known in Polish literature as the "exodus." Many soldiers and couriers, like Olgierd B——, quoted in the preceding pages, joined civilians and were able to pass in this manner. However, passing as a civilian only brought some measure of safety, for in agreeing to the terms of capitulation, which included the evacuation of the populace of Warsaw, the leaders of the uprising had agreed to place the residents of Warsaw into German hands. In the following passage, Basia recalls how her sister, Sławka, managed to avoid being taken to the detention camp at Pruszków.

> Later, there were various other adventures, and passages, and different experiences. But the uprising ended, and there was an evacuation, the capitulation. My sister [Sławka] was almost the last to be wounded and in the knee at that. I remember how in a fury I said, "Couldn't you have gotten wounded some place other than the knee?" because she had to be carried. So we carried her walking and so on. Later we escaped from the column, later other things. I was not taken captive because, as you know, my father was killed, and mama fell ill and was in a very bad state of nerves. Sławka was wounded, and it was not clear what was happening with her, so I had to sort of take care of things. I became head of the household. So, well, we carried her out, and we took her to the hospital, and there outside the hospital it was drizzling. You know, there were not even proper stretchers, just two broom sticks and a blanket. The Germans were chasing us out; there was no way to stay. Well, in any case, she was put on a wagon with some major, and she

could not escape because of her knee. Well, then the major began to negotiate his way out [*kombinować*] with the peasant because Sławka told him that some acquaintances of our former seamstress lived in Pruszków. So, they began to talk the peasant into [going there], saying that they would pay him, that there would be money there, dollars to be exact because, after all, there wasn't anything else. Actually, I could have gone with my backpack to Bank Polski, which was lying in little pieces and money covered the ground, [but] it didn't enter anyone's head—well, maybe somebody's but not mine, because it was—You know there was terrible hunger, it was cold, right? Well, they succeeded, and that peasant turned, and within a minute they were taken off the cart, the peasant took his horse and left.

ELT: But you were not there with Sławka then?

Basia: I was. I was with my mother and aunt there. In general there was a whole group of people, but we were there already. We had walked there on foot, and we were living with the seamstress, and Sławka and the major were brought from Warsaw by wagon, and they talked that peasant into pulling up to the house, and we took them off the cart, it lasted a minute, and there was neither peasant, nor goat, nor anything. Well, that's what those adventures were like.

Warsaw was emptied of virtually all its inhabitants save those who opted to hide in the ruins rather than risk an unknown fate determined by the Germans—a choice made by many Jews who had been in hiding up until that point.[2] This was an option rejected by Janina R——'s mother, who decided to take with her Piotr, the Jewish child whom she and her daughters had been hiding, and to leave the city with the rest of the civilian population. Janina recalled:

Mama sat in the basement with Todzia and Piotrek. When the uprising fell, the Germans threw everyone out of Warsaw. Mama left with Piotrek, but Piotr looked in such a way that if somebody saw him, there wouldn't be a discussion, they would have just said that this was a Jew. So Mama bandaged his entire head, except for one eye, which she left uncovered so that it would look like he was wounded when they walked out of Warsaw in that crowd. They left Warsaw, except that our neighbor who lived next door, when she saw Piotr—that was the time of the conspiracy, the occupation, nobody told anybody anything so as not to increase the risk, simply nobody—she looked at Piotrek and said, "Jesus and Mary! It's enough to see one eye to know that he's a Jewish child." Well, but nothing went wrong.

Mama went to the camp, and at the camp she said that he was her child.

And they let women with small children go. And he called her Mama. And they sent Mama to some estate, and Mama even had some acquaintances there—it was outside of Kraków, but she couldn't [risk] go[ing] there with Piotrek. So she went to a village. She went to a village, and she stayed there with Piotrek. So, she took off the bandages, and this village woman said, "Lady, dear lady"—because Mama was a very light blonde just like we were— "You are so fair, and here your son is so [dark]." And Mama said, "Yes, my husband was Georgian, and I am afraid that someone will think he is a Jewish child." And Mama stayed there the whole time with him. Except that she went to Kraków and sold mushrooms, herbs, something—she went to Kraków to make money. Later, when the Russians came, they returned to Warsaw.

While the terms of the capitulation stipulated that Polish soldiers and civilians were not to be sent to forced labor or concentration camps and that they were to be treated humanely and not starved, these narratives illustrate the meaninglessness of such agreements in practice. Once at the transitional detention camp at Pruszków, Germans "selected" Polish civilians for transportation to villages in the area around Warsaw, as was the case for Janina's mother and Piotr. However, many people were selected for deportation to labor camps in Germany—or to concentration camps. Eugenia described the conditions and one such selection at Pruszków, where she arrived with her elderly mother, her brother, and her sister-in-law in early September of 1944:

That camp was at a railroad yard . . . and they ordered us to stay there. We were there for three days. I told my sister right away that she had a right to go free and that she should go to the Red Cross. There was a Red Cross unit, and she could have reported that she was pregnant so that she wouldn't be taken for labor in Germany because they were going to send us somewhere in Germany to work. . . . Aha, and they were taking a lot of people away. They were taking them constantly, and so I would hide Mama so that she could get better, because a lady gave me some [anti-diarrheal] tablets for Mama. And I wanted her to have more time to get better so she would be a bit stronger. We would hide a little so that they wouldn't catch us. So please imagine that they separated us, they divided us.

And so there was a selection: one group for work and the other back to the General Government. Older people to the General Government and younger people to work. So I said to my brother's wife, "You absolutely must go and get released [zwolnij się] because otherwise they'll catch you for work." She looked so beautiful as she never had before when she was pregnant. . . . But she said, "I'm staying with Józef, I'm staying with Józef." She went with Józef, my brother, he was standing there. He looked awful because he hadn't shaved, because he was tired, and he had been pulling the dead from the church. However, they took him for work. Later, it turned out that they sent him to a concentration camp.

And I went with Mama. . . . Of course, they separated us. But they shoved and pushed me to the left, and Mama was to go to the right, along the tracks. And Mama said, "Please, sir, that is my only help." So, just like a German he tore Mama away from me, and I was to jump to the left. But when I looked, I saw that he was busy with the next group of people. Then I saw those who were supposed to stay in the General Government and in the other line those who were sent to the camps and between them was a group of Germans armed with machine guns, dividing one group from another. And so I thought to myself, I'll go with that group, and I hid behind those Germans and I walked behind them, and I got to the third [German] and I said, "Please, sir, I see my mother is staggering, she is suffering from the cold." Indeed I had a pelisse, you know a fur muff for her hands. "I just want to give this to her, please allow me to do so." They checked to see what I had and said, "Gut, gut." He even helped me with the baggage and allowed me to go to Mama. I went to Mama. She said, "You are here!" I took her hand, and I tied a scarf around my head as if I had been wounded, and I limped. I walked and I limped as if I was wounded, and I walked with Mama, and in that way I was saved.

But my sister-in-law went with my brother to the [line for the] camps. . . . After some time my brother's wife came and found us. I said, "How is it you are here by yourself?" She said, "I went and was released." I said to her, "You couldn't do that before? You just led him there?" Because if he had been alone he would not have been sent there, because he looked so old. So I felt an enormous bitterness toward my brother's wife, enormous. Well, it happened that they [Józef and the others in the line] were sent to a concentration camp. . . . She joined us, and she stayed with us the whole time; I took care of her, right? They sent us some place by train, who knows where. They didn't tell us where. In the end we arrived at Opoczno . . . and there we were divided and sent to different villages.

Joanna's account about her stay at Pruszków is equally revealing:

Those are things that a human being is not in a state to forget but at the same time not in a state to convey to others, because someone who didn't live through it [*przeżył*] doesn't have the level of understanding. . . . For example, I remember as if through a fog the camp. The camp in Pruszków. It was called *dulag,* because it was a transitional camp, *dulag,* in Pruszków.

They packed those of us from Warsaw in there. I remember a great factory hall and through the center was a gutter, which was full of dried-out human excrement. There they gave me hot food for the first time in two months. It was soup made from grass, stewed grass. Yes. I was there for about a month because I was lying there sick from typhus.

ELT: Were there doctors there?

Joanna: And how? No, there were not, proszę Pani! It was wet straw on concrete so that one's back was cold. [My] head was shaved because of the fever. Not just me, because there were hundreds lying there like that. And that's how we came out of the uprising, and afterward that nightmarish road [back] to Warsaw and life here in the ruins.

Health-care Workers

Because of their responsibilities to their patients, health-care workers experienced the expulsion from Warsaw somewhat differently from civilians, soldiers, and couriers, though the danger of deportation to a labor camp was the same. Soldiers and couriers had the opportunity to try to blend in with civilians. In contrast, medical personnel, who for the most part were also members of the Home Army, did not have this option because they could not abandon the patients in their care, whose lives were also in danger. Janina K——, the secretary for a field hospital in Żoliborz, recalled spending a night at the end of September rewriting the medical records of Polish soldiers in order to render them civilians, if only on paper.

> Just before the capitulation we got an order to hide the patients' records where we had written pseudonyms. We did not have first and last names, just addresses and army units: this unit, this leader, and so on. All the military patients were to be described as civilians. That meant we were to write their real last names. After all, the wounded could be found everywhere, so there was a lot of writing to do to make them all civilians because we took everybody. After all, if someone had been shot in the leg or arm, we would not tell him or her to go and heal by themselves. We also had German wounded. We also had to care for them. . . . So it was quite urgent, and I was writing all night . . . and I finished just as the sun began to rise.

Once the hospital staff had done all they could to ensure the patients' safety, they turned their attention to their own plight and decided to attempt to recast the hospital as an institution affiliated with the Red Cross in an attempt to give the staff that international protection. Janina K—— describes the steps taken to do so in the passage that follows.

Later there was a whole series of events after the capitulation, that means after the uprising actions stopped. We began to consider what to do here. They hadn't taken us yet because they didn't take hospitals in the same way they took the whole population. The rest of the population had already been moved out, but we hadn't been yet. But maybe there were ways to work out a way to avoid our wounded and young people, especially girls who were very young, eighteen- and nineteen-year-olds, being taken to Germany to camps or, in general, to no one knew where. To this end we came to the conclusion that, despite the fact that this is a Home Army hospital, in other words AK, we would try to make it a Red Cross hospital. To give everyone, all the workers, papers identifying them as employees of the Red Cross. But, at that time, the Red Cross was located near the Polytechnic on Naukowska and we were in Żoliborz in the park. What to do? Who was going to go? This Pani Patkowska and I said, "We'll go." We went on foot together. We left in the morning and walked to Old Town, to Marszałkowska near the Saxon Gardens, and along Marszałkowska to Naukowska, so that we could walk a bit along Koszykowa. Warsaw was already without residents. It was empty, and one house after another was burning. If it was already destroyed then maybe not, but those which were whole were being burnt. The Germans would throw in a stick, and on the end was a sort of rag that was wet, most likely with benzene, that they lit and threw it into the basement. And within seconds with a great glow it burned, and because often there was coal or people's things which they threw in, well, it all burned beautifully. And in this way we walked to the Red Cross. We walked from early in the morning around eight or something. It was the 15th of October exactly. We walked together. Well, she was a lot older than I; she had a daughter who was my age, but I was only 34 years old, so. We arrived there. They were still in charge there, so we asked politely, prettily, we requested so many IDs, these books, that we had a list of our workers, and so on. And he answered very politely, "Wait until tomorrow, and in the morning we'll prepare everything." And where were we to wait? How? Instead of saying stay here for the night, and we'll also stay and we'll write—because it was 60-some IDs to write. But the fact is that none of our patients, not one of our personnel went to a German camp.

ELT: Not even one?

Janina: We were successful in saving them all. Because the patients were taken to Tworek, and those who were young and healthy then—hey, let's go and manage on your own however you can, and they got along as well as was possible. No one went to a camp.

Janina took great pride in the fact that the efforts she described had not been in vain and that none of the hospital personnel or their patients was deported to Germany for forced labor.

Olgierd Z—— was one of the medics who accompanied patients to Tworek; he recalls his experiences there as well as the need to evacuate (as he put it) to avoid deportation to Germany:

> I was in Tworek. I worked because there was a hospital there, and the conditions there were very poor because we worked in a hospital for the mentally ill. So, the mental patients were taken to the basement, and the first-floor rooms were all occupied by the wounded. Of course, there were no sheets, there was only straw. There were some blankets, pillows stuffed with straw or hay. So primitive, difficult conditions. . . . I worked there until the middle of November. Through all of October until the middle of November, then I escaped. I escaped in the night with a group of friends, except that, of course, before that we tried to enable the escapes of those who were lightly wounded. So, only those who were badly wounded, who couldn't move on their own, were left at the hospital. Of course, some of the personnel stayed, but we young people, I would say, we evacuated. That means at night we escaped. Well, and it was a good thing because the next day an SS unit came, and they took all the remaining able-bodied young people to a labor camp, to a stone quarry, in Germany. So, in this way, we saved ourselves.

Avoiding arrest and deportation to work and concentration camps was an ongoing problem for Warsovians, who after all were homeless at that point. While adult women with young children and the elderly were placed in villages with families, as was the case for Janina R——'s mother and Piotr, as well as Eugenia, her mother, and her sister-in-law, young people from Warsaw were threatened with incarceration. Since their documents identified them as Warsovians, they were in particular danger. Consequently, many found themselves wandering from place to place in search of surviving family members or friends. Janina R—— and Krystyna, for example, both went to Zakopane, a resort town in the mountains to which many Warsovians had fled, and volunteered with a Polish relief organization (RGO) until the Soviets liberated the area and they could return to the capital. Jerzy was not so lucky; he was sent to a labor camp in Germany that was eventually liberated by American troops.

Displacement

Just as each person's experience of the war is unique, so is each of their paths following the capitulation. However, their narratives of these wanderings illustrate that there are commonalities in what is inscribed in memory. It is not possible to recount the wanderings of each of my informants here, so I offer Olgierd Z——'s experiences as a displaced person in an effort to highlight some of these common themes.

> If it's about what happened to me later, I escaped from Tworek. Later I learned that I escaped at the last possible moment because the next day an SS unit came, and they took all the able-bodied young people to work in a quarry, to a labor camp. After a few days of traveling by cargo wagon, because they didn't have normal wagons, I arrived in Kraków. I looked for my mother, but I had not seen her or had contact with her, and so I thought, well, maybe she is somewhere in Kraków, because Kraków is a big city. There was a Red Cross unit there so it was easy to contact her. Of course, after some inquiries through the Red Cross, I found out that Mama was in Kielce.

Olgierd was one of five informants who escaped from detention camps or transports to the Reich. Others either avoided going to Pruszków altogether, as did Basia and Sławomira, or managed to avoid selection for work once there, as did Todzia/Irena, Janina's mother, and Eugenia. While explanations of avoiding the camps or selections were often elaborately explained in informants' narratives, escapes were usually simply stated—as is the case in the preceding passage from Olgierd. After hearing of several such escapes, I asked how it was possible. Several of my informants who had been there told me that the camp at Pruszków was poorly guarded and that, given the vast numbers of Warsovians detained there, escape was relatively easy.

The search for family members, friends, and former neighbors is also a frequent theme in recollections of the post-uprising wanderings, as well as in narratives about the return to Warsaw. Prior to the uprising some families had planned to leave word with friends and family in other cities as to their whereabouts. Many others could only guess as to where their loved ones might have fled, and many more were uncertain as to whether they had survived or not. Olgierd Z——'s experiences are revealing:

> In Kraków I stayed at this boarding house for a while. Later I came upon some extraordinary people, the Dydo family, who, I would say, took me under their wing and even gave me a room, and I lived with them, working as a nurse in a public clinic. I was successful in finding work as a nurse, and I lived with the Dydos.
>
> ELT: Were they acquaintances from before the war?
>
> Olgierd: No, no. There was this situation. When I was on a transport, I joined a group at night. I remember I got on a train—a cargo wagon—in Pruszków, and a woman came to me. She said, "Please, sir, I have here a package, and

I would like to send it to Wrocław because there is a camp in Wrocław"—Wrocław was still under the Germans, it was a German city—"and my son is there and my husband. And I would like to send this package. Where are you going, sir?" And I told her, "I'm trying to go to Kraków." And to that she said, "Apparently it is possible to send packages to the Reich, to Germany, from Kraków." Because it was not allowed from the area around Warsaw. "Could you, sir?" I told her, "All right, if I arrive in one piece, if they don't catch me!" She asked me, "Do you have friends in Kraków?" I told her, "I have no one. Maybe somebody will be there; I'll look for them when [the Germans] stop looking for me." To that she said, "Just in case, I'll give you the address of my very good friends," precisely the Dydos. I still remember: Filip Street, number 5. "You can turn up there, and they will certainly take care of you."

When I arrived in Kraków, I was staying in that boardinghouse, which was constantly being searched by the Germans, so it was dangerous because if the Germans found someone with an ID card [*kenkarte*] from Warsaw, they arrested him. So it was not safe there. So I went to the post office to send the package, but I see that they are in charge there, and in front of me there was someone whose ID they checked. Because I had a Warsaw ID, I couldn't show myself there because the clerk could give me up to the Germans, and they would arrest me on the spot. So I went to the Dydos, thinking maybe they could send the package. I wasn't thinking that they would help me, no, simply that they could send the package. So, I introduced myself, and when they learned that I was from Warsaw, that that lady, Pani Górska—later I looked for her, but unfortunately I could not find her after the war; I don't know what happened to her—in any case, when they learned that I am from Warsaw, they took me under their roof. Extraordinary people, wonderful!

As Olgierd mentioned, the Germans suspected young Warsovians, especially men, of having taken part in the uprising and therefore arrested them. Yet, in general, my informants were fortunate in finding other Poles sympathetic to their plight. Many related stories of strangers' hospitality, kindness, and solidarity to displaced Warsovians. Olgierd continued:

> Later, when I learned where Mama was, I brought her from Kielce to Kraków, and so later we were there together until the liberation of Kraków, we were there. So I lived through the liberation of Kraków, together with my mother there at the Dydos' apartment. Extraordinary! Extraordinary! Whatever can be said about Krakowians that they were, right—well, people vary, but I happened upon exceptional people.[3]
>
> So, if it's about Kraków, we were in Kraków until sometime in January,

when Kraków was liberated. Later I registered at Jagiellonian University; of course, one had to turn in the necessary papers in order to get credit, right? So, I accomplished that later in the spring when it was possible to go to Warsaw, and I succeeded in getting there. There were some papers, some documents, some transcripts, among others Pani Professor Dąbrowska and other professors who were saved, who were alive, and on the basis of those documents, I was accepted into the third year of medical school in Kraków. I was there for the third year, in the fall of 1945, just after the end of the war. And then I transferred to Warsaw for the fourth year. So, I finished my degree in medicine in Warsaw, I got my diploma in Warsaw.

The liberation of Kraków by Soviet troops brought with it new dangers for Warsovians, as Olgierd's attempts to return to Warsaw illustrate:

ELT: When did you first return to Warsaw after the war?

Olgierd: I tried for the first time in March 1945, but unfortunately, Soviet units stopped our train in a tunnel near Kraków. I found out later that they wanted to catch Warsovians. Because they knew that those Warsovians from the uprising were primarily young people, and, later, a lot of those people who were caught in that tunnel were sent to Russia, to Siberia. Along with Mama, I succeeded in escaping from there, thanks to a railroad worker who told us that some freight train with coal was leaving at night from a different part of the tracks. Because the area was entirely surrounded by Soviet army units, and otherwise there would have been no way out. So, when the train with the coal came, we jumped in and laid on the coal, and the train pulled away. And in this way we escaped from that tunnel. So, it was one of those kinds of adventures, by a hair's breadth we could have found ourselves somewhere in Siberia.

Like Olgierd, many Warsovians came to realize during the course of their post-capitulation wanderings that there was relatively little difference in the way their participation in the uprising was viewed by the German occupants and by their allies, the Soviets: both viewed them as criminals, and while the former sought to deport them to the west for forced labor, the latter sought to deport them east to the gulag.[4] Because young men from Warsaw were in particular danger of arrest, Olgierd's mother initially made the trip to their home alone.

Afterward, we returned to Kraków, and Mama wouldn't let me go to Warsaw; instead she went by herself. Well, because our house was destroyed, she stayed with some neighbors. Mama worked at the Bureau of Public Transportation, and she reported to the director, and they put her to work immediately. The office was in Praga then, so she had to walk there across a pontoon bridge because there was no transportation from [Żoliborz]. Later in the fall I came to Warsaw and was with Mama, and we began little by little to rebuild the house, to remodel it.

Like many people his age, Olgierd's return to Warsaw as a permanent resident of that city was delayed by his studies, which initially could only be undertaken in Kraków due to the destruction of the University of Warsaw.

Returning to Warsaw

In the preceding chapter I have suggested that for my informants, perhaps even for most elderly Warsovians, the memory of the Warsaw Uprising is inscribed in the city itself: in bullet-scarred buildings left standing, in the verisimilitude of the reconstructed Old Town, in what remains and what was rebuilt, and also in the empty expanse that marks the site of the Warsaw Ghetto and the ruins of Pawiak, the Gestapo prison. The evidence of this lies in the close attention to place that characterizes these narratives, in informants' invitations for walking tours both literal and photographic, and more recently, in the proliferation of plaques on both publicly and privately owned buildings. The traumatic nature of that past raised the question in my mind of how my informants went about rebuilding a sense of normalcy when their experiences of death and loss are embodied in the city itself. My vantage point on the way that war impinges on people's lives comes from working with elderly people who experienced the war as children and young adults. I knew from the outset of each interview that, whatever they had suffered under the German occupation, my informants had somehow managed to live lives characterized in many cases by personal achievement. Most had married, many had children, most had completed their studies at university, and several had long and sometimes distinguished careers in their chosen professions. The people I met were reminiscent of none of the dire predictions so often made about young people who witness, experience, and take part in war. Thus, I felt free to assume that my informants had regained normalcy, and I have focused instead on how they were able to do so.

In an attempt to discover how the people with whom I worked were able to reconstruct the familiar, I began by asking three basic questions: When did they return to Warsaw and how? What were their initial impressions of the city? What was the mood in Warsaw at the time? These questions led to others about the specifics of their experiences, about encounters with the Red Army who liberated the city, and attitudes to Poland's postwar authorities. However, in the following pages I focus almost exclusively on narratives offered in response to my three initial questions and save the others for the following chapter. In some ways, from the moment they are marched out of Warsaw by the Germans, many Warsovians were planning their return to their city, and I sense that, for my informants at least, the war did not end until they returned to Warsaw. What follows is an exploration of informants' accounts of returning to Warsaw, from which I have attempted to glean some clues not only about the lived experience of that time but of how the people with whom I worked went about reconstructing lives that had been interrupted, altered, and damaged by war.

First Impressions

> **ELT:** When did you return to Warsaw?
>
> **Olgierd B——:** The day after the occupation [ended]. The front had advanced, and I was already close to Warsaw. I was living 44 kilometers from Warsaw in a place called Żyradów, and there I was waiting for the Russians to come. The moment they left, I left on foot for Warsaw. I walked for several hours, the whole day. I walked, and I arrived here in Żoliborz so that I could see. It was almost completely empty except for people with bundles carried on hooks; you know, they came with backpacks to the city, and already people were drawn back. Sometimes one saw a person someplace, but very few. I saw how the apartment where I lived looked. It was very much destroyed; it was without windows, without anything. Naturally, I'm not even talking about electricity or other things—that goes without saying. Nothing was there. Despite that, there had not been bombardments. It had not been reduced to rubble, because if it had been in the Old Town, for example, or in another neighborhood in Warsaw, it would have been in ruins. Żoliborz was partially saved. That means it was burned, gutted, but a house that is burned is not the same as one that is destroyed to its foundations. If one says that 85 percent of Warsaw's material substance was destroyed, then I would say that Żoliborz was maybe 50 to 60 percent destroyed. So, a very big difference.

Olgierd alludes to the fact that many buildings and homes in Żoliborz had been burned; however, because they were constructed of brick, concrete blocks, or poured cement rather than wood (as was the case in Marymont, a neighborhood that was almost totally destroyed), many buildings were gutted but still standing. Warsovians, who like Olgierd B—— were living in the villages and towns surrounding the capital, were able to return to Warsaw without the risks of deportation faced by those who came by train.

ELT: Could you describe what it was like when you returned?

Olgierd B——: So, Warsaw was occupied by the Russian army and Polish units who fought with the Red Army or alongside the Red Army. It was occupied beginning on January 17, 1945. I cannot tell you at this moment if I returned on the 18th or the 19th; I don't remember any more, but almost as soon as it was possible. One had to take care because the roads were mined after all. So, that wasn't particularly pleasant either. You know, I don't really remember everything exactly because I cannot even recall where I spent that first night here, but I suppose that I had some sort of hideout or something. Later, I began to hammer boards to the windows [of his family's apartment in Plac Wilsona], because there was frost. It was winter. Worse than what we have now. There was snow. So, it was very cold, and one must take that into consideration because, returning in that kind of frost or snow, that was not terribly pleasant. So, it was about just coming back, in order to return and, you know, shut the door for example.

Irmina and her parents also returned to Warsaw the day after the liberation:

ELT: When did you return to Warsaw?

Irmina: Well, immediately when Warsaw was conquered when the Germans were forced out in January, the 17th of January, 1945. The next day we came back in a wagon. Right away, my parents walked here on ice, over a bridge that was nearly destroyed. You had to jump over the holes in it. They somehow got here to see what was going on. It happened that the house had not been burnt. However, the second house on the other side of the wall had been [Irmina's home is a semi-detached house]. Because the Germans systematically burnt one house after another, but they didn't see that there is a wall here that actually didn't catch fire. So, ours didn't burn, except that there was nothing here. Everything had been taken except the fortepiano because it was too heavy. But everything else had been taken away.

Bogumiła: But by whom? The Germans or looters?

Irmina: Well, the Germans maybe. I don't know who else could have done it. Nobody else was here. Everything was taken: the furniture and the pots—everything, even the toys and the baubles for the Christmas tree. The only thing left was the piano and broken windowpanes. There was glass lying everywhere and some books with their pages scattered. So, it was difficult . . .

Given the living conditions, Irmina's parents decided to take her back to Radość, where she stayed while her mother found work in a newly organized government ministry and her father took up the task of making their home livable again. Irmina recalled that she joined them in June or July of 1945, some six months after the liberation and that they were one of the first families to return to their street.

> **ELT:** When you returned to Warsaw, what were your first impressions of the city?
>
> **Irmina:** Well it was terrible, it was terrible. Warsaw looked terrible. . . . Well, it was really in a very tragic state. The houses looked all shot up, and everywhere there were holes in the walls, windows without panes. I don't know how they were able to turn on the water supply so fast. However, there was an enormous enthusiasm to rebuild.

After recovering from typhus, Joanna S——returned to Warsaw in March of 1945 and made her way through the city to the apartment building where she and her mother had lived throughout the entire war. Indeed, she was still living there when I met her in 1996. She remembered:

> I returned to Warsaw by myself, Mama came earlier. I was 11 years old when I returned to Warsaw alone. And what were my first impressions? That I not get lost among the ruins. To return home I had to walk the entire day. Here the park was a cemetery. The whole park. The squares, all of them were cemeteries; it took two years to exhume them all and bury them at Powązki. It would be difficult for you to imagine how it looked. You know, when I remember it and close my eyes, I am not even able to recollect how I made it [home]. It happened that in 1946 already nearly a million people had returned to Warsaw.

Like Olgierd B——, Joanna was unable to remember exactly how she found her way home. One of the most striking features of the narratives of return is this absence of specific references to place. This is in stark contrast to other narratives, particularly those about the uprising. It is clear that the ruined city left an imprint in memory, but the violence done to it left Warsaw unfamiliar and without points of reference to describe it. Perhaps this, coupled with the lack of people, meant that the ruins were not distinguishable one from another and had yet to become meaningful as places. It seems equally possible that it is neither a problem of memory or place but of finding the words to describe the fact that Warsaw was literally reduced to rubble.

Olgierd Z——also returned to Warsaw in the spring of 1945, but while he described the city in terms that can only be described as desolate, his own mood was quite different, and he found reason for hope in the ruins.

> **ELT:** What were your first impressions of Warsaw when you returned here?
>
> **Olgierd:** First impressions. . . . So I remember the moment when the train arrived—a freight train, of course, because there weren't passenger trains yet, just the freight trains. The train arrived at West Station. Central Station was still ruined. Here everything was rubble. One got off the train there and went on foot.
>
> So, my first impression was feeling fortunate that I was finally in Warsaw again, that I had returned to Warsaw. I went along, walking through the ruins, when I saw a tiny window in a ruined house. I sensed that somebody was already living there. It was an unbelievable sight as one walked through those little streets, little hills, because they weren't really streets but hills of rubble that had been opened through the gravel so one had to climb up, then walk down, and on and on. All around just gravel, so it was an unbelievable impression, right? Only that tiny window showed that somewhere someone was still living. So, that was a big experience. I remember the first time it was a big experience, and I was glad that I was here, back in Warsaw.

The desire to see Warsaw again drew thousands of Warsovians back to the capital in the months following the liberation. They came to assess the damage and to reclaim their homes. As Joanna noted, by 1946 nearly a million people had come to the city. Knowing the conditions they returned to did not, however, make it any easier for me to understand the process of rebuilding normalcy. In rereading these narratives, however, it seems as if the demands of daily life itself created the impetus to move forward. Thus, while Olgierd B——'s comment that it was about returning to "shut the door, for example" may be understood as sort of a symbolic reclaiming of space, it was also a statement about the very real need for shelter. Similarly, he mentions that one of the first things he did upon returning to his family's home was to put boards on the windows to protect himself from the cold.

In regard to housing, living in Żoliborz proved to be advantageous after the war, not so much because it was a middle-class suburb but because it was a new neighborhood and, as such, lacked sites of historical and cultural significance and industry. As a result, it was low on the Germans' list of areas to destroy, and though it had been burned and to some degree mined, it had not been dynamited. This is important because it is possible to live in a burned-out building, and there is much less involved in rebuilding such a structure than one that has been shelled or deliberately demolished. Thus many, though not all, who lived in Żoliborz had the advantage of returning to homes that, though damaged, were structurally sound and still in possession of roofs and doors, if not windows and furnishings. The same cannot be said for most Warsaw residents who returned to neighborhoods that were literally in ruins.

Recollecting his return to Warsaw, Olgierd Z—— described immediately being caught up in the demands of fulfilling everyday needs, as well as redressing the suspension of certain social norms.

> Later when I walked to Żoliborz, I took part. I helped in carrying water and in finding the graves of my friends. Some of my friends' mothers came to me looking for their sons, thinking that maybe I had had contact with them and that they would learn where they were buried. I told them what I remembered. And there were the exhumation actions. I would again like to emphasize the huge role Father Trószyński played here. From the first moment he arrived, he returned here. He was the provost of the Parish of Królowej Koronej Polskiej in Marymont. He exhumed those soldiers who were killed in Żoliborz so that they could be buried in the cemetery. That was in 1945–46. In the autumn of 1945 and later in '46, I was here all the time.

After returning to Warsaw, Janina R—— took up similar work with an exhumation detail, as she described her work to me. "That means that I worked with a group of 20 people, and when they dug somebody up, I described all the bodies and recorded any identifying signs or marks so that later it would be possible to identify the remains."

One factor that we did not discuss explicitly but that clearly played a role in my informants' ability to rebuild normalcy was socioeconomic position. My informants' parents were for the most part professionals, and prior to the war my informants themselves were raised in middle- and upper-middle-class homes. This meant that they had more resources going into the war in 1939 than did the majority of their compatriots. However, many of their fathers were officers in the Polish army, which made them targets of both the Nazi and Soviet regimes. Joanna and Janina R—— both lost their fathers, not in battle but in the mass murder of Polish officers by the Soviets in Katyń. Others were part of a social milieu specifically targeted by the Nazis, the Polish intelligentsia. In this way my informants belonged to groups that, though socioeconomically advantaged, were disadvantaged in terms of the ruling regimes during the war. Moreover, several had parents who had participated in the uprising. Zofia, Sławomira, and Basia's fathers were killed during the uprising, and three others lost a parent during the occupation. The most extreme example of how the war impacted families is that of Zofia, whose father, two brothers, sister, sister's husband, and brother's wife were all killed during the occupation and the uprising. Clearly these losses had a major impact on the emotional lives of surviving family members and also on their resources for rebuilding their homes. This forced some of my informants, such as Basia and Janina R——, to return to work immediately after the war rather than continue their studies, as did the majority of my informants. It is no coincidence that both women lost fathers, and their homes were either entirely destroyed, as was the case for Basia, or in need of major repair to the roof and foundation to render them livable again. Both women were also in their early twenties in 1945. Basia's sister, Sławomira, in contrast was still in school in 1945, and by the time she graduated, the family's financial situation had stabilized, allowing her to continue her studies at the University of Warsaw.

Remembering Loss

Just as the violence of the occupation and the uprising were inscribed in the city, so too was the suspension of social norms reflected in the cityscape, with the dead buried in city parks, public squares, and backyards. Exhuming the dead was an important part of returning the city to normal, but, of course, it also brought with it reminders and confirmation of loss. Separated during the uprising or at civilian detention centers, many Warsovians did not know whether their loved ones had survived, let alone where they might be. As a result they covered buildings and ruins throughout the city with messages for the missing, communicating the locations where they could be found. When I asked Eugenia about the mood in Warsaw when she returned in May of 1945, she focused primarily on dealing with separation and uncertainty about one's loved ones: "You know, well . . . it was terribly hard, because people still had not learned about their nearest. That dispersion—when I was among young people and adults, families that had been separated, that was terribly difficult because they were always asking didn't one know, hadn't one seen a message someplace. They looked for those messages on walls: 'Look for me here and there.' When someone returned from a camp, the young people always asked one another, 'Who's looking for you?' There was always that questioning, that searching."

Olgierd recalled that the prolonged period of shared suffering had created a certain sense of solidarity, one reflected in the joy that people felt at meeting other Warsovians. This is something he described in the following terms when I asked him about the mood in Żoliborz: "So, people were glad when they met, that someone was still alive, that they were still [living]. There was joy. It was like finding one's closest family. People who were apparently strangers were at the same time very close. It was because of everything that had happened. Each was happy that they could come upon—that they had a bit of roof over their heads. That it was theirs, no! No one felt that they were among strangers, but that they were secure and that they could return."

Janina R—— and her mother faced a number of challenges upon their return to Warsaw, among them dealing with the damage to her family's home and locating Piotr's surviving relatives.

> I returned to Warsaw, to Felinski Street, where our house had been hit and had three huge holes. Mama was already there with Piotrek. That was in March of 1945. Mama was here with Piotrek already and Todzia—Irena—had gone to Łódz, where she was waiting for her husband to return from the POW camp, and indeed he returned fairly quickly. My sister was taken with others who fought in the uprising to a camp in Germany, and later she was in an oberlangen [a labor camp]. I went to Praga with Mama because Praga was almost undamaged. The Jewish gmina [city administration] was there. And we went to the gmina to register that we had Henryk T—— [Piotr] with us, thinking that maybe some of his relatives would be found. The gmina took the advertisement [that Piotr was with the R—— family], and after a very short time, in fact, Piotr's family answered. His mother's sister with her husband and two sons, who had been in Russia, returned here, and an uncle in America also responded.
>
> And here began what was actually a tragedy. Mama had started working. The house was destroyed, it was full of holes, and so, to work. I also started to work in an exhumation detail. And Piotr actually should have gone to his family, and he didn't want to. He had become attached to us. But there weren't the conditions, he had to go to school. Here's the best part because the one from America, that uncle, wrote asking Piotr to come, and Piotr wrote to his uncle that he would but only if Pani Jasia [Janina] or Auntie, because he called Mama that after the war, Auntie would come. But neither Mama nor I wanted to go. And as a result a few months passed, and he went to Kraków and later to Wrocław to his family to go to school there, and in 1953 he emigrated to Israel.

While in Wrocław, Piotr's relatives placed him in an orphanage. Though they took him with them when they emigrated to Israel, they ultimately placed him in a children's home there, as well, something that still seemed to upset Janina when I talked to her fifty-some years later.[5]

Reflecting on the mood of Warsaw in 1945, Irmina turned her attention to the deeper consequences of the loss of so many people, particularly young people, during the war.

> **ELT:** What was the mood like in Warsaw when you returned?
>
> **Irmina:** Well, for one thing it was after the fall of the uprising so, in general, many families lost their nearest relatives, especially youth. I remember that before the uprising I was going to church, and a group of mostly girls came out. Such a lot of boys were killed, and especially boys at such a young age. Of my friends I remember these two lovely Martynowski brothers: Marek was 15, and Andrzej was 16 when they were killed. Włodek Wołosiewicz was also only 16, and he also died. Cześ Liczbak, who had very bad grades and did not do well at school, and he turned out to be a hero. He also died in the attack on the Glass House Complex. A kind of a change of the value system took place. The notion that this one is a good student, or clever—everything took on an entirely different value in light of their heroism during the uprising. After all they were very young boys.

Irmina's reflections suggest a shift in values driven by the loss of life, while seeking to validate it as heroic sacrifice. We might expect the deaths of so many young people to be greeted with a rejection of war borne of grief. Instead it seems that grief is assuaged and death sanctified once again by the notion that to die fighting for one's country is a noble and honorable death. In this way the insurrection myth is upheld, and those lost in another failed uprising regarded as heroes.

Returning to Normalcy

The persistence of the insurrection myth raises the question of how individuals transition from wartime values and models for living to those that will sustain them in times of peace in conditions where war has left its mark deeply on the psyche, society, and the landscape. Michael Watts (1992) has pointed out that the landscapes we inhabit are ways of seeing both culturally constructed realities and ideas of self and identity. Quoting geographer Stephen Daniels, Watts emphasizes that "place is inseparable from the consciousness of those who inhabit it" (1992: 122, cited in

Nordstrom 1997: 179). Carolyn Nordstrom has interpreted Watts's notion of the interconnection of landscape and self as it relates to the experience of warfare as implying that with the destruction of place comes the destruction of life worlds, of identity and the self (1997: 179). The stories my informants told me of returning to burnt-out apartments emptied of virtually all the things they had owned, of exhuming and reburying the dead and looking for the missing, and of clearing the rubble off the streets with nothing but their hands brought me to the conclusion that the restoration of normalcy to their personal lives was inextricably intertwined with the reconstruction of the city itself. There is a tendency to psychologize the reconstruction of normalcy, to assume that, in order to carry out the activities essential to everyday life, an individual must somehow deal with the emotional pain of loss first and only engage in rebuilding the community or the city after this is well underway. Yet, this process is not one that my informants emphasized or even mentioned; instead they tended to focus their narratives on meeting more immediate needs for housing and income, as well as on the task of restoring the city to conditions more suitable for habitation. These narratives seem to suggest that everyday needs for shelter, warmth, water, and food pulled them back into the rhythm of the familiar (see also Valent 1998: 524–25). Nordstrom (1997: 178) sees the obliteration of life worlds in the destruction of place, but for my informants, attachment to place and identification with the city as co-victim is what drew them back. Simultaneously they reclaimed and reconstructed their personal lives and public space from the ruins. This difference in perspective may come from the fact that Nordstrom conducts her research in active war zones, with people for whom loss is recent and the war ongoing. Perhaps the feeling expressed by many of her informants that war had taken everything from them, including who they were, is one that fades with time as new experiences overlie those of violence. My informants were able to rebuild lives interrupted, altered, and damaged by war; it was just a question of discovering and describing how.

In my last months of research, I began asking informants directly how they went about rebuilding normalcy. Their answers were not particularly satisfying. Several laughed and asked me, "What was the alternative?" When I asked Joanna, she told me, "We had to build a normal life, because it was necessary to work. There was great enthusiasm to rebuild because somehow we weren't aware that man falls from one prison into another. It was a longing for life like [she takes a deep breath and exhales to illustrate], and later it happened that it was like removing one tick and being caught by another." In other words: life chooses life, and in order to live in a ruined city, the dead must be reburied, water must be carried for washing, boards need to be hammered into empty sills to keep out the cold. This work, whether it is undertaken on behalf of oneself or others, is a path leading those who take it from the violence of the war, the uprising, and the destruction of the city toward the re-creation of the everyday. "It reformulates everyday life through collective action, enabling a resumption of normality and the remoralizing of local communities" and in this way gives rhythm to daily life marking reentry into normal time. (Mehta and Chatterji 2001: 213). Eugenia also pointed me toward an answer, with her observations about her pupils after the war:

> Because those first years after the war were difficult, but the youth were so wonderful, so joyful, and they were so happy that they had returned to Żoliborz. They were so glad about Żoliborz, you have no idea. They just sang those songs from the uprising. . . . The youth, I must say that in those difficult conditions they learned very well. There were no textbooks, after all, those were all burned. Books had been burned and libraries. Our school library was also destroyed. There were no books. They learned, and as I recall, the classes were overflowing, but they learned.
>
> I started a Red Cross club at the school. You know, around 80 girls took part, and the leader was so small, the very short daughter of our doctor. But there was such silence during those meetings. She just developed that charity work. And they didn't have anything either. They organized soup; they organized their parents to cook it. They didn't have anything either; however, you know, they conducted that volunteer work among the poorest of the populace, those who came from Marymont and were living in basements [without houses above them]. It was something awful. They went everywhere to the elderly and to people who were sick. They worked wonderfully.
>
> So, because they were doing such wonderful work, I was an eager leader. I organized a course in first aid. The doctors here in Żoliborz were so giving, really wonderful doctors, those longtime Żoliborzians, and they gave those lessons, and afterward there were regular exams. It was nursing: how to wash, how to give shots, and they did it all so eagerly.
>
> And I was fresh from my pedagogical studies, you know. I was very interested in the psychology of pedagogy and in psychology in general. So they asked me to do a course in psychology! So we made a course in psychology. I still have as a souvenir this laurel wreath that they made for

me. One of them who had a lot of talent made two ornaments from their silhouettes, black silhouettes. And, you know, it was possible to recognize each student in the course from her silhouette. The likenesses of those silhouettes were so well captured! I've kept it until today. They thanked me so beautifully, and they were so interested in that psychology; they remembered it for the rest of their lives.

Even now, still now, once in a while one of them will call me and reminisce about that time when we were working on that psychology, or about the nursing course, and all. That youth was very engaged. You know, it was so moving. After all, they had just returned from labor camps in Germany.

Pani Eugenia saw her students' enormous desire to learn and encouraged it, opting to stay in the ruined city though jobs and more comfortable living conditions were offered her in other places. In learning, developing the self, and service to others these girls created links with one another and with those around them, forging community out of chaos. Nordstrom (1997: 206–8) cites similar examples of creative community building in her work, and she sees such activities not as re-creation but creation anew, old models having been rendered irrelevant by violence (ibid. 198–99). However, I see in these activities the reengagement of models for dealing with hardship that were enacted during the occupation as forms of resistance, such as learning in secret schools and training in first aid or communications to work as medics and couriers. The roots of these actions can be found in the dedication to social service that characterized the neighborhood before the war. Edward Sapir has noted, "Invention takes place within a field of culturally available possibilities, rather than being without precedent. It is as much a process of selection and recombination as one of thinking anew. Creativity emerges from past traditions and moves beyond them; the creative persona reshapes traditional forms" (Sapir 1924: 418, quoted in Rosaldo, Lavie, and Narayan 1993: 5). Rosaldo, Lavie, and Narayan (1993: 5), drawing on Sapir, note, "Members of a society's younger generations always select from, elaborate upon, and transform the traditions that they inherit." As Eugenia recalled, "They just sang those songs from the uprising," and in doing so, they cloaked themselves in the moral authority that the conspiracy still carried, despite defeat, and translated wartime resistance into peacetime service. "So, those young people who returned to Żoliborz gave the neighborhood the kind of enthusiasm it used to have, even though it wasn't the same young people [in my classes], and the conditions weren't the same [as before the war] because things were difficult. But maybe, maybe because of that it was better. They weren't pampered by servants, because those young ladies were primarily governors' or officers' daughters, higher officers, generals' daughters. They did not need all those various things. But here in those modest conditions they settled in wonderfully in Żoliborz." Children went back to school, and young people who like Olgierd B—— and Olgierd Z—— had begun their studies during the war in secret courses went to Kraków to complete their degrees. Others, like Jerzy, who had not been able to start their studies, gathered the documents necessary and took the entrance exams. Wiesława, whose incarceration in three different concentration camps had prevented her from finishing secondary school, began a course for adults. There she met the man she would later marry, Adam, who she discovered had been on the same transport to Auschwitz.

Irmina answered my question about normalcy with a desciption of Warsaw in the summer of 1945:

> Very quickly little stores began to open, and trade began, despite the fact that so much had been destroyed [and was in] ruins. There was a wonderful book that showed this on the outskirts—that in a completely ruined neighborhood somehow life started to take shape. There was trade. There were stores. Life likes to return to norms quickly. Somewhere I have a picture of the Royal Palace Square completely destroyed, and there is one existing corner house and in it is a café [she laughs]. You understand? Because that was more pleasant than all those misfortunes. People want what is pretty, no?

Jerzy told me a story about a woman living in the ruins of Old Town who became known for feeding the pigeons; a sculpture over a doorway on Piwna Street in Old Town now marks the spot where she lived.

Joanna offered me this narrative about re-creating normalcy:

> I remember very well, and I am going to remember to the end of my life, how the Polish Theater was rebuilt. It must have been in 1947; I don't remember exactly. There was a premiere. Though Warsaw was entirely ruined, and that reconstructed theater did not fit into Warsaw at all. It was entirely as if it had been brought from another world, right? I had never been to the theater because when the war started I was so little. During the war no one went to the theater because it wasn't done. So my mother went, and she took me to the premiere, to the theater. Now, when one goes to the theater, they dress elegantly. When I recollect how people were dressed then! I remember my mother wore army pants, and she had a blazer of my father's that she had

saved—so, she was beautifully dressed! Someone there had a pair of elegant shoes, but each was a different color. Yes. I remember exactly and, you know, I cannot forget those things. Like the moment when they raised the curtain, and I flew from my chair. For me that was such an impression. I lasted until the end of the performance, and then I became terribly ill. Because it made such an impression on me—after the war, after those tragedies, after all we had been through—to go to the theater that I became ill. It was such a shock. It was the shock of returning to normalcy.

Returning to normalcy entailed reengaging the prewar past, remembering the city, life, and oneself as it had been, and imagining what it could be again. This involved literally reburying the dead and cleaning the rubble from city streets. In this way informants enacted the tradition of social activism that they recalled as characteristic of the neighborhood in the opening chapters of this book. Rebuilding a sense of normal life, however, also entails reactivating life worlds: knowledge of life without war and that "unreflected upon experience of the way things are which cultures of terror so often erode" (Nordstrom 1997: 178). This is what Joanna described as she recalled the audience dressed for the premiere in mismatched shoes, the ladies in men's jackets, all in an effort to recall a vision of elegance that reconnected them to the past and to normalcy. Informants' memories of Warsaw, of life as it existed before the uprising and before the war, were essential to the maintenance of life worlds, making it possible for them to reinvest a place made foreign and threatening by violence with familiarity, security, and beauty.

These stories of resilience and creativity in the face of destruction—of cafés in ruins, of schoolgirls with nothing making soup for others, of a woman living in the ruins of Old Town saving bread crumbs for pigeons—are hopeful and somehow comforting. Hundreds of thousands of people can be marched out of a city, separated from their families and dispersed, their city turned into rubble, and yet people return. Adults go to work, children go to school, people take care of one another, life resumes. But Joanna's memory of the premiere illustrates that the normalcy that was re-created was patched together and fragmentary. Like Joanna, whose father had been murdered at Katyń, six of my informants lost a parent during the war, one lost a child, another a brother and sister as well as a sister and brother-in-law, and all lost close friends. Few lost their homes, but their neighborhood was altered by physical reminders of war and the absence of neighbors who never returned.

Joanna's memory of the premiere at the newly reconstructed Polish Theater also reminds us that the return to normalcy can be jolting, even shocking. Was it the excitement of the premiere, with its spectacle of improvised elegance, that stunned Joanna? Or the contrast of the beauty of the theater and the play to her daily life in the ruins? Both explanations seem plausible. But Joanna was only six years old when the war began; she had never been to the theater or the cinema or anything like it. It seems to me that maybe what was so upsetting for Joanna was the realization of what life could have been had there been no war. Perhaps the evening brought the recognition of what life should have been like to a young girl who could remember little besides violence and loss.

Conclusion — *Memory and Its Discontents*

THE HARDEST TOPIC OF ALL to persuade my informants to talk about was not the war, for all its tragedies, or contemporary politics of the postcommunist era, but their lives during the nearly 50 years of communist rule. Many would sum up whole careers in a few brief sentences. Others shrugged away the difficulties they faced due to their wartime involvement in the underground and dismissed them as nothing compared to what an acquaintance had suffered. A few described in minutiae the humiliations they had suffered, the residual bitterness of this era as palpable as other guests in the room. Some protested that for 50 years they had lived under communist occupation, while others took pains to outline the benefits of the system they had helped to build and mourned its demise. Though their responses to the early years of the Polish People's Republic were diverse, they agreed that once again, as with the defeat of the uprising, they were on the losing side of history. This stems from several factors, among them the outcome of Yalta and the West's disengagement from Poland's fate as a Soviet satellite state. Perhaps more salient, though, was the way that the Warsaw Uprising of 1944 was interpreted by Poland's Soviet-backed postwar leaders. In the pages that follow, I examine how the generation who came of age during the war was represented in state-sanctioned media in the early years of the Polish People's Republic. I argue that the misrepresentation of the defining event of their generation motivated their desire to share their memories with others as a challenge to official representations. In doing so, I explore sanctioned representations of the uprising that appeared in a variety of publications during the communist era, paying particular attention to how Warsaw youth who participated in the uprising were depicted in political discourse and popular culture. I then consider how my informants have constructed their memories of the war so as to imbue their lives with meaning. Finally, I explore the ways that their generations' wartime experiences have been institutionalized in order to be transmitted to younger generations of Poles.

Official Histories of the Warsaw Uprising

Even before Poland's postwar leaders were in power, the communist press in Poland reacted to the uprising. Its approach was initially to denigrate the Home Army for launching the attack, then to assign credit for successes to their own Armia Ludowa (the People's Army), and finally to denounce the capitulation as an act of treason on the part of Home Army leaders. Poland's postwar rulers treated the Warsaw Uprising as an aggressive response to Soviet intervention in the governance of Poland, rather than to German occupation. Though the Polish forces were clearly fighting German troops, the Soviets were not entirely unjustified in this view. Home Army leaders saw the uprising as serving the dual purpose of ridding the capital of Nazi troops and of counteracting Soviet attempts to rule after liberation. On July 14, 1944, General Bór-Komorowski (Bór-Komorowski 1951: 201), commander of the Home Army in Warsaw, wrote a report to the Polish commander-in-chief, stating the goals of the uprising: "The guiding thought of our final encounter is: (a) To show the world our undaunted attitude against the Germans and our will to fight them till the end; (b) To deprive the Soviets of the spiteful propaganda argument for putting us into the category of silent allies of the Germans or into that of neutrals; (c) To take under our auspices that part of the community which does not form part of the Home Army, but nevertheless wishes to vindicate its wrongs at German hands—in order to draw it into mutual action toward independence and not let it fall under Soviet influence." Bór-Komorowski continued with the warning that, should the Home Army remain passive, the communist underground in Poland would most likely take action against the Germans and that "less-informed citizens" might join them (ibid.). This, he argues, would lead the country toward collaboration with the Soviets and ultimately to integration as the 17th republic of the USSR (ibid).

Poland's communist clandestine press revealed the Soviet Union's attitude toward the uprising shortly after the fighting started on August 1, 1944, when articles and communications appeared in publications of the Soviet-backed Polish Workers' Party (Polska Partja Robotnicza), decrying the uprising as a reactionary action launched by the leaders of the Home Army against their lower-ranking members and the civilian populace. The Polish Workers' Party alleged that Warsaw residents were not only far more progressive than the Home Army leadership but were also politically oriented toward Moscow, in spite of the fact that in the interwar era communist organizations in Poland had little popular support (Żebrowski 1995: 9). One month into the uprising, on September 1, 1944, Edward Osóbska-Morawski, the leader of the Polish Committee of National Liberation (PKWN), wrote that the contemporary movement for an independent Poland (in effect the uprising) was the work of a clique of prewar leaders who "without consulting our allies, motivated by base desire to rule over the nation, gave a signal for a premature, unprepared, hopeless insurrection" (*Powstanie w Warszawie. Fakty i dokumenty,* [b.m.w.] maj 1945, s4).

Yet, while communist leaders denigrated the uprising as a crime perpetrated on the general populace by an indifferent elite bent on independence at any cost, they simultaneously sought to take credit for its successes. They did so with propaganda that claimed it was the Moscow-backed People's Army (Armia Ludowa) and its volunteers, rather than the Home Army, who fought courageously in the most brutal battles, including those in the Old Town and Wola (*Rzeczpospolita* nr.44, 1944). That the communist press claimed credit for the battle in the Old Town had great symbolic significance. It suggests that the People's Army struggled to save the very heart of the capital and by extension the nation. By claiming Wola, a neighborhood where Ukrainian units under German command executed civilians en masse, the People's Army situated itself in what was perhaps the bloodiest battle in the city. There is no reason to doubt the courage and commitment of those who fought with Armia Ludowa; however, there is quite a difference in the number of people who participated. Historians estimate that 800 Armia Ludowa soldiers participated in the uprising, a figure boosted as high as 5,000 members by the communist-era Ministry of Public Safety (Ministerstwo Bezpieczenstwa Publicznego) (Davies 2004: 183; Żebrowski 1995: 9). In contrast, historians estimate the ranks of the Home Army numbered between 36,500 and 40,330 soldiers at the beginning of the uprising (Curry 1984: 335; Davies 2004: 183).

Just days after Home Army leaders negotiated and signed the Act of Capitulation, the communist paper *Rzeczpospolita* denounced the surrender as an act of treason (October 5, 1944). The paper also exaggerated the number of fatalities incurred, from an estimated 200,000 (Karski and Friszke 1997) to 700,000 and laid the responsibility for these deaths at the feet of Home Army leaders (Żebrowski 1995: 11). More damaging still was the assertion that Home Army leaders had conspired with the Nazis in both the planning and the implementation of the uprising, as well as the conditions of surrender. Such allegations are counterintuitive and contradict the experiences of thousands of Warsovians. Later, Stalin cited the failure of the Home Army to act during the Red Army's liberation of the city some three months after capitulation as proof that the Polish underground army had collaborated with the Germans; he used this claim to back up Soviet propaganda justifying intervention in Poland (Roszkowski 1997: 138). This in spite of the fact that, at the time of liberation on January 17, 1945, Home Army members were dispersed in various detention, labor, and concentration camps in Poland and Germany.

The claim that the Home Army had collaborated with the Germans was disseminated long after the war had ended. In the introduction to *Eight Days on the Left Bank,* published in Poland in 1950, Piotr Jaroszewicz, who later became the premier of Poland, wrote: "The plan for the uprising was made in agreement with Nazi intelligence. . . . The Nazis, counting on a Soviet offensive with the evacuation of Warsaw, agreed to deliver the city into the hands of their reactionary business partners, in exchange gaining a pledge not to attack the German army and the possibility of exiting Warsaw. The Polish reactionaries loyally fulfilled their obligations to the Nazis" (cited in Żebrowski 1995). Much postwar literature embellished these accounts by portraying Home Army leaders such as General Bór-Komorowski as members of the Polish aristocracy who had made a pact with the Nazis against the Soviets. Moreover, this literature depicted these "reactionary class agents" as heartlessly luring the youth of Warsaw to their deaths in a hopeless and futile battle in order to secure their own selfish goals. Kazimierz Brandys's depiction of Bór-Komorowski in his story *Man Does Not Die* is a telling example: "On the fifth of October Count Bór-Komorowski, horrified by the results of his crimes, scurrying like a rat in the smoke flowing from the city, the view insidiously awash with blood spilled at his behest, at last enraged by the unpleasant situation and in fear of blowing the cover of the London leadership, who under the banner of an uprising against the Nazi occupants forcibly pushed the youth of Warsaw against the liberating Peoples Army, both Soviet and Polish—terrified, frightened and enraged with it all, Count Bór went to Ożarowa. There in the quarters of SS leader von dem Bach, after a friendly chat during which the generals discovered mutual ancestors on the distaff side—he signed the act of capitulation" (Brandys, cited in Żebrowski 1995). Brandys not only portrays the uprising as a disaster, something many would agree with regardless of political ideology, but he also makes Bór-Komorowski into a count and portrays him not only as the political partner of the fascists but also a blood relative of an SS leader. According to state-sanctioned histories, the vast majority of those fighting in the uprising were not fighting German troops but had been tricked into fighting their liberators, the Soviets. Clearly this interpretation contradicts the memories of my informants. Given that the Soviets were absent from the site of the uprising until three and a half months after capitulation, the claim was generally dismissed by Poles as propaganda.

The allegation that Home Army leaders duped the youth of Warsaw is more complex and has had a more lasting impact in postcommunist era debates about the legacy of the uprising. In postwar representations of the war, young Warsovians were portrayed as pawns in a political game in which they were forced or tricked into attacking those on the side of social justice. However, the claim that young Warsovians were exploited for political ends is not entirely lacking in merit. Consider this statement from a report that Bór-Komorowski wrote to the Polish commander-in-chief just weeks before making the decision to launch the uprising: "The Home Army expresses the will of the nation to gain independence. This forces the Soviets to have to break us by force and hinders their working against us from within. *I agree that coming out into the open involves the grave danger of annihilation of our most spirited elements.* Nevertheless, the Soviets will not be given the opportunity of doing it in secret, and they will have to report to open acts of violence; that on the other hand may evoke the protest of well-wishing allies" (Bór-Komorowski 1951: 202, emphasis added).

Bór-Komorowski seems to acknowledge that, in the wake of the uprising, there would inevitably be repercussions against those who participated and that it was the youth of Warsaw, "our most spirited elements," who were the most vulnerable. He seems to view this as a necessary sacrifice if Poland is to gain the attention of the world and, in doing so, independence. Postwar literature and film accentuate the moral ambiguity of relying on the youth of Warsaw to take on the German army. Representative of this genre are works such as *Ashes and Diamonds*, a novel by Jerzy Andrzejewski that was later made into a film by Andrzej Wajda. The hero, Matthew, a veteran of the Home Army, longs to resume normal life but is persuaded by Home Army leaders and by his own sense of loyalty to his fallen comrades to assassinate the local district secretary of the Communist Party, a decent and compassionate man who has himself suffered in a variety of prison and concentration camps (Andrzejewski 1991 [1948]; Wajda 1958). Though the film captured the rapidly shifting landscape of postwar Poland, it depicted those who came of age during the war, particularly young Home Army members, as a generation deceived by false heroes, confused by conflicting ideologies, and unable to find its place in a new socialist society, a sort of "lost generation."

In the following section I explore my informants' memories of the early years of the Polish People's Republic. In doing so I focus on their attitudes toward the Soviets and narratives of repression in an effort to understand how the ban on public commemoration and attempts to limit even private discussions about the uprising impacted both individual memory and my informants' attitudes toward the new socialist system.

During the communist era in official media and popular culture, the Soviets were celebrated as the liberators of Poland. Most of my informants use the terms "Russian" and "Soviet" interchangeably or simply use the former, which suggests that they see Soviet domination of Poland as a continuation of tsarist policy. While the degree to which the Soviet presence was welcomed and the duration of that welcome are debatable, there is no question that it was the Red Army that forced German troops out of Poland, bringing about the end to the war in that country. In the case of Warsaw, however, the Soviets' role as liberators is contested history. Joanna explains why this is so.

> **ELT:** Did people see them as some kind of liberators?
> **Joanna:** Were they liberators? You know, in some ways they were. . . . One could say they were and they weren't. Because at the moment when there was the uprising in Warsaw, the Russian army stood at the banks of the Vistula, and they watched as we were killed, and they did not help us. And those Poles who wanted to swim the Vistula to help the uprising, well, the Russians simply shot at them. And afterward, they freed Warsaw when there was nobody here and it was already destroyed.

As Joanna and many others pointed out in reply to this question, the Red Army neither joined in the battle to drive the Germans from the city nor acted to prevent the Germans from destroying Warsaw in the months that followed the capitulation. Since the city was literally in ruins and virtually uninhabited when the Red Army entered on January 17, 1945, many Warsovians do not see this as a "liberation" as much as a betrayal from a dubious ally. Jerzy also expressed this view:

> So, chiefly, we bothered them [the Nazis] and they bothered us, because the main goal of the uprising was to occupy the city in advance of the Russians. And they [the Soviets], unfortunately when they realized that the uprising

had broken out, they stopped the offensive. In effect, we were left for those two months doomed to failure. Because according to the AK leadership's plans, the uprising was to last for two or three days, and they were prepared for that with the appropriate weapons and ammunition and units. And indeed, in those first days, the city was actually under [our] control, and if the Russians had hit, if they had crossed the Vistula, well, we would have pushed the Germans out without a problem. Well, unfortunately, here politics took its course. It was not comfortable for the Russians to enter a city that was already liberated of Germans, and that is why they left us here, with the Germans killing and destroying the city, and so on. Well, unfortunately, that is always what happens when politics mix in with war: it all plays out on somebody's skin. And it played out terribly—those are indescribable things.

Irmina recalled that she was not at all relieved, but terrified, at the news that the Russians were coming:

So, I remember that I was terribly afraid and that I asked my mother and my aunt, who was awfully brave as well, I said, "They [the Polish insurgents] will beat the Germans and the Russians will come. And what will happen to us?" And my mama [answered], "Somehow we will have to live well!" She was brave; she said, "Well, listen, somehow we must survive and get through it all." Even though we already knew what the Russians were all about from part of our family who lived outside of Vilnius. They had to flee from Vilnius in order to escape being sent east [to Siberia]. They managed to come here during the war and told us that all the residents of Vilnius were sent to Siberia. So it was terror and fear, but where to escape? There was nowhere to go! Here the Nazis sent us out through the chimney, and they [the Russians] would have roasted us, too, if only they could have. So people simply wanted to survive, knowing that it was going to be very difficult. That's how it is to be born in this place in Europe.

While many informants remember having low expectations for a Soviet liberation, Olgierd remembered things a bit differently. When I asked him about the mood in Warsaw when he returned in the spring of 1945, Olgierd recalled having high hopes:

Well, we were very happy that the war was over, and we thought that there would be normal conditions, that everything was going to get better and better; so there was an enormous civil action from the whole of society in cleaning up Warsaw. There was enthusiasm, an enormous enthusiasm for rebuilding. Later, unfortunately, those political changes were introduced. It was a blow to people, especially those who had been engaged with the AK; well, they were on the index as enemies, and that was the most hurtful [*przykre*]. The most hurtful because Poles were all treated like traitors, or like enemies. In the same way, I personally had a lot of unpleasantness for that reason. But all those ordeals, it is difficult to talk about it, actually, but it was a very difficult time.

Poland's postwar authorities considered participation in the Home Army and the uprising a crime against the people. Fearing repression, most of my informants did not disclose their participation in the Home Army. This was the case for Olgierd who, following his completion of medical school, was drafted into the Polish army.

> **ELT:** But at the beginning was it a problem that you had taken part in the uprising?
>
> **Olgierd:** Well, so, at the beginning I couldn't speak of it. I couldn't acknowledge that. There was a time when it was not permitted to admit to that, so I hid [my participation]. Only little by little, in certain situations these issues became clear.
>
> **ELT:** Did that start right after the war or . . .
>
> **Olgierd:** No. I remember a time at the very beginning when in units of Polish soldiers there were army chaplains, and later that was all liquidated. Soldiers were forbidden to attend church. So, that is how it was. At the beginning, I would say, it was more Polish. Later, there were actions, one could see that those were the actions of the second enemy, whom we actually had not considered an enemy, because we thought that the Russians were our liberators. That they liberated us. . . . Later, I came in contact with Russians who held higher positions in the army, for example, and those were Russians, and they were very decent people. Very decent people. They understood our situation, but there were those who wanted to beat, who wanted to destroy. So, this was for me as a young man—I was still green one could say—that was a shock. An enormous shock that—how could it be! We offered our hand in cooperation and they persecuted us.
>
> **ELT:** So, at the beginning it seemed to you that the Russians were in some sense liberators?
>
> **Olgierd:** At the beginning, yes! After all, during the uprising when Soviet units arrived in Warsaw [in Praga, on the left bank], they were welcomed like something extraordinary, right? It was when they wouldn't leave that it was like a bucket of cold water over the head.

Though he describes his shock at the new situation as akin to being doused with cold water, what Olgierd describes in the preceding passages evokes the sense of continuous and ever deeper disillusionment. His narrative is inscribed with different types of alienation. His near arrest in Kraków, which is described in detail in the previous chapter, marks his alienation from Poland's Soviet liberators, while the potential for his work as a medic to be treated as treason rather than service to country marks his alienation from the postwar government. Finally, his experiences as a devout Catholic in a Polish army that did not permit religious observances marks his alienation from the ideological goals of the system and the permeation of repression from his public life into his private life. If alienation from the system is characterized by the erosion of the state's legitimacy, then repression is experienced as a threat to different facets of identity: as a patriot fighting for Polish independence, as a doctor-in-training serving his country, as a Catholic and a person of faith.

Jerzy's low expectations for the liberation and the regime that followed were only confirmed when he returned to Warsaw in 1946 from American-occupied Germany:

> Just like now, people liked to write on the walls, and the first inscription that I saw in Dziedzice—well, this immediately froze us because the inscription was, "Death to the Home Army bandits." That was my welcome in my homeland. So, that is what my return looked like.
>
> Well, [we were] a bit concerned about how we would be received.
>
> So, I can tell you because, you know, I returned sufficiently late that those first numerous arrests that took place directly after the war did not affect me. I simply did not keep in touch. Really, at least for the first year, I did not keep in touch with my colleagues from the war. I did not engage in any politics. And somehow I had good fortune, because really I did not have occasion to sit in jail like many of my friends.

Jerzy showed me a list of people from his Home Army battalion who had been arrested for their wartime activities. His unit originally numbered some three hundred people, many of whom died during the uprising. Some survivors stayed abroad after the war and never returned. However, among those who lived in Poland after the war, some 50 people had been arrested and sentenced to prison by postwar authorities. A few had been sentenced to death, though after the death of Stalin some of their sentences were commuted. Jerzy chose one case—that of a friend—and elaborated.

That man I told you about, Tadeusz, they let him go in 1956. Released him in Figury. He didn't have an apartment, he didn't have clothes, because during those few years those clothes that they arrested him in, they fell right off him. And what next? Well, he continued to be under surveillance; he had to report to the *milicja* [the police] once a week, or every two weeks, in any case he was under surveillance. Because his name day[1] was approaching, those of his friends who were in Warsaw then, well, they got together and bought him some coupons for material, for a suit, and they agreed that they would meet with Tadeusz for a name-day party. I was supposed to go too, only at the last minute they changed the place, and I didn't know the new address, so I didn't go. But those who went had hardly sat down and started to talk when three sad men, those Security Bureau agents, came. And [they asked] who? And why? And what are they doing there? And so on. Well, they [Tadeusz's friends] explained to them that this was Tadeusz's name day, that they wanted to meet with him because he had just been released and so on, and that all the rest worked, lived normal lives, and so on. Well they took it all down, and in the end they said: Well, okay. They did not have anything against this type of meeting, except that it came from above that the next meeting of that kind should take place under the auspices of the Union of Freedom and Democracy Fighters [the Party-sanctioned veterans' organization], not in a private home because that's how they wished it. So you know, it was nothing. Nothing further happened, but it was simply the pleasure of being investigated, one had to report who was who, what they did, because right away they asked about work, what did one do, etcetera. So, that's how we lived in that first period of the Polish People's Republic.

Just as Olgierd's narrative illustrates how repression followed a person from public to private life, Jerzy's illustrates the contagion of repression from Tadeusz, who was arrested and imprisoned, to his friends. Others experienced repression not as a result of their own activities or those of the people they chose to spend time with but because of a close relative's fate or choices. This was the case for Joanna, whose father was one of the 4,255[2] Polish officers who were captured as prisoners of war and murdered in the Katyń forest in the Soviet Union. Throughout the communist era, official accounts attributed the mass murders to the Nazis in spite of the overwhelming evidence that this was an act committed by the Soviets. Joanna and her mother learned that her father had been killed in Katyń in 1943 when the Germans discovered the graves and published lists of those buried there. It was only in 1990 that Yeltsin brought to Poland documents acknowledging Soviet responsibility for the Katyń murders.

ELT: Did you have any doubts then [in 1943] that it was the Soviets who were responsible?

Joanna: Oh, no! No! Nobody doubted it! Absolutely everybody knew that it had been the Russians! Naturally! Nobody had any doubts whatsoever. Only one couldn't say it.

Joanna's conviction that it was the Soviets all along may seem incredible to readers unfamiliar with this history; however, the Soviets had allowed the Polish officers to write letters home and had made no secret about holding them captive.

Joanna: You know, one couldn't talk about it because, for example, the director of my school, who was zealously pro-Party, she found out that my father was killed at Katyń. If you please, two weeks before the *matura* [graduation exam] she threw me out of school. Yes. When she found out that he had died at Katyń. Because I wasn't allowed to write it, I could only say that he was killed. It was such a huge secret, that they threw me out of school.

ELT: Because you told somebody that—

Joanna [**interrupting and offended**]: Well, hmpf [in other words: No!]. She found out. Yes! That's what it was like here! People were afraid to talk about it.

ELT: So you couldn't take the exam?

Joanna: No, no. Later they accepted me. I had to take all the exams, they accepted me, and I finished my studies at the university. But what I lived through [*przeżyłam*] is mine.

It is important to note that Joanna was barred from taking the exam not because she had talked or written about her father's murder, but because the facts of his death themselves presented a challenge to the myth of Polish-Soviet friendship. Similarly, Hanna had difficulties continuing her studies at the University of Warsaw. She told me that although she passed her entrance exams with high scores she was not initially accepted. A professor intervened on her behalf and secured her the identity papers of a former student so that she could begin classes, albeit under a false name, while she appealed to the ministry of education for permission to begin her studies. In December of her first year of studies, she was officially admitted, something Hanna credits to the intervention of her professor. I wondered whether her difficulties were the result of her own involvement in the Home Army or a reaction to her family connections: her brother had flown for the Royal Air Force and had remained in England after the war. When I asked her what she thought, she replied, "I don't know! I never did learn, but you see, in life that's how it is. Things always work out and you have to hang in there." Experiences such as these fomented fears of surveillance and far-ranging repercussions and caused many to avoid not only public meetings with other veterans but also private contact with their friends and fellow combatants in the years immediately after the war. This drove shared remembrance into hiding and private recollection underground.

Of course, not everyone experienced this type of repression firsthand or through the contagion of remaining in contact with someone who had been declared an enemy of the people. Janina K——, who had been the secretary at a Home Army hospital in Żoliborz during the uprising, declared that not only had she not experienced any repression, but neither had any of the people associated with the hospital.

> **ELT:** Did you have any problems after the war because you were in the AK?
>
> **Janina:** No, no, I didn't, but don't forget—please, make sure the recorder is on. A girl with the pseudonym "Krysia" and an AL [*Armia Ludowa,* People's Army] armband was brought to us at the hospital. She had been wounded in the knee in Old Town. And from Old Town she came to us through the sewers, which—pardon my language—were full of crap—to the hospital. Her wounded knee had to be disinfected and washed because it was a terrible thing. Just before the capitulation we got an order to hide the patients' records. We had written pseudonyms; we did not have first and last names, just addresses and army units, so this unit, this leader, and so on. All the military patients were to be described as civilians, that meant we were to write their real last names, because after all the wounded could be found everywhere. So there was a lot of writing to do to make them all civilians. It was very urgent, and I was writing all night, and I go to Krysia, who was much better . . . and I ask her, "Krysia, give me your surname and your address." And she says to me, "Oy, please ask my mother instead."
>
> [Krysia's mother, who was also named Janina, volunteered at the hospital and at one of the villas in which patients were housed.]
>
> So I say, "What, you don't know what your name is?" I'm thinking what's this all about? Maybe she has a very ugly name or something. So I go to her mother, "Pani Janina, what is your surname?" "Oy, do I have to tell you?" Well, yes, and I tell her why. "Ahh, my name is Bierut." That was the wife of Bierut. But at that time we still knew nothing of Bierut; he was in Lublin and we were in Warsaw so we knew nothing about him!
>
> [Bolesław Bierut was the first postwar premier of Poland, trained in the USSR and selected for the post by Stalin.]
>
> **ELT:** You had never heard of him?

Janina: I hadn't heard of him. And so I, well, I have a sharp tongue, I said, "Why be embarrassed? Bierut, or Gajut, or Ryba [fish]?" I meant, what's the difference if one takes or is given one or the other, right? And the saying stayed. And on the first anniversary of the uprising, Pani Bierut together with Krysia organized a meeting. And I have the impression that they kept an eye on things so that none of ours were arrested. No one from our group had problems. Well, that's the way it is; it's a hospital, one has to save the patients. It's the health service; that's what we do. So, I never had any unpleasantness ever.

I later learned of an exception to Janina's claim that no one from the hospital at the fort ever experienced any problems. Janina R——, who was a member of the Home Army and served as a medic for the hospital on Śmiała Street before joining the staff of the hospital in the fort, did have difficulties finding a job after the war. She had spent some time in Germany after the war, and her sister, also a member of the Home Army, had emigrated to England. Additionally, their father, an officer in the Polish army, had been murdered at Katyń. However, Janina R—— simply refused to lie about her involvement in the Home Army. She explained:

All of Żoliborz knew me. Everybody knew, so I thought that hiding it would be worse than writing it on the form. Well, the personnel manager saw that and said, "Proszę Pani, I am very sorry, but we cannot offer you a job." I put in my application at I don't know how many institutes, and everywhere it was the same: "We are sorry, we can't." So even though people in high places vouched for me, unfortunately I could not be employed. And I remember I went to Wola to apply at Central Agricultural Supply, and the director read my application and read it again. [He was] an older man, he looked and looked at it and said, "Did you have to write that bit about being in the AK?" "Well, I had to because everyone knew me, and they all knew perfectly well that I took part in the uprising, and they knew what went on in our house," and so on. "Alright," he said, and he called the personnel manager and told her, "This lady is hired." She saw it and asked, "You'll take responsibility?" [He said,] "Yes, yes, she's hired." I found out later who that director was. It so happened that he was in London. He was a test pilot on planes from the U.S. so he himself had a background just as rotten [as mine], and so when he saw that, he hired me.

As memory is always a product of the present, it is difficult to know to what extent informants' claims that they viewed the Soviet liberation negatively in 1945 are colored by the subsequent actions of Poland's postwar government. It is possible that Olgierd was correct in his impression that people were initially optimistic that the end of war would bring with it a return to normalcy and that only later their experiences with the regime led them to alter their expectations and the way they recalled the early days of the Polish People's Republic. For example, in light of the arrests of Home Army members and the denunciations of its leaders in the press, perhaps they chose to highlight and recount those events that best demonstrated the injustices of the new system. However, we must also consider their experiences prior to the liberation. The Soviet Union invaded Poland on September 17, 1939. Mass arrests and deportations to Siberia followed in those areas under Soviet control, something Irmina alludes to when she states, "We already knew what the Russians were all about from part of our family who lived outside of Vilnius." The mass murder of Polish officers at Katyń was well-known, and if that was not enough to make Poles doubt the intentions of the Soviets, there was the latter's lack of involvement in the uprising. Whether this knowledge resulted in Warsovians' lackluster response to the liberating Red Army or not, it certainly colored my informants' perceptions of the postwar regime, leading to their alienation from the government, which lost legitimacy in their eyes by colluding with the Soviets. When Poland's postwar authorities adopted the Soviet attitude toward the uprising, my informants' feelings of alienation from the new socialist government only deepened. In response, my informants took their memories of the uprising to the only place they could: underground.

However, while my informants were disappointed in their desires for a free Poland that recognized and valued their contributions during the war, they did not react by disengaging from society as a whole. On the contrary, though some were slowed by repressive measures, most persevered in their efforts to rebuild normalcy, using social networks when necessary to continue their studies and find work. They started careers as doctors, lawyers, journalists, scholars, editors, and artists, and they found jobs at research institutes, pharmaceutical companies, colleges and schools, hospitals, and in city administration. Though modest about the accomplishments of their working lives, many made significant contributions to Polish society through their work. Though they lost their battle for Polish self-determination, they were by no means a lost generation.

Composing Memory

The question of personal continuity is central to issues of identity, narrative, and memory. This is a topic of particular concern, in studies both of aging and of survivors of war. Carolyn Nordstrom (1997: 185) argues that "experience is not something that happens to the self, *experience becomes the self*—it is that through which identity is forged," and in this sense "the new relationships thrust on war's victims (soldier and civilian alike) begin to define them as much as the lifelong ones did." As a result, she posits, "people exist in a continual process of re-formation," in which the self is constructed, enhanced, and rebuilt (ibid. 188). Informants' assertions that a person cannot wholly understand if he or she has not experienced war personally can be read as a testament that war changes those who survive it. As Joanna explained to me:

> Those are things that a person is not able to forget, but at the same time is not able to pass on to others, because someone who hasn't lived through it does not have a basis for understanding. It's just like when I talk to my friend. We were both in Calcutta. She was in one part of the city and I in another, and when we talked about it, it was as if we had been in two different cities, despite that we were there at more or less the same time, and in Calcutta. It is so hard to come to an understanding because it's not just the generational difference but also the difference of experiencing something on one's own skin. Yes.

Some scholars have interpreted survivors' convictions that others are incapable of understanding as a demand that survivors' experiences be granted special reverence (cf. Clendinnen 1999). I prefer to see such assertions as a testament to how their experiences have altered the way they interact with and understand the world. Basia warned me that "some things you just can't scrub off," an idiom that captures the indelibility of wartime experiences. She continued by explaining that since the war, although she loves dogs, she is terrified of German shepherds and cannot stand the sound of a whistle. Similarly, Sławomira told me that whenever someone is more than fifteen minutes late to meet her she falls into an uncontrollable panic and is convinced that some terrible fate has befallen them, regardless of how unlikely this is. However, those things that cannot be scrubbed away cannot be taken away either. At gatherings, old friends would agree with a sort of conspiratorial defiance: "What I lived through [*przeżyłam*] is mine, and no one can take that from me." This was a refrain I heard at the end of many an interview too, as if to imply that the memories of these experiences and by extension my informants' narratives of them are something organic and intrinsically a part of themselves (see Skultans 1998: 22).

However, the path from experience to memory is not a direct one: from the totality of our experiences we only record some in memory, and there is a whole range of ways in which individuals express memories of the same event, as the narratives I have presented in the preceding pages illustrate (Thomson 1994: 8). Constructing a self from the raw material of remembered experience is a creative process of narrating the past to ourselves and others (Ochs and Capps 1996: 21). Because public representations of any given war change over time, so too do the memories and identities of those who were caught up in it (Thomson 1994). This is apparent in my informants' narratives when they talk about the early years of the Polish People's Republic, describing it as a time when they did not publicly commemorate the uprising, seek out wartime contacts, or even discuss the past, save with those with whom they were on the most intimate terms. This is in sharp contrast to the years following the downfall of communist rule in eastern Europe, when many were involved in various types of memory work. Olgierd Z——, for example, lobbied to have a small street in Marymont renamed in honor of a Home Army chaplain (Tucker 1998); Wiesława contributed to a volume of remembrances from Majdanek prisoners; Krystyna volunteered at the Pawiak Prison Museum; Jerzy compiled a list of individuals who were arrested or investigated for their Home Army activities after the war. That they had the time to do so as retirees and the freedom to do so after 1989 only partly explains this surge in memory work. My informants' own understanding of memory suggests that remembering is a matter of choosing: to embrace memory or to avoid it, to imbue an event with meaning, rendering it memorable and part of oneself, or to deem it inconsequential, anomalous, and forgettable. Most of all, creating meaning from experience and forging a self that is whole and integrated demands choosing how to retell one's remembered past to oneself and others.

Hanna, for example, is someone who tries to avoid remembering. As a result her voice is often subdued and her narratives disjointed. After showing me the medals she received for her work as a courier, she told me, "I return to all this reluctantly because for me it is all too fresh. As a result of our reality here, well, it is [too fresh], because I was in Solidarity, you know, and so on. Well, it was too—I have had enough of it. Already it should be enough." Hanna drew a connection between the German occupation and the repressions faced by Solidarity activists in the 1980s, fearing that these might recur under the leadership of the then new president Aleksander Kwaszniewski, who represented the reconstructed communist party, Social Democratic Party (SLD). Hanna may have experienced this new government as threatening because of her experience with more extreme forms of repression during the war and in the years immediately following it. As I described in the introduction, Hanna actively avoids remembering and steers clear of places that might remind her of her wartime losses.

For the vast majority of my informants, however, it was not a question of choosing whether to remember—or even whether to share these memories—but of choosing how to talk about the past. This was something Krystyna made clear to me. I learned from Krystyna that, just as one can choose to lock certain memories away by actively avoiding the people involved or the places where an event took place, so one can choose to remember and retell certain experiences in a particular way.

> ELT: Could you tell me how your daily life changed during the occupation?
> Krystyna: Well, you know, there's little I can tell, I mean certainly it changed like everything, but I have a rather weak memory, maybe because of the war, I don't know. Certainly, there wasn't food, there weren't a lot of things. I rather look for the humorous things in life and not the tragic. I like to take things like Svejk: cheerfully . . .

Svejk, sometimes transliterated from the Czech as Schweik, is the title character in Jaroslav Hasek's *The Good Soldier Svejk*. Through Svejk's hilarious antics, Hasek satirizes the pomp and grandeur that characterized the military institutions of the Great War. In the following passage Krystyna recounts an incident that illustrates this cheerfully ironic stance:

> Aha, another thing, which I just recalled at this moment, this tiny café on Grochów. I remember how I sold cakes to earn money, and I carried them in a huge box to this little café. And in this way I earned some money. That was a bit of a trek with such a big box, and in the winter it was rather slippery. Those were very tasty pastries with cream. You know, very crumbly pastries with cream, and I slipped and I fell on the box with all those pastries. Never in my life have I eaten so many pastries as when I had to eat that whole box! But, you see, I remember cheerful things. I don't like tragic heroics.

Following Svejk, however, involves not just focusing on humorous events, or looking for humor in the tragic, but rejecting certain types of narrative frames.

> ELT: What were those first days like in Żoliborz?
> Krystyna: No, I don't have that registered, those first days, nothing. Somehow I don't have any specifics. Of course, it was a terrible thing that happened, but I don't have a lot of memories about it. . . . In 1939 during the bombardment

I was here, in the courtyard. Yes, I have shrapnel in my leg from the time in that staircase near the gates [when the building was hit by a bomb]. Of course, I have a photo of how I lay wounded in the basement, but I rather dislike pathos. I really don't like it, so I answer with sufficient nonchalance because I really do not like getting carried away or dramatic at all. I believe that everything was tragic, but also somehow I do not like to make a hero of myself, even though the times were very . . . dramatic.

Krystyna has composed her memories to reject the heroic. Instead, her narratives highlight what was humorous in her experiences. Rather than glorifying her own activities as a courier and a medic in the Home Army, or romanticizing the underground, her stories are critical, mostly of herself and her immaturity, but they also show an appreciation for absurdity and irony. For example, the Gestapo arrested Krystyna under suspicion that she was a courier for the Polish underground; in fact, she carried messages to Władysław Bartoszewski who later became the first postcommunist foreign minister, one of the founding members of Żegota. As a result, Krystyna was held for a time in Pawiak, the Gestapo prison. However, when she told me about this, she did not emphasize the appalling conditions or the suffering but rather how well she was cared for by other members of the underground who were imprisoned and knew her. For example, she remembers that somehow someone managed to smuggle in ham sandwiches to her. Thus, she underscored the irony that she ate ham in Pawiak when people outside the prison could not legally buy meat. This is not to say that Krystyna was incapable of recollecting other aspects of her stay or that she was indifferent to the suffering in Pawiak. The fact that she volunteered at the Pawiak Prison Museum suggests that the experience was a significant one for her. The story does illustrate well the constructed nature of memory.

I suspect that Krystyna has also composed her memories to forget certain events or aspects of them that do not fit into the antiheroic narrative frame that she favors. On some occasions this has distanced her from others. In the following passage, she recounts an illustrative example:

Recently when there was the 50th anniversary of the uprising, a person came to me and said, "Duszka [her pseudonym], good morning. You don't remember me?" I said I didn't. "But I did time with you in Cyril and Metody!" Cyril and Metody, you know, in Praga next to the Orthodox Church, there used to be a prison [called] Cyril and Metody. That must have been—I don't remember when—in the 40s. [She said] "I sat with you in Cyril and Metody." There were some riots. You know, youth. But I, for one, do not remember that. And that one caught me in an embrace [and said], "I did time with you in Cyril and Metody. You don't remember that we returned to Żoliborz together that night from Cyril and Metody?" I answered, "I don't remember a thing."

"What can be done about it?" she asked me, laughing. She explained that in the late 1940s, while studying at the university, she was regularly followed and questioned by a Security Bureau agent. Though she is not sure, she suspects that it had something to do with attending English classes that were sponsored by the Methodist Church. However, she insisted that she did not really see it as repression:

> So, I don't register those things in a political way: he investigated me, he sat and I told him, he always sat in a particular place and checked if I was going to lectures or to class, but it didn't awaken a sense of threat in me. A strange reaction—no—cynical. This nonchalance shows that I am not good informant material. Of course, those were Stalinist times, but I was not personally engaged and didn't have any troubles because fortunately I wasn't outed anywhere. But it was an era when there were repressions against the Home Army. 1948. Maybe it was then that I was in the Cyril and Metody prison; it certainly must have been then. But, you see, I'm not even sure. I don't remember. I have a mental block, I don't have that experience [*przeżycie*] encoded, but maybe that was what it was. But in the arms of some general action, not an action against me personally.
>
> ELT: You still do not remember if you were there with your friend, or you don't remember if you were there at all?
>
> Krystyna: I don't remember it at all. I am so busy with everyday life that I very rarely look back at all. I am not very engaged with the past.
>
> ELT: But you were in jail after the war?
>
> Krystyna: Well, exactly, one or two nights, but I don't remember it, others remember though.

In an effort to understand, I asked Krystyna if perhaps she did not remember because for her the experience was not meaningful and was not really a *przeżycie* in the usual sense of the word. She answered:

> Maybe everything depends on the degree. I have a friend who at this moment is going to court. Her father was killed before her eyes, precisely during those times, for his involvement with the Home Army. She saw him in prison, saw them kill him in the prison in Praga. It was that same time. I didn't [*przeżyłam*], it's true, maybe it's because of my attitude. It would be terribly

tragic to be in jail and look through the bars and see how they killed one's father there, right? Those trials are now being carried out against the crimes of the Stalinist government. She was very active. She would answer your questions completely differently. It depends on with whom you talk. I am not very interesting. . . . At this moment I look at things differently. It's a different perspective when a person is mature and has more knowledge because more is known now about those times. She knew [then] because she saw them kill her father, and my father worked, and I didn't have that personal experience, right?

In general my informants who, like Krystyna, embrace antiheroic narratives offer a critical view of the past that is open to reinterpretation as they gaze back on history and their own role in it from different vantage points of time and self. The antiheroic stance that Krystyna has adopted toward her war experiences is not common among my informants, nor is it the one that has been adopted for public representation of this period of history. My informants for the most part have composed their memories in the romantic-heroic tradition, emphasizing not their own heroism but rather the nobility of their cause. This way of remembering is most clearly represented in the narratives of Olgierd and Sławomira. Reflecting on our many conversations about her experiences during the war, Sławomira commented:

But somehow people adapted, because human beings have that ability to adapt to a variety of things. Of course, it was a time when friendships among young people were very strong, because it was a time of tension, danger, mutual interest. Of course, people were enormously strongly attached to one another, and equally, right, girls among themselves, from one group or company of medics, as well as with boys. Besides, the boys with whom we were on the friendliest terms were veiled in romantic legends because the majority of them also worked in the underground. I was in that sort of milieu [*środowisku*]. The majority of them were involved [in the conspiracy]. So that also awakened a variety of shy feelings. But all of it in general was very important, very romantic, except that often those boys at some point had to disappear because they were in danger either from some specific threat, or they were arrested, or they had to go to the forests to the partisans. "To the forest," in other words, "to the partisans." Yes. It was very, very strong friendship and a feeling of connection. Very strong feelings of connection, and I must tell you that, in spite of everything, that youth was in some sense very beautiful. I remember it as a time that was in some sense wonderful because first of all everybody's attitude was—I don't want to say exalted, not exalted because much of it was everyday life. But our goals overrode everything and were very, very important.

Sławomira imbues her memories of the past with meaning derived from her participation in the underground, casting a glow of solidarity, adventure, and romance on many of the events she remembers and retells. It is a vision of the past that is beguiling in its tale of beauty found in relationships based on service, sacrifice, and courage for the sake of a cause larger than oneself. However, in our interviews and informal conversations Sławomira recounted events in which fear and pain crept in, revealing human frailty and moral ambiguity. Sławomira's recollections about moving into the apartment that had been in the Little Ghetto after it was liquidated and the time her family hid the Jewish poet when the Gestapo came to their apartment building are just two examples. Once, at the end of a conversation, she told me, "You know, we went off to the uprising singing, 'We'll fight until the streets run red with our blood and Poland is free!' And that is what happened, only we were not free, and we were left with nothing."

Just as Krystyna has composed her memories to highlight the ironic and absurd, Sławomira has for the most part composed her memories to create a past that is salvific, a life lived as moral document (Myerhoff 1992: 240). Those who have adopted heroic memory and narrative tend to have a greater sense of connection with others from their own generation, who share their perspective, but they also draw connections with opposition activists in the 1970s and 1980s (Tucker 1998). Though not universally accepted, many Home Army veterans and Solidarity activists drew parallels between anti-Nazi resistance and the Solidarity movement. Indeed, as I have described elsewhere, some of my informants saw Solidarity as continuing their own struggle for Polish independence, despite the radical differences in armed insurrection and nonviolent protests. Heroic memory lends itself to claims of moral authority, bringing with it the possibility that their lives will be recognized as worthy of memory and public commemoration.

Remembering World War II in the Post-Socialist Era

My informants who have constructed their memories as moral documents have done so in response to a variety of factors. For example, as I described in chapter 3, many of them recalled learning in underground schools as an act of resistance aimed at demonstrating to the Germans that they could learn and achieve far beyond the roles the Germans envisioned for them as slaves in the new Reich. In this sense their memories are constructed to challenge an oppressive occupying force that attempted to dehumanize them. The careful attention to destruction of place and loss of life in narratives of the uprising can be understood as an accusation of betrayal to the Soviets, who accused the Polish insurgents of collaboration with the Nazis while the Red Army halted their advance, failing to cross the Vistula River to save the residents of Warsaw or the city itself. Narratives that focus on recriminations for Home Army involvement, for fathers murdered at Katyń, and family members in the West are constructed in response to a regime that rejected and denigrated their attempts to restore Polish sovereignty. Narratives like those of Olgierd and Sławomira emphasize that, despite everything, this was in some ways a beautiful youth, sanctified by suffering and the injustice of defeat, and are constructed for their children and offered to younger generations of Poles as a model on which to pattern their own lives. Narratives such as these, which focus on secret schools, clandestine activities, and the like, convey the message that, even in the worst of times and perhaps because of them, we have an obligation to care for our own development, while stories that highlight social solidarity suggest we must act toward others so as to preserve and create community. The stories themselves may have taken on a luster that the original events lacked, but the messages they convey are worth our attention.

With the fall of communism in Poland in 1989, Warsovians finally had the opportunity to commemorate the past and to publicly remember this episode of their history in ways not open to them during the communist era. However, commemorations of the uprising in the early 1990s did little to convince my informants that younger generations would remember or wholly accept their heroic vision of the past. Anniversaries in the 1990s were primarily Warsaw—even neighborhood—affairs, with each battalion holding its own ceremonies, often in the form of a memorial mass, and one large commemorative ceremony in the military section of Powazki beginning at five in the evening, the moment at which the uprising officially began. The only national ceremony was the sounding of sirens throughout Poland at five o'clock, signaling a moment of silence. On many occasions these small-scale public commemorations were accompanied by debates about the necessity of the uprising, its consequences, and the like in the major newspapers (cf. Karski and Friszke 1997) and articles with revelations about less than heroic behavior on the part of some Home Army units to Polish Jewish soldiers who attempted to join their ranks. In the year 2000 I went online, expecting more of the same in all the main Polish papers, only to be reminded that it was the twentieth anniversary of the Solidarity movement. Retrospectives on Solidarity leaders and commemorations of the movement's accomplishments had pushed coverage of the uprising commemorations to the inside pages of most major papers.

In 2004 I returned to Poland for the sixtieth anniversary of the Warsaw Uprising. In contrast to previous years, the city of Warsaw, under the leadership of the president of the city of Warsaw, Lech Kaczyński (who later became president of Poland), had greatly expanded the ceremonies honoring the uprising. Scouts from all over the country came to Warsaw to take part in the commemorations. These young people were in uniform and present en masse at every event. Among other things they helped elderly veterans to their seats, passed out bottled water, and took surveys of audience members' and pedestrians' knowledge about the uprising. In addition to the usual comemorative ceremonies at the cemetery, there were other events: staged reenactments, concerts of insurgent songs, and dramatic readings from the wartime memoirs of Polish literati such as Krzysztof Kamil Baczyński, Maria Dąbrowska, and Miron Białoszewski. One group of Boy Scouts took a walk through the city's storm sewers as an homage to the insurgents. Basia described the news of their feat as "absurd!" while her friend Lala declared it "a beautiful gesture." The sight of so many young people in scouting uniforms intermingled with a few hundred elderly veterans at these events was for me a powerful reminder that it was the youth of Warsaw who had fought and died in this battle.

At the same time that the city of Warsaw engaged the youth of Poland in remembering the Warsaw Uprising, it established a new institution to ensure that the uprising and those who fought during it would have a permanent place in Polish memory. The Museum of the Warsaw Rising opened its doors for the first time on the sixtieth anniversary of the Warsaw Uprising. It chronicles the wartime history of Warsaw with an emphasis on the Polish underground. Permanent exhibits depict the German occupation of Warsaw, the outbreak of the uprising, everyday life during urban warfare, major battles and massacres, the capitulation of the Polish underground to German troops, the deportation of the populace from the city, the city's destruction, and the fates of those who took part in the uprising in the Polish People's Republic. The museum also houses a café, classrooms and lecture halls, special exhibits for young visitors, the Wall of Memory, and Freedom Park. It is both the first interactive, technologically savvy museum in Poland and, at present, the country's most popular museum among people under the age of 30.

On my most recent trip to Warsaw, in the summer of 2008, I asked some of my informants about the museum. All had visited. When I asked Sławomira what she liked best about the museum, she said, "Just the fact that it exists." When I pressed her to be more specific, she said the Wall of Memory was particularly moving because it lists the names of all who died, including her father and several friends. I asked about her thoughts on the exhibits themselves or what was on display, and she reminded me that the museum is dimly lit and her vision is very poor. There are also very few places for visitors to sit. This was the pattern I noticed with most of the elderly Warsovians I talked to about the museum: they were overjoyed that it existed and pleased by its popularity, but it was not for them. Some said, "I lived through it, I do not need to go to the exhibits." Others admitted that even if they wanted to visit, the lighting, lettering, technology, stairs, and lack of benches were impediments. Most elderly visitors to the museum visit the meeting room for combatants, where veterans can gather to talk over a cup of tea, not the exhibit halls. It is a museum that commemorates the seminal events of my informants' youth, but it is a museum designed for and marketed to the youth of contemporary Poland.

Similarly, the commemorative ceremonies of 2008, organized for the most part by the Museum of the Warsaw Rising, combined somber state ceremonies geared toward veterans with a variety of youth-oriented activities. Among the latter were family picnics in Freedom Park, part of the museum complex, a puppet show that required the audience to stand for long periods of time and then to follow performers on foot for several kilometers through various Warsaw neighborhoods, outdoor theater performances, a concert featuring heavy-metal reduxes of songs from the uprising, and a bicycle race through Warsaw. Contemporary Warsaw youth in great numbers enthusiastically attended these events, many of which sold out. Clearly the museum has made this difficult history appealing to its core audience, Warsovians under thirty. Whether this was because young Warsovians sought a connection with the past or because these events brought relief from the dog days of summer is a question for further exploration.

Visiting the museum for the first time, I reflected on the times that informants had worried aloud that all they had shared with me would be forgotten, about their worries that no one would remember, or care. It was with some satisfaction that I visited the three-story structure and the park surrounding it. The historians, exhibit designers, and curatorial staff have strived to balance the political-military history of the uprising with the experiences of the individuals who took part as soldiers, health-care workers, and civilian relief workers. Though the narrative arc of the museum is about planning and launching the uprising, various battles, the capitulation, and the consequences for the insurgents and the city, this battle-oriented account is interspersed with panels, videos, and audio recordings of individuals recounting their experiences, which personalizes the history.

While the narrative offered by the museum's exhibits is for me a familiar one, it is not the story I have set out to tell here nor the one that I tell myself about the people who have shared their lives with me. For me, the story of their lives is remarkable not just because of what they did during the war but what they achieved in its aftermath, in the years of rebuilding their city and re-creating normalcy, and also in old age, in the work of constructing meaning from memories. Though memory may be the source of trauma for some, for most of my informants it has been the source of healing as well. By constructing their memories to make sense of the past, they have constructed lives that are serviceable both in living with trauma and loss and also in navigating the present.

Perhaps reconstructing everyday life, familiarity, and normalcy in the wake of war is not unlike the process, undertaken in old age, of constructing a sense of wholeness from a life characterized by radical disruption and loss. If narrating our lives is as basic a need as food, shelter, and sex, then it is the force of our desire to understand the self and to gain the understanding of others that pulls us into the intertwined processes of remembering and retelling. Sifting through memory for the experiences that best convey who we feel ourselves to be or who we want to become involves making choices about what to remember or forget—and most important, about how to remember. This involves finding narrative frames that are true to ourselves and the understandings of our lives that we construct from experience as well as finding a voice that will carry that meaning to others.

Notes

Introduction

1. My informants would first associate any reference to an "uprising" with the Warsaw Uprising of 1944, rather than the Warsaw Ghetto Uprising of 1943. This is most likely because they were participants in the former and only witnessed the latter from outside the walls of the Warsaw Ghetto.

2. Manor houses (*dworki*), villas (*willi*), semidetached pair of homes (*bliźniaki*—literally "twins").

3. Born in 1798 in Nowogrodek in the Grand Duchy of Lithuania, Adam Mickiewicz was the preeminent Polish poet of the Romantic era. His most famous poem, *Pan Tadeusz,* opens with the lines "Lithuania, my homeland." (See Miłosz 1983: 208–32.)

4. Jan is using the term "ghetto" to describe the neighborhood as an ethnic enclave. Prior to the war this area was a predominantly Jewish area, but it was not closed; its residents and others could come and go, no one was forced by law to live there, and in fact Polish Jewish residents of Warsaw lived in other neighborhoods, too. It became the mandatory residence of Jewish Warsovians and was walled only during World War II as a result of German policy.

5. Józef Piłsudski was a politician active in the Polish Socialist Party and a military leader in the movement for an independent Poland as well as the Russian-Polish War of 1920. In May of 1926, he launched a successful military coup. As a result, parliament appointed him president. Piłsudski, however, refused the position and made Ignacy Moscicki president in his place, preferring to exercise his own influence as commander of the military forces. Half a year later he was made prime minister. To this day he is regarded by many as a national hero.

6. Two notable exceptions, though they are entirely different in approach, perspective, and tone, are Jan Tomasz Gross's *Polish Society under German Occupation: The Generalgouvernement, 1939–1944*, published in 1979, and Richard Lukas's *The Forgotten Holocaust: The Poles under German Occupation, 1939–1944*, published in 1986.

7. Anti-Jewish pogroms did not take place after the war in Żoliborz or Warsaw as a whole. Because my informants know of them only through postwar reports on the news and in papers, rather than through firsthand accounts, they are not a part of this study.

1: Identity Politics in Interwar Poland

1. In Stanisław Wyspianski's play *The Wedding* (*Wesele*, 1901) and Władysław Rejmont's *The Peasants* (*Chłopi*, 1904–1909), the peasantry was idealized and romanticized.

Similarly, folk art from the Zakopane region in particular was popularized as the inspiration for home decor and architectural design by the well-known artist Stanisław Witkiewicz (Jedlicki 1995; Miłosz 1983: 370).

2. The general was Ivan Paskievitch (Davies 1984: 166–67).

3. This metaphor was the creation of Mickiewicz in his play *Forefathers' Eve* ("*Dziady*," 1832). He developed this theme further in *Books of the Polish Nation and of the Polish Pilgrims* (*Księgi Narodu Polskiego i Pielgrzystwa Polskiego*, 1832).

4. For other examples, see Ponichtera 1997: 28–29.

5. It is no coincidence that 1864 is also the date often given as the end of Polish romanticism (see Miłosz 1983).

6. For more on Russification in Poland, see Walicki 1991.

7. This was part of an attempt to Russify the Polish population, which was motivated by a Pan-Slavic movement popular with the tsar at that time. For more on this subject, see Walicki 1991.

8. The volunteers of one such organization, the Riflemen's Union (Związek Strzelecki), which was affiliated with the PPS, had plans to spend the summer of 1914 expanding their membership and recruiting working-class and peasant women, but the outbreak of the war rendered such plans impossible to realize (Ponichtera 1997: 22–23).

9. Indeed, I often found that those who displayed such photos romanticized interwar-era politics for, after all, Piłsudski had led a decidedly undemocratic military coup in 1926.

10. For a general overview on the impact of this and other anti-Semitic campaigns on Jewish communities in Poland, see Steinlauf 1997, Melzer 1989; for more detailed accounts, see Cała 1994, Heller 1977, Polonsky 1989.

11. I became aware of this contest when I read an article by the Polish historian and ethnographer Alina Cała published in *Polin*; the quotations I use here are taken from her article and are cited with reference to her article as well as to the record numbers assigned to the diaries by YIVO. More recently, a selection of diaries submitted to the competition was edited by Jeffrey Shandler and published by Yale University in a volume entitled, *Awakening Lives: Autobiographies of Jewish Youth in Poland before the Holocaust.*

12. It should be noted that neither he nor any of the other diarists claimed affiliation with the Assimilationist movement (Cała 1994: 42).

13. Though not Orthodox himself, Abraham Rotfarb resided in a predominantly Orthodox Jewish neighborhood in Warsaw (ibid. 52).

14. Mehta and Chatterji follow Feldman (1991: 14), who argues that the event of violence is what can be narrated and thus such narration is characterized both by "semantic excess" and an instrumental imagination of violence as it impinges on material culture (Mehta and Chatterji 2001: 245).

2: Memories of the Invasion

1. The Molotov-Ribbentrop Non-Aggression Pact was a pact made between the USSR and Germany, in which they agreed not to attack one another's territory.

2. It is worth noting that, while Polish authorities may have chosen to turn their attention to higher levels of political organization than the Hitler Youth, the Germans saw the Polish Scouts as a potential threat from the very beginning of their campaign to dominate Poland. So much so that when the Germans invaded Bydgoszcz, a city in central Poland, their first action was to execute a group of scouts (*harcerstwo*) ranging in age from 12 to 16 in that city's marketplace (Lukas 1986: 3).

3. Where I do see evidence for Gross's analysis is in postwar representations of young people's lives during the war, particularly in Andrzej Wajda's war trilogy *Generations: Pokolenia*, 1956; *Kanał*, 1958; and *Ashes and Diamonds* (*Popiół i Diamente*), 1958.

4. The battle of Kock was the last in the September campaign, ending on October 6.

3: Memories of the Occupation

1. Nazi racial ideology was codified into law and presented to the wider public in the form of the Nuremburg Laws beginning in 1933. The First Decree for Implementation of the Law for the Restoration of the Professional Civil Service, codified into law on April 11, 1933, stated, "A person is to be regarded as non-Aryan if he is descended from non-Aryan, especially Jewish, parents or grandparents. It is enough for one parent or grandparent to be non-Aryan. This is to be assumed especially if one parent or one grandparent was of the Jewish faith" (cited in Dawidowicz 1976: 41). In September of 1935, the Law for the Protection of German Blood and German Honor was passed, banning marriage between Jews and Germans and criminalizing all sexual relations between the two groups. Finally, in November of 1935, the Reich Citizenship Law stated that "a Reich citizen is only that subject of German or kindred blood who proves by his conduct that he is willing and suited loyally to serve the Reich. . . . The Reich citizen is the sole bearer of full political rights as provided by law" (cited in Dawidowicz 1976: 45). The implementation decree accompanying this law also defined "anyone who is descended from one or two grandparents who are fully Jewish as regards race" as a "Jewish *Mischlinge*," a person of mixed race and subject to the same restrictions as Jews.

2. The so-called Nuremburg Laws, which changed the definition of German citizens, not only denied Jews their basic civil rights but also disenfranchised those identified as Gypsies. A category that included Sinti and Roma, as well as their descendents, Gypsies were also defined as a dangerous, alien race (*Fremdrasse*), perceived as posing a threat to the racial purity of Germans (Fraser 1995: 257). Gypsies in general were considered by the Nazis to be "asocial," a race of criminals, while those in the "part-Gypsy" category, in effect 90 percent of those living in Germany, were considered to be the most dangerous in terms of criminal behavior (Fraser 1995: 258–59). Individuals were considered to be "part Gypsy" (*Zigeunermischling*) if they had two great-grandparents who were Gypsies, this in contrast to the policy on the definition of Jews, which considered an individual non-Jewish if none of the grandparents were Jewish. As early as 1933, those defined as Gypsies by the Reich were subject to forced sterilization and, by 1937 in Germany and in 1938 in Austria, to internment in concentration camps (ibid.).

3. Historian Richard Lukas suggests that these methods are best described as genocide and argues that, had the war continued, once the Nazis had murdered all the Jews of Europe, their sights would have been set on eliminating the Poles. As an anthropologist, I am not concerned by the "what might have beens" of history, nor is my goal to sift the documentary evidence in order to declare whether the way in which the Germans treated Poles can be classified as genocidal or not. Rather the task, as I see it, is to illustrate how Nazi policy in Poland impacted the lives of those who had to live within its narrow confines.

4. Mikołaj Kopernik was born in 1473 in Toruń, a Polish town, and is considered by Poles to be Polish.

5. To the north the Warsaw Ghetto bordered on Stawki and Żoliborska Streets, on the northeast Bonifraterska and Tłomacki, on the southeast Żelazna Brama Square, on the south Złota and Siena Streets, and on the west Leszno Street and the Jewish cemetery.

6. In Poland the names of shops, cafés, restaurants, and the like in older sections of cities will often take their names from some sort of architectural feature of the building. In this case there must have been a star in the frieze above the doorway.

7. For an insider's account of the "resettlement" of the Little Ghetto, see Władysław Szpilman's *The Pianist*.

8. Dorothy Macardle (1951: 75–76), who was in Europe after the war conducting research for UNICEF, reported that "at Warsaw thousands of women fought for a trainload of children with such fury that the Germans afterwards arranged that transports should in future be sent by a different route." Richard Lukas (1986: 22) also reports that in Warsaw women met these transports and successfully ransomed some of the children they carried.

9. Schools in interwar-era Poland were not coeducational and were divided into primary school for the first through fifth grades, followed by a four-year gimnazjum, and a two-year liceum.

10. Pan Olgierd rejects the word *Państwo,* conveying formality and social distance, in favor of the word *znajomy* (acquaintances) in order to convey a closer relationship.

4: The Conspiracy

1. Sławomira met Stefan through her work with the Żoliborz hospice. I am not sure exactly how it came about, but at some point the two discovered that Stefan had known Sławomira's father from the underground and was able to tell her about a part of her father's life that, because of his death during the Warsaw Uprising of 1944, she knew very little about. Save for her sister Basia, there were few people still living who remembered Sławomira's father, making Stefan a rare link with the past. In the spring before Stefan's death, Sławomira spent many hours at the couple's apartment helping his wife, Lidia, care for him.

2. Jurek is a nickname for Jerzy. Whenever Pani Basia has news for me about Pan Jerzy, she refers to him as Jurek.

3. The paper with the widest circulation was reportedly *Biuletyn Informacyjny,* which is said to have reached 43,000 readers (Rzepecki 1983).

4. Members of the Gray Ranks wore gray uniforms, thus the reference to the gray brotherhood.

5. Courses for troop leaders are also revealing. One course discussed the issues of developing moral and intellectual values through contact with the arts. Courses for scoutmasters were divided into four thematic groups including "The Concept of Poland," "Silhouette of a Modern Woman," "History of Polish Girl Scouts," and "New Directions in Psychology" (Zawadzka 1995: 125–27).

5: Reflections on Helping Polish Jews

1. For eyewitness accounts of these executions, see Tec 1986: 66–67.

2. David Engel (1993) posits that the leadership of the Polish government-in-exile viewed the wider Jewish community abroad as an advocate for the Polish Jewish community. As a result the Polish state did not view itself as responsible for the fate of its Jewish citizens and therefore considered the impact that efforts on behalf of Polish Jews would have on the ethnic Polish population. While he uses correspondence to demonstrate this quite clearly among the leadership, this is not a position that any of my informants ever voiced about Polish Jews.

3. Engelking-Boni (2003: 52) contends, "The many Poles who actually saved Jews, at risk to themselves, did so in the face of general indifference among most Poles to the fate of the Jews."

4. The interview continues:

Olgierd: A little later, after the war and until today, there are still a few Jews, but because in general there are very few Jews in Poland, of course the percentage [of Jews in the neighborhood] has been greatly diminished.

ELT: Were there a lot of Jews living in Żoliborz before the war?

Olgierd: Before the war there were some but mainly in the WSM blocks, but it was comparatively a small percent [of the population]. Of course the intelligentsia was here, and in the intelligentsia there were some Jews. During the war, a lot [of Jews] flowed in—escapees from the ghetto. The ghetto bordered on Żoliborz, it was just on the other side of the train tracks. A lot escaped from there and went into hiding in Żoliborz, so it seems to me that maybe there were more Jews here during the occupation than before the war, I don't know. I haven't done the statistics.

5. The Home Army did provide the Jewish Fighting Organization with 20 pistols between December 1942 and January 18, 1943, as well as directions on how to make Molotov cocktails and instruction in diversionary action as noted in Lukas (1986: 174).

6. Janusz Korczak was an internationally renowned pediatrician known throughout Poland for his radio broadcasts about raising children. He was also the author of numerous books about and for children, some of which are still required reading in Polish schools. Dr. Korczak also ran an orphanage for Jewish children in Warsaw. When the orphans were sent to the Warsaw Ghetto, Korczak went with his children though there were many who offered to help him escape. Later he accompanied his orphans to Treblinka, where he shared their fate. He is the only person who died at the Treblinka death camp who is commemorated by name at the monument that marks the site.

7. The other, Wiesława, was arrested and sent to Majdanek in 1942 for her activities as a courier for the Polish underground, and our interviews focused on these events.

8. Oliner and Oliner (1988) also report that "Aryanizing" or "de-Judaizing" Jews with regard to their physical appearance, gestures, walking, or speech was a concern noted by many of the rescuers whom they interviewed.

6: Remembering the Warsaw Uprising

1. In eastern Poland the AK sought to cooperate with and, indeed, fought alongside the Red Army to liberate key cities like Wilno, Grodno, and Białystok. In the wake of these battles, Polish soldiers were given the option to join General Berling's army or to disband and go home. While the AK continually sent emissaries to negotiate with the Soviets, these emissaries never returned from their missions and, in fact, an estimated 50,000 Polish soldiers from the Home Army were arrested and deported to the Soviet Union when they opted not to join Berling (Roszkowski 1997: 131–32).

2. According to historian Richard C. Lukas (1986: 185), German efforts to fortify a few key points across the city with machine-gun posts and tanks was taken as evidence that the German authorities were planning to implement a plan for the removal of the entire male population of the capital. Lukas cites the September 25, 1944, issue of *Biuletyn Informacyny* in support of both the existence of the plan and Warsovians' belief that it was about to be carried out.

3. For such an account, see Davies 2004.

4. All of my informants were members of the Home Army; there was, however, another group called Armia Ludowa (the People's Army) that was also involved.

5. To contextualize the Warsaw Uprising with other twentieth-century conflicts: in World War I, over 80 percent of those who died as a result of battle were soldiers; in contrast 50 percent of World War II casualties were civilians. At present, nearly 90 percent of all war-related deaths are civilians. In other words, there has been an ever-increasing trend for battles to take place, not in trenches and battlefields, but in villages, towns, and cities, making the local populaces that inhabit them not collateral damage but tactical targets (Nordstrom and Martin 1992).

6. Many of them eventually returned just days before the uprising began when the Germans took measures to strengthen their forces in Warsaw (Dunin-Wąsowicz 1984: 198).

7. In reference to the uprising, most Warsovians who lived through it describe all enemy soldiers who spoke Russian as "Ukrainians." The units responsible for the mass murders, rapes, general pillaging, and destruction that took place in Wola and the neighboring suburb of Ochota were the Kamiński Brigade, which numbered 1,700, and the Dirlewanger Brigade, which was comprised of 16 officers and 865 soldiers; they were joined by SS, Wehrmacht, and a German police group (Lukas 1986: 196). Byelorussians and Ukrainians constituted more than 50 percent of some of these groups (ibid. 199).

8. Norman Davies (2004: 252) groups Ochota and Wola together and cites the number of noncombatant casualties as being 20,000–50,000.

9. For survivors' accounts, see Harris (1954: 201–4).

10. Basia explained how the area looked different during the war than in the reconstructed Old Town: "Things looked a little different there than they do now, there where the medieval wall has been excavated at the royal palace, there were regular houses, and only part of the wall was there simply as a component of those houses because they were built right onto it, and there was so-called Ślepa (Blind) Street because it didn't have an entrance onto the square."

11. For a similar observation in a different context, see Mehta and Chatterji (2001: 208).

12. Mehta and Chatterji (2001: 208), who conducted research in an Indian town devastated by interethnic riots, found that on narrated walking tours "it is almost as if walking is an act of remembrance being embodied in speech, but an act also that establishes the boundary between Hindus and Muslims."

13. See also DesPres 1976, Nordstrom 1997: 75–110.

7: Aftermath: Exodus and Return

1. I am not entirely sure why Olgierd laughed at this point, but *pierwotnie* can mean both "original" and "primitive."

2. Many Jews who had been in hiding in the city chose to stay rather than venturing out where they might be recognized and denounced by their Polish neighbors or discovered by Nazis. For one such account of life in Warsaw after capitulation, see Władysław Szpilman's memoir, *The Pianist*.

3. Warsovians are quick to note that Krakowians have never launched an uprising while Warsaw has launched, lost, and subsequently paid the price for several. It is also my

understanding that Warsovians view Krakowians as a bit aloof and pretentious, an attitude that, among other things, is connected to a sort of competition between the two cities based on Kraków's status as the former capital and the conviction of many Krakowians that it is still the cultural center of the country. Note the emphasis that Olgierd places on receiving his degree from the newly opened University of Warsaw, rather than Jagiellonian University, which is one of the oldest institutions of higher learning in Europe.

4. Eugenia told me that, while she was in Opole looking for work, she had to hide from Soviet troops who were arresting Warsovians. Opole is a town in what is now western Poland that prior 1945 had been in Germany.

5. Janina and her family stayed in touch with Piotr until 1968 when, due to an anti-Semitic campaign that resulted in the majority of Jews then living in Poland losing their jobs and being given exit visas, they lost touch. Later, Piotr managed to contact Janina again, and she made several trips to Israel to visit him and Irena before Piotr's death from a heart attack in the early 1990s. Janina, her sister Wanda, and their mother all received the Yad Vashem designation of Righteous Gentiles. A tree has been planted in their honor on the Avenue of the Righteous in Jerusalem.

Conclusion: Memory and Its Discontents

1. In Poland many people celebrate name days, the day dedicated to the saint for whom they have been named. In my experience these celebrations are not religious but more like our birthday parties.

2. This number is from the 4,255 bodies that were recovered from Katyń; the remains of an additional 10,000 officers imprisoned at Starobielsk, Kozielsk, and Ostawków are missing and presumed to have been killed in a similar manner (Allen 1991).

Bibliography

Allen, Paul
  1991 *Katyń: The Untold Story of Stalin's Polish Massacre.* New York: Charles
        Scribner's Sons.
Andrews, Molly
  2007 *Shaping History: Narratives of Political Change.* Cambridge: Cambridge
        University Press.
Andrzejewski, Andrzej
  1991 [1948] *Ashes and Diamonds.* Translated by D.J. Welsh. Evanston, IL:
        Northwestern University Press.
Aretxaga, Begonia
  1997 *Shattering Silence: Women, Nationalism, and Political Subjectivity in
        Northern Ireland.* Princeton, NJ: Princeton University Press.
Argenti, Nicolas, and Katharina Schramm
  2010 Introduction. In *Remembering Violence: Intergenerational Perspectives on
        Transmission.* New York: Berghahn Books.
Aristotle
  1962 *Poetics.* New York: Norton.
Assuntio, Rudi, and Władek Goldkorn
  1999 *Strażnik: Marek Edelman Opowiada.* Kraków Społeczny: Instytut Społeczny.
Bakhtin, Mikhail
  1981 *Dialogic Imagination: Four Essays.* Translated by C.M. Emerson and M.
        Holquist. Austin: University of Texas.
Ballinger, Pamela
  2003 *History in Exile: Memory and Identity at the Borders of the Balkans.*
        Princeton, NJ: Princeton University Press.
Bartoszewski, Władysław
  1968 *Warsaw Death Ring, 1939–1944.* Translated by Edward Rothert. Warsaw:
        Interpress.
  1984 [1859] *Dni Warszawy.* Krakow: Znak.
  1989 *Dni Walczącej Stolicy: Kronika Powstania Warszawskiego.* Warszawa:
        Wydawnictwa ALFA.
  1990 *Warto Być Przyzwoitym: Teksty Osobiste i Nieosobiste.* Poznań: W Drodze.
Bartoszewski, Władysław, and Zofia Lewin
  1970 *The Samaritans: Heroes of the Holocaust.* New York: Twayne Publishers.
Bax, Mart
  1963 Mass Graves, Stagnating Identification, and Violence: A Case Study in
        the Local Sources of "the War" in Bosnia Hercegovina. *Anthropological
        Quarterly* 70 (January): 11–19.

Berdahl, Daphne
   1999 *Where the World Ended: Re-Unification and Identity in the German Borderland*. Berkeley: University of California Press.
Białoszewski, Miron
   1977 *Memoir of the Warsaw Uprising*. Edited and translated by Madeline Levine. Ann Arbor, MI: Ardis.
Bilu, Yoram, and Eli Ben-Ari
   1992 The Making of Modern Saints: Manufactured Charisma and the Abu-Hatseiras of Israel. *American Ethnologist* 19(4): 672–87.
Bloch, Maurice
   1992 *Prey into Hunter: The Politics of Religious Experience*. New York: Cambridge University Press.
Borecka, Emilia, and Leonard Sempoliński
   1985 *Warszawa 1945*. Warszawa: Państwowe Wydawnictwo Naukowe.
Bór-Komorowski, Tadeusz
   1951 *The Secret Army*. London: Victor Gollancz.
Borneman, John
   1991 *After the Wall: East Meets West in the New Berlin*. Boston: Basic Books.
   1992 *Belonging in the Two Berlins: Kin, State, Nation*. Cambridge: Cambridge University Press.
Brandys, Kazimierz
   1964 *Listy Do Pani Z*. Warszawa: Panstwowy Instytut Wydawnictwo.
Bratkowski, Stefan
   1998 *Najkrótsza Historia Polski*. Warszawa: Krajowa Agencja Wydawnicza.
Bronsztejn, Szyja
   1994 Polish Jewish Relations as Reflected in Memoirs of Interwar Poland. In *Polin: Studies in Polish Jewry* 8: 66–88. London: Institute for Polish-Jewish Studies.
Browning, Christopher
   1993 *Ordinary Men: Reserve Police Battalion 101 and the Final Solution in Poland*. New York: Harper.
Bruner, Jerome
   1990 *Acts of Meaning*. Cambridge, MA: Harvard University Press.
Burke, Peter
   1989 History as Social Memory. In *Memory: History, Culture, and the Mind*, edited by T. Butler, pp. 97–113. Oxford: Blackwell.
Cała, Alina
   1994 The Social Consciousness of Young Jews in Interwar Poland. In *Polin: Studies in Polish Jewry* 8: 42–65. London: Institute for Polish-Jewish Studies.
Caruth, Cathy
   1995 Introduction to Trauma and Experience. In *Trauma: Explorations in Memory*, edited by C. Caruth. Baltimore, MD: Johns Hopkins University Press.
Chojnowski, Andrzej
   1995 Polish National Character, the Sanacja Camp, and the National Democracy. In *National Character and National Ideology*, edited by Ivo Banac and Katherine Verdery, pp. 23–38. New Haven, CT: Yale Center for International Studies.
Clendinnen, Inga
   1999 *Reading the Holocaust*. Cambridge: Cambridge University Press.

Cole, Jennifer
    2001   *Forget Colonialism? Sacrifice and the Art of Memory in Madagascar.*
        Berkeley: University of California Press.
Connerton, Paul
    1989   *How Societies Remember.* Cambridge: Cambridge University Press.
Curry, Jane Leftwich (editor)
    1984   *The Black Book of Polish Censorship.* New York: Vintage Books.
Danieli, Yael (editor)
    1998   *International Handbook of Multigenerational Legacies of Trauma.* 1st ed.
        New York: Plenum Press.
Daniels, Stephen
    1985   Arguments for a Humanistic Geography. In *The Future of Geography,* edited
        by R.J. Johnston. London: Metheun.
Das, Veena
    1985   Anthropological Knowledge and Collective Violence. *Anthropology Today*
        1(3): 4–6.
Das, Veena, and Arthur Kleinman
    2001   Introduction. In *Remaking a World: Violence, Social Suffering, and Recovery,*
        pp. 1–30. Berkeley: University of California Press.
Davies, Norman
    1984   *Heart of Europe: A Short History of Poland.* Oxford: Oxford University Press.
    2004   *Rising '44: The Battle for Warsaw.* New York: Viking Books.
Davis, Natalie Zemon, and Randolph Starn
    1989   Introduction, Special Issue: Memory and Counter Memory. *Representations*
        0(26):1–6.
Dawidowicz, Lucy
    1976   *A Holocaust Reader.* West Orange, NJ: Behrman House.
DesPres, Terrence
    1976   *The Survivor: An Anatomy of Life in the Death Camps.* Oxford: Oxford
        University Press.
Drozdowski, Marian M., and Andrzej Zahorski
    1972   *Historia Warszawy.* Warszawa: Państwowe Wydawnictwo Naukowe.
Dunin-Wąsowicz, Krzystof
    1984   *Na Żoliborzu, 1939–1945.* Warszawa: Wydawnictwo Książka i Wiedza.
Dunin-Wąsowicz, Krzystof, Benon Lisowski, Andrzej Liszek, and Tadeusz Targowski (editors)
    1981   *Z Dziejów Liceum i Gimnazjum im. Ks. Jozefa Poniatowskiego w Warszawie.*
        Warszawa: Państwowy Instytut Wydawniczy.
Duraczyński, Eugeniusz
    1974   *Wojna i Okupacja Wrzesień, 1939–1943.* Warszawa: Wiedza Powszechna.
Dzikiewicz, Lech
    1994   *Zbrodnia Stalina Na Warszawie.* Warszawa: Wydawnictwo Bellona.
Elder, Glen H. Jr., Michael J. Shanahan, and Elizabeth Colerick Clipp
    1994   When War Comes to Men's Lives: Life-Course Patterns in Family, Work and
        Health. *Psychology and Aging* 9 (March): 5–16.
Elkind, David
    1967   Egocentrism in Adolescence. *Child Development* 38(4): 1025–34.
    1985   Egocentrism Redux. *Developmental Review* 5(3): 218–26.

Engel, David
    1993   *Facing a Holocaust: The Polish Government in Exile and the Jews, 1943–1945.*
            Chapel Hill: University of North Carolina Press.

Engelking, Barbara
    2001   *Holocaust and Memory: The Experience of the Holocaust and Its*
            Consequences: An Investigation Based on Personal Narratives. Translated by
            Emma Harris. London: Leicester University Press.

Engelking-Boni, Barbara
    2003   Psychological Distance between Poles and Jews in Nazi-Occupied Warsaw.
            In *Contested Memories: Poles and Jews during the Holocaust and Its*
            Aftermath, pp. 47–53. New Brunswick, NJ: Rutgers University Press.

Eriksen, Anne
    1994   Memory, History, and National Identity. *Ethnologia Europaea* 27: 129–38.

Erikson, Erik
    1959   *Identity and the Life Cycle.* New York: Norton.

Farmer, Sarah
    1999   *Martyred Village: Commemorating the 1944 Massacre at Oradour-sur-Glane.*
            Berkeley: University of California Press.

Feld, Steve, and Keith H. Basso (editors)
    1996   *Senses of Place.* Santa Fe, NM: School of American Research Press.

Feldman, Alan
    1991   *Formations of Violence: The Narratives of the Body and Political Terror in*
            Northern Ireland. Chicago: University of Chicago Press.

Fentress, James, and Chris Wickham
    1992   *Social Memory.* Oxford: Blackwell.

Fischer, Michael M.J.
    1993   Working through the Other: The Jewish, Spanish, Turkish, Iranian,
            Ukrainian, Lithuanian, and German Unconscious of Polish Culture. In
            Perilous States: Conversations on Culture, Politics and Nation. Chicago:
            University of Chicago Press.

Foucault, Michel
    1977   *Discipline and Punish: The Birth of the Prison.* New York: Vintage Press.
    1980   *Language, Counter-Memory, Practice: Selected Essays and Interviews.* Ithaca,
            NY: Cornell University Press.

Frankl, Viktor E.
    1962   *Man's Search for Meaning: An Introduction to Logotherapy.* New York: Simon
            and Schuster.

Fraser, Angus
    1995   *The Gypsies.* 2nd edition. Oxford: Wiley-Blackwell.

Gal, Susan
    1991   Bartok's Funeral and Representations of Europe in Hungarian Political
            Rhetoric. *American Ethnologist* 18(3): 440–58.

Garlicki, Andrzej
    1995   *Józef Piłsudski, 1867–1935.* Translated by John Coutouvidis. Hants, UK:
            Scolar Press.

Głowacka, Dorota, and Joanna Zylinska (editors)
    2007   *Imaginary Neighbors: Mediating Polish-Jewish Relations after the Holocaust.*
            Lincoln: University of Nebraska Press.

Goffman, Erving
   1974   *Frame Analysis: An Essay on the Organization of Experience.* New York: Harper and Row.
Goldson, Edward
   1995   The Effect of War on Children. *Child Abuse and Neglect* 20 (September): 809–19.
Gross, Jan Tomasz
   1979   *Polish Society under German Occupation: The Generalgouvernement 1939–1944.* Princeton, NJ: Princeton University Press.
   2001   *Neighbors: The Destruction of the Jewish Community of Jedwabne, Poland.* New York: Penguin Books.
   2006   *Fear: Anti-Semitism in Poland after Auschwitz.* New York: Random House.
Grupińska, Anka
   1991   *Po Kole: Rozmowy z Żydowskimi Żołnierzami.* Warszawa: Wydawnictwo Alfa.
Grzymala-Siedlecki, Bogdan
   1988   *Powstanczym szlakiem walczącego Żoliborza.* Warszawa: PTTK "Kraj."
Gumkowski, Janusz, and Kazimierz Leszyński
   1961   *Poland under Nazi Occupation.* Warsaw: Polonia Publishing House.
Gushee, David P.
   1994   *Righteous Gentiles of the Holocaust.* Minneapolis, MN: Fortress Press.
Gutman, Israel
   1994   *Resistance: The Warsaw Ghetto Uprising.* Boston: Houghton Mifflin.
   2003   Some Issues in Jewish Polish Relations during the Second World War. In *Contested Memories: Poles and Jews during the Holocaust and Its Aftermath,* pp. 212–17. New Brunswick, NJ: Rutgers University Press.
Hacking, Ian
   1994   Souls in One Body. In *Questions of Evidence: Proof, Practice, and Persuasion across Disciplines,* edited by James Chandler, Arnold Davidson, and Harry Harootunian. Chicago: University of Chicago Press.
Hanson, Joanna K.M.
   1982   *The Civilian Population and the Warsaw Uprising of 1944.* Cambridge: Cambridge University Press.
Harris, Whitney R.
   1954   *Tyranny on Trial: The Evidence at Nuremberg.* Dallas, TX: Southern Methodist University Press.
Hayden, Robert M.
   1994   The Rediscovery and Redefinition of Wartime Massacres in Late- and Post-Communist Yugoslavia. In *Memory, History, and Opposition under State Socialism,* edited by R.S. Watson, pp. 167–84. Santa Fe, NM: School of American Research Press.
Heer, Nancy
   1971   *Politics and History in the Soviet Union.* Cambridge, MA: MIT Press.
Heller, Celia Stopnicka
   1977   *On the Edge of Destruction: Jews of Poland between the Two World Wars.* New York: Columbia University Press.
Herbst, Stanisław (editor)
   1975   *Encyklopedia Warszawy.* Warszawa: Państwowe Wydawnictwo Naukowe.

Herling-Grudziński, Gustaw
   1986 [1951]   *A World Apart*. Translated by Andrzej Ciokosz. New York: Arbor
      House.
Hermann, Rauschning
   1939   *Hitler Speaks*. London: Thornton Butterworth.
Heyman, Łukasz
   1976   *Nowy Żoliborz 1918–1939: Architektura—Urbanistyka*. Wroclaw: Polska
      Akademia Nauk-Instytut Sztuki.
Hillebrandt, Bogdan
   1973   *Konspiracyjne organizacje młodzieżowe w Polsce, 1939–1945*. Warsaw:
      Książka i Wiedza.
Hirsch, Marianne
   1997   *Family Frames: Photography, Narrative, and Postmemory*. Cambridge, MA:
      Harvard University Press.
Hobsbawm, Eric, and Terrence Ranger (editors)
   1992   *The Invention of Tradition*. Cambridge: Cambridge University Press.
Hogman, Flora
   1994   Some Concluding Thoughts. *Psychoanalytic Review* 85(4)(August): 659–72.
Holubowicz-Gadkowska, Anna "Iwona"
   1992   *Pamiętnik Łaczniki Kapelana*. London: Nakladem Fundacji Armii Krajowej.
Hrabar, Roman
   1981   *The Fate of Polish Children during the Last War*. Translated by Bogdan
      Buczkowski and Lech Petrowicz. Warsaw: Interpress.
Janion, Maria
   1984   *Osoby: Wybór opracowanie i radakcja M. Janion*. Gdańsk: Wydawnictwo
      Morskie.
Jaworski, Rudolf, and Bianka Pietrow-Ennker (editors)
   1992   *Women in Polish Society*. Boulder: University of Colorado Press.
Jedlicki, Jerzy
   1995   Polish Concepts of Native Culture. In *National Character and National
      Ideology*, edited by Ivo Banac and Katherine Verdery, pp. 1–22. New Haven,
      CT: Yale Center for International Studies.
Jezernik, Bozidar
   1997   Monuments in the Winds of Change. *International Journal of Urban and
      Regional Research* 22(4): 582–88.
Kaminsky, Marc
   1992   Introduction. In *Remembered Lives: The Work of Ritual, Storytelling, and
      Growing Older*, edited by M. Kaminsky. Ann Arbor: University of Michigan
      Press.
   1993   A Table with People: Storytelling as Life Review and Cultural History.
      In *YIVO Annual*, edited by J. Kugelmass. Evanston, IL: Northwestern
      University Press and the YIVO Institute for Jewish Research.
Karaszkiewicz, Jerzy
   1993   'Krzywa' Rośnie. *Gazeta Stołeczna*. 27 Oct., pp. 4. Warszawa.
Karski, Jan, and Andrzej Friszke
   1997   Czy Powstanie Warszawskie Było Potrebne? O sensie Powstaniia
      Warszawskiego dyskutują historycy Jan Karski i Andzej Friszke. *Gazeta
      Wyborcza*. 26 August. Warszawa.

Kaufman, M.T.
   1989   *Mad Dreams, Saving Graces: Poland, a Nation in Conspiracy.* New York: Random House.
Kertzer, David I.
   1996   *Politics and Symbols: The Italian Communist Party and the Fall of Communism.* New Haven, CT: Yale University Press.
Khazanov, Anatoly
   1998   Post Communist Moscow: Re-building the "Third Rome" in the Country of Missed Opportunities? *City and Society.* Annual Review, pp. 269–314.
Krakowski, Shmuel
   2003   The Attitude of the Polish Underground to the Jewish Question during the Second World War. In *Contested Memories: Poles and Jews during the Holocaust and Its Aftermath,* edited by J. Zimmerman, pp. 97–106. New Brunswick, NJ: Rutgers University Press.
Krall, Hanna
   1992   *The Subtenant/To Outwit God.* Evanston, IL: Northwestern University Press.
Królikowski, Lech, and Bolesław Orłowski
   1995   *I Warszawę Nie Od Razu Zbudowano.* Warszawa: Wydawnictwo Instytutu Historii i Nauki.
Kubik, Jan
   1994   *The Power of Symbols against the Symbols of Power: The Rise and Fall of State Socialism in Poland.* University Park, PA: Pennsylvania State University Press.
Kugelmass, Jack
   1986   *The Miracle of Intervale Avenue: The Story of a Jewish Congregation in the South Bronx.* New York: Schocken Books.
   1995   Bloody Memories: Encountering the Past in Contemporary Poland. *Cultural Anthropology* 10: 279–301.
Kundera, Milan
   1981   *The Book of Laughter and Forgetting.* Harmondsworth, UK: Penguin Books.
   1985   *The Unbearable Lightness of Being.* New York: Harper and Row.
Kurek, Ewa
   1996   *Your Life Is Worth Mine: How Polish Nuns Saved Hundreds of Jewish Children in German-Occupied Poland, 1939–1945.* New York: Hippocrene Books.
Kuroń, Jacek, and Jacek Żakowski
   1996   *PRL Dla Początkujących.* Wrocław: Wydawnictwo Dolnośląskie.
Kurski, Jarosław
   2002   Chrzanowski: Byłem przeciwny, ale walczyłem. *Gazeta Wyborcza.* August 1, p. 2.
Labouvie-Vief, Gisela
   1990   Toward a Psychology of Wisdom and Its Ontogenesis. In *Wisdom: Its Nature, Origins and Development,* edited by Robert J. Sternberg. Cambridge: Cambridge University Press.
Labov, Willliam
   1972   *Language in the Inner City: Studies in the Black English Vernacular.* Philadelphia: University of Pennsylvania Press.
Lambek, Michael
   2006   Memory in a Maussian Universe. In *Memory Cultures: Memory Subjectivity and Recognition,* edited by Susannah Radstone and Katherine Hodgkins, pp. 202–16. New Brunswick: Transaction.

Langer, Lawrence L.
1991 *Holocaust Testimonies: The Ruins of Memory*. New Haven, CT: Yale University Press.

Lass, Andrew
1994 From Memory to History: The Events of November 17 Dis/membered. In *Memory, History, and Opposition under State Socialism*, edited by R.S. Watson, pp. 87–104. Santa Fe, NM: School of American Research Press.

Levi, Primo
1989 *The Drowned and the Saved*. Translated by Raymond Rosenthal. New York: Vintage Books.
1995 *Survival in Auschwitz: The Nazi Assault on Humanity*. Translated by Stuart Woolf. New York: Simon and Schuster.

Lifton, Robert Jay
1967 *Death in Life: Survivors of Hiroshima*. New York: Random House.
1986 *The Nazi Doctors: Medical Killing and the Psychology of Genocide*. New York: Basic Books.

Long, Kristi
1996 *We All Fought for Freedom: Women in Poland's Solidarity Movement*. Boulder, CO: Westview.

Lukas, Richard C.
1986 *The Forgotten Holocaust: The Poles under German Occupation, 1939–1944*. New York: Hippocrene.

Macardle, Dorothy
1951 *Children of Europe: A Study of the Children of Liberated Countries: Their War-time Experiences, Their Reactions, and Their Needs, with a Note on Germany*. Boston: Beacon Press.

Majdaczyk, Czesław
1970 *Polityka III Rzeszy w Okupowanej Polsce*. Warszawa: Państwowe Wydawnictwo Naukowe.

Malinowski, Bronisław
1961 *Argonauts of the Western Pacific: An Account of Native Enterprise and Adventure in the Archipelagos of Melanesian New Guinea*. New York: Dutton.

Marten-Finnis, Susanne
1995 Collective Memory and National Identities: German and Polish Memory Cultures: The Forms of Collective Memory. *Communist and Post-Communist Studies* 28(2): 255–61.

Martin, Emily
1987 *Woman in the Body: A Cultural Analysis of Reproduction*. Boston: Beacon Press.

Martin, JoAnn
1992 When the People Were Strong and United: Stories of the Past and the Transformation of Politics in a Mexican Community. In *Paths to Domination, Resistance, and Terror*, edited by Carolyn Nordstrom and JoAnn Martin, pp. 177–89. Berkeley: University of California Press.

Mazur, Elżbieta
1993 *Warszawska Spółdzielnia Mieszkaniowa, 1921–1939: Materialne warunki bytu robotników i inteligencji*. Warszawa: Instytut Archaeologii i Etnologii Polskiej Akademii Nauk.

Mehta, Deepak, and Roma Chatterji
  2001   Boundaries, Names, Alterities: A Case Study of a "Communal Riot" in
          Dharavi, Bombay. In *Remaking a World: Violence, Social Suffering, and
          Recovery*, edited by Veena Das and Richard Kleinman, pp. 201–49. Berkeley:
          University of California Press.
Melzer, Emanuel
  1989   Anti-Semitism in the Last Years of the Second Polish Republic. In *The
          Jews of Poland between Two World Wars*, edited by Yisrael Gutman, Ezra
          Mendelsohn, Jehuda Reinharz, and Chone Shmeruk, pp. 126–37. Hanover,
          NH: University Press of New England.
Michlic, Joanna Beata
  2006   *Poland's Threatening Other: The Image of the Jew from 1880 to the Present.*
          Lincoln: University of Nebraska Press.
Miłosz, Czesław
  1983   *The History of Polish Literature.* Berkeley: University of California Press.
Mink, Louis O.
  1978   Narrative Form as a Cognitive Instrument. In *The Writing of History:
          Literary Form and Historical Understanding*, edited by R.H. Canary and H.
          Kozicki. Madison: University of Wisconsin Press.
Morawski, Karol, and Wiesław Głębocki
  1982   *Warszawa Przewodnik Turystyczny.* Warszawa: Krajowa Agencja
          Wydawnictwa.
Myerhoff, Barbara
  1978   *Number Our Days.* New York: Simon and Schuster.
  1992   *Remembered Lives: The Work of Ritual, Storytelling, and Growing Older.* Ann
          Arbor: University of Michigan Press.
Nagengast, Carole
  1994   Violence, Terror, and the Crisis of the State. *Annual Review of Anthropology*
          23: 109–136.
Nałkowska, Zofia
  2000   *Medallions.* Translated by Diana Kuprel. Evanston, IL: Northwestern
          University Press.
Nora, Pierre
  1989   Between Memory and History: Les Lieux de Mémoire. *Representations* 26,
          Special Issue Memory and Counter-Memory 25 (Spring): 7–24.
Nordstrom, Carolyn
  1992   The Backyard Front. In *Paths to Domination, Resistance, and Terror*, edited
          by Carolyn Nordstrom and JoAnn Martin, pp. 260–74. Berkeley: University
          of California Press.
  1997   *A Different Kind of War Story.* Philadelphia: University of Pennsylvania Press.
Nordstrom, Carolyn, and JoAnn Martin
  1992   The Culture of Conflict: Field Reality and Theory. In *The Paths to
          Domination, Resistance, and Terror*, edited by Carolyn Nordstrom and
          JoAnn Martin, pp. 3–15. Berkeley: University of California Press.
Novick, Peter
  1999   *The Holocaust in American Life.* Boston: Houghton Mifflin.
Nowak, Jan
  1992   *Courier from Warsaw.* Detroit, MI: Wayne State University Press.

Ochs, Elinor, and Lisa Capps
    1996   Narrating the Self. *Annual Review of Anthropology* 25: 19–43.

Olick, Jeffrey K.
    1999   Genre Memories and Memory Genres: A Dialogical Analysis of May 8,
           1945 Commemorations in the Federal Republic of Germany. *American
           Sociological Review* 64(3): 381–402.

Olick, Jeffrey K., and Daniel Levy
    1997   Collective Memory and Cultural Constraint: Holocaust Myth and
           Rationality in German Politics. *American Sociological Review* 62(6):
           921–36.

Olick, Jeffrey K., and Joyce Robbins
    1998   Social Memory Studies: From "Collective Memory" to the Historical
           Sociology of Mnemonic Practices. *Annual Review of Sociology* 24: 105–40.

Oliner, Samuel P., and Pearl M. Oliner
    1988   *The Altruistic Personality: Rescuers of Jews in Nazi Europe.* New York: Free
           Press.

Ortner, Sherry B.
    1973   On Key Symbols. *American Anthropologist* 75(5): 1338–46.

Osowski, Jaroslaw
    1993a Stołeczna Połwieczna. *Gazeta Stołeczna.* 19 Oct., p. 3. Warszawa.
    1993b Bez Stołecznej i Lumumby. *Gazeta Stołeczna.* 31 Dec.–2 Jan., p. 4. Warszawa.

Paulsson, Gunnar S.
    2002   *Secret City: The Hidden Jews of Warsaw, 1940–1945.* New Haven, CT: Yale
           University Press.

Pawlikowski, John T.
    2003   Polish Catholics and the Jews during the Holocaust: Heroism, Timidity, and
           Collaboration. In *Contested Memories: Poles and Jews in the Holocaust and
           Its Aftermath*, edited by J. Zimmerman, pp. 107–19. New Brunswick, NJ:
           Rutgers University Press.

Piłsudska, Aleksandra
    1929   *Wspomnienia Uczestniczek Walk o Niepodległoście, 1915–1918.* Warszawa:
           Głowna Księgarnia Wojskowa.

Plath, David
    1980   *Long Engagements: Maturity in Modern Japan.* Stanford, CA: Stanford
           University Press.

Plewa, Barbara Tornquist
    1992   *Wheel of Polish Fortune: Myths in Polish Collective Consciousness during the
           First Years of Solidarity.* Lund, Sweden: Lund University Press.

Podlewski, Stanisław
    1957   *Przemarsz Przez Piekło.* Warszawa: PAX.
    1979   *Rapsodia Żoliborska.* 2 vols. Warszawa: Instytut Wydawniczy PAX.

Poliakov, Leon
    1979   *Harvest of Hate: The Nazi Program for the Destruction of the Jews of Europe.*
           New York: Holocaust Library.

Polonsky, Antony
    1989   Failed Pogrom: The Demonstrations in Lwów, June 1929. In *The Jews
           of Poland between Two World Wars*, edited by Yisrael Gutman, Ezra

Mendelsohn, Jehuda Reinharz, and Chone Schmeruk, pp. 109–25. Hanover, NH: University Press of New England.

Polonsky, Antony, and Joanna B. Michlic (editors)

2004 *The Neighbors Respond: The Controversy over the Jedwabne Massacre in Poland.* Princeton, NJ: Princeton University Press.

Ponichtera, Robert M.

1997 Feminists, Nationalists, and Soldiers: Women in the Fight for Polish Independence. *International History Review* 19 (February): 16–31.

Popiełuszko, Jerzy

1986 *The Way of My Cross: Masses at Warsaw.* Translated by Michael J. Wrenn. Chicago: Regnery Books.

Pospieszalski, Karol

1946 *Polska pod Niemieckim Prawem.* Poznań: Wydawnictwo Instytutu Zachodniego.

Povrzanovic, Maja

2002 Identities in War: Embodiments of Violence and Places of Belonging. *Ethnologica Europaea* 27: 153–63.

Prazmowska, Anita J.

1997 The New Right in Poland: Nationalism, Anti-Semitism and Parliamentarianism. In *The Far Right in Western and Eastern Europe*, pp. 198–214. New York: Longman.

Prekerowa, Teresa

1982 *Konspiracyjna Rada Pomocy Żydom w Warszawie, 1942–1945.* Warsaw Państowy Instytut Wydawniczy.

1987 "Sprawiedliwi" i "bierni." *Tygodnik Powszechny* March 29, 1987, reprinted in A. Polonsky, *My Brother's Keeper? Recent Polish Debates on the Holocaust.* New York: Routledge. 1990: 73–74.

Protacio-Marcelino, Elizabeth

1991 Working Papers: First International Seminar Workshop on Children in Crisis. Quezon, Philippines: Children's Rehabilitation Center.

Proust, Marcel

1970 *Swann's Way.* Trans. C.K. Scott Moncrieff. New York: Vintage Press.

Punamaki, Raija Leena

1987 *Childhood under Conflict: The Attitudes and Emotional Life of Israeli and Palestinian Children.* Jyvaskyla, Finland: Tampere Peace Research Institute.

1996 Can Ideological Commitment Protect Children's Psychosocial Well-Being in Situations of Political Violence? *Child Development* 67(February): 55–69.

Punamaki-Gitai, Raija Leena

1990 *Political Violence and Psychological Responses: A Study of Palestinian Women, Children and Ex-Prisoners.* Jyvaskyla, Finland: Tampere Peace Research Institute.

Radstone, Susannah

2001 *Memory and Methodology.* New York: Berg Publishers.

Rapacki, Marek

1993 Całe życie Stołecznej. *Gazeta Stołeczna.* 20 Oct., p. 3. Warszawa.

Rev, Istvan

1995 Parallel Autopsies. *Representations* 49: 15–39.

Ricoeur, Paul
  1981   Narrative Time. In *On Narrative*, edited by W.J.T. Mitchell, pp. 165–86.
         Chicago: University of Chicago Press.
Ries, Nancy
  1997   *Russian Talk: Culture and Conversation during Perestroika*. Ithaca, NY:
         Cornell University Press.
Rosaldo, Renato, Smadar Lavie, and Kirin Narayan
  1993   Introduction: Creativity in Anthropology. In *Creativity/Anthropology*,
         edited by Smadar Lavie, Kirin Narayan, Renato Rosaldo. Ithaca, NY: Cornell
         University Press.
Rosenberg, Tina
  1995   *The Haunted Land: Facing Europe's Ghosts after Communism*. New York:
         Random House.
Roszkowski, Wojciech
  1997   *Historia Polski, 1914–1996*. Warszawa: Wydawnictwo Naukowe PWN.
Rybarczyk, Marek
  2000   Esesmani na Wyspach. *Gazeta Wyborcza*. 27 December.
Rzepecki, Jan
  1983   *Wspomnienia i przyczinki historyczne*. Warszawa: Czytelnik.
Rzepniewska, Danuta
  1995   Kobieta w rodzinie ziemianskiej w XIX wieku: Królewstwo Polskie. In
         Kobieta i Społeczeństwo na Ziemiach Polskich w XIX Wieku, edited by Anna
         Żarnowska and Andrzej Szwarc, 2nd ed. Warszawa: Wydawnictwo DiG:
         Instytut Historyczny Uniwersytetu Warszawskiego.
Sapir, Edward
  1924   Culture, Genuine and Spurious. *American Journal of Sociology* 29: 401–29.
Savage, Kirk
  1994   The Politics of Memory: Black Emancipation and the Civil War Monument.
         In *Commemorations: The Politics of National Identity*, edited by John R.
         Gillis, pp. 127–49. Princeton, NJ: Princeton University Press.
Scarry, Elaine
  1987   *The Body in Pain: The Making and Unmaking of the World*. Oxford: Oxford
         University Press.
Schuman, Scott
  1989   Generations of Collective Memories. *American Sociological Review* 54: 359–81.
Schwarcz, Vera
  1991   Strangers No More: Personal Memory in the Interstices of Public
         Commemoration. In *Memory, History, and Opposition under State Socialism*,
         edited by R.S. Watson, pp. 45–64. Santa Fe, NM: School of American
         Research Press.
Scott, James C.
  1985   *Weapons of the Weak: Everyday Forms of Peasant Resistance*. New Haven,
         CT: Yale University Press.
  1992   Domination, Acting, and Fantasy. In *The Paths to Domination, Resistance,
         and Terror*, edited by Carolyn Nordstrom and JoAnn Martin. Berkeley:
         University of California Press.
Sereny, Gitta
  1983   *Into That Darkness: An Examination of Conscience*. New York: Vintage.

Sinnott, Jan D.
    1998   *The Development of Logic in Adulthood: Postformal Thought and Its Applications*. New York: Plenum Press.
Skultans, Vieda
    1998   *The Testimony of Lives: Memory and Narrative in Post-Soviet Latvia*. New York: Routledge.
Sluka, Jeffrey A.
    1992   The Anthropology of Conflict. In *Paths to Domination, Resistance, and Terror*, edited by Carolyn Nordstrom and JoAnn Martin, pp. 18–36. Berkeley: University of California Press.
Snyder, Timothy
    2002   Memory of Sovereignty and Sovereignty over Memory: Poland, Lithuania and Ukraine, 1939–1999. In *Memory and Power in Post-War Europe: Studies in the Presence of the Past,* edited by Jan-Werner Muller, pp. 39–58. Cambridge: Cambridge University Press.
    2009   Holocaust: The Ignored Reality. *New York Review of Books* 56(12).
Sokolewicz, Zofia
    1991   National Heroes and National Mythology in 19th and 20th Century Poland. *Ethnologia Europaea* 21: 125–36.
Stebelski, Adam
    1964   *The Fate of Polish Archives during World War II*. Translated by Barbara Przestepska. Warszawa: Państwowe Instytut Wydawnictwo.
Steinlauf, Michael C.
    1997   *Bondage to the Dead: Poland and the Memory of the Holocaust*. Syracuse, NY: Syracuse University Press.
Stola, Dariusz
    2003   The Polish Government in Exile and the Final Solution: What Conditioned Its Actions and Inactions? In *Contested Memories: Poles and Jews in the Holocaust and Its Aftermath*, edited by J. Zimmerman, pp. 85–96. New Brunswick, NJ: Rutgers University Press.
Sturken, Marita
    1997   *Tangled Memories: The Vietnam War, the AIDS Epidemic, and the Politics of Remembering*. Berkeley: University of California Press.
Sutton, David E.
    1998   *Memories Cast in Stone: The Relevance of the Past in Everyday Life*. Oxford: Berg.
Swedenburg, Ted
    1993   *Memories of Revolt: The 1936–1939 Rebellion and the Palestinian National Past*. Minneapolis: University of Minnesota Press.
Szarota, Tomasz
    1973a Jawne wydawnictwa i prasa okupowanej Warszawie. In *Studia Warszawskie* 10, Warszawa lat wojny i okupacji: Zeszyt 2: 140–66.
    1973b *Okupowanej Warszawy dzień powszedni; studium historyczne*. Warszawa: Czytelnik.
Szpilman, Władysław
    1999   *The Pianist*. New York: Picador.
Szwankowski, Eugeniusz
    1963   *Ulice i Place Warszawy*. Warszawa: Państwowe Wydawnictwo Naukowe.

Szymczak, Kazimierz
    1948   "Dni Grozy i Walki o Wolność." In *Pamiętniki Robotników z Czasów Okupacji*, edited by Centralna Rada Związków Zawodowych w Polsce. Warszawa: Książka i Wiedza.

Taussig, Michael
    1985   *Shamanism, Colonialism, and the Wild Man: A Study in Terror and Healing*. Chicago: University of Chicago Press.

Tazbir, Janusz
    1998   *Polska Na Zakrętach Dziejów*. Vol. 7. Warszawa: Wydawnictow Sic!

Tec, Nechama
    1986   *When Light Pierced the Darkness: Christian Rescue of Jews in Nazi-Occupied Poland*. New York: Oxford University Press.

Ten Dyke, Elizabeth A.
    2001   *Dresden: Paradoxes of Memory in History*. London: Routledge.

Thomson, Alistair
    1994   *Anzac Memories: Living with the Legend*. Melbourne: Oxford University Press.

Todorov, Tzvetan
    1996   *Facing the Extreme: Moral Life in the Concentration Camps*. Translated by Arthur Denner and Abigail Pollak. New York: Henry Holt.

Tomaszewski, Jerzy
    1989   The Role of Jews in Polish Commerce, 1918–1939. In *The Jews of Poland between Two World Wars*, edited by Yisrael Gutman, Ezra Mendelsohn, Jehuda Reinharz, and Chone Shmeruk, pp. 141–57. Hanover, NH: University Press of New England.

Tucker, Erica L.
    1998   Renaming Capital Street: Competing Visions of the Past in Post-Communist Warsaw. *City & Society*. Annual Review, pp. 223–44.

Turner, Victor
    1978   Foreword. In *Number Our Days*, by Barbara Myerhoff. New York: Simon and Schuster.

Valent, Paul
    1998   Resilience in Child Survivors of the Holocaust: Toward the Concept of Resilience. *Psychoanalytic Review* 85 (4) (August): 517–35.

Verdery, Katherine
    1991a *National Ideology under Socialism: Identity and Cultural Politics in Ceaucescu's Romania*. Berkeley: University of California Press.
    1991b Theorizing Socialism: A Prologue to the "Transition." *American Ethnologist* 18(3): 419–39.

Vromen, Suzanne
    1993   The Ambiguity of Nostalgia. In *YIVO Annual*, edited by Jack Kugelmass. Evanston, IL: Northwestern University Press and the Yivo Institute for Jewish Research.

Wajda, Andrzej
    1958   Popiół i diament. Zespół filmowy KADR. Screenplay by Jerzy Andrzejewski and Andrzej Wajda.

Walicki, Andrzej
 1991 *Russia, Poland, and Universal Regeneration: Studies on Russian and Polish Thought of the Romantic Epoch.* Notre Dame, IN: University of Notre Dame Press.
Walzer, Michael
 1992 *Just And Unjust Wars: A Moral Argument with Historical Illustrations.* New York: Basic Books.
Wandycz, Piotr S.
 1974 *The Lands of Partitioned Poland, 1795–1918.* 11 vols. Seattle: University of Washington Press.
Watson, Rubie S.
 1994a Making Secret Histories: Memory and Mourning in Post-Mao China. In *Memory, History, and Opposition under State Socialism,* edited by R.S. Watson, pp. 65–86. Santa Fe, NM: School of American Research Press.
 1994b Memory, History, and Opposition under State Socialism, An Introduction. In *Memory, History, and Opposition under State Socialism,* edited by R.S. Watson, pp.1–20. Santa Fe, NM: School of American Research Press.
Watson, Rubie S. (editor)
 1994c *Memory, History, and Opposition under State Socialism.* Santa Fe, NM: School of American Research Press.
Watts, Michael
 1992 Space for Everything (a Commentary). *Cultural Anthropology* 7(1): 115–29.
Welch, David
 1983 Educational Film Propaganda and the Nazi Youth. In *Nazi Propaganda: The Power and the Limitations,* p. 228. London: Croom Helm.
Wertsch, James V.
 2002 *Voices of Collective Remembering.* Cambridge: Cambridge University Press.
Wessells, Michael G.
 1998 Children, Armed Conflict, and Peace. *Journal of Peace Research* 35(5): 635–46.
White, Hayden
 1981 The Value of Narrativity in the Representation of Reality. In *On Narrative,* edited by W.J.T. Mitchell, pp. 1–23. Chicago: University of Chicago Press.
Young, James E.
 1993 *The Texture of Memory: Holocaust Memorials and Meaning.* New Haven, CT: Yale University Press.
Żarnowska, Anna, and Andrzej Szwarc (editors)
 1995a *Kobieta i Edukacja na Ziemiach Polskich w XIX i XX wieku.* Warszawa: Wydawnictwo DiG: Instytut Historyczny Uniwersytetu Warszawskiego.
 1995b *Kobieta i Społeczęstwo na Ziemiach Polskich w XIX Wieku.* 2nd ed. Warszawa: Wydawnictwo DiG: Instytut Historyczny Uniwersytetu Warszawskiego.
Zawadzka, Anna
 1998 *Harcerstwo Żenskie w Warszawie w latach 1911–1949: Pamięci warszawskich harcerek i instruktorek.* Warszawa: Municipium S.A.

Żebrowski, Leszek
    1995   *Paszkwil Wyborczej: Michnik i Cichy o Powstaniu Warszawksiem*. Warszawa: Burchard.

Zerubavel, Yael
    1994   The Historic, the Legendary, and the Incredible: Invented Tradition and Collective Memory in Israel. In *Commemorations: The Politics of National Identity*, edited by John Gillis, pp. 105–23. Princeton, NJ: Princeton University Press.

Zimmerman, Joshua D.
    2003   Introduction: Changing Perceptions in the Historiography of Polish-Jewish Relations during the Second World War. In *Contested Memories: Poles and Jews during the Holocaust and Its Aftermath*, edited by Joshua Zimmerman, pp. 1–18. New Brunswick, NJ: Rutgers University Press.

Zimmerman, Joshua D. (editor)
    2003   *Contested Memories: Poles and Jews during the Holocaust and Its Aftermath*. New Brunswick, NJ: Rutgers University Press.

Zubrzycki, Geneviève
    2006   *The Crosses of Auschwitz: Nationalism and Religion in Post-Communist Poland*. Chicago: University of Chicago Press.

Index

National Socialists, 75
Nationalist Independent Camp, 34
Naukowska Street, 210
Nazi executions, 73–75, 164, 178
Nazi policies, 73, 79, 88
Nicholas I, Tsar, 31
Niedzielski, Mieczysław. *See* Żywiciel
Nordstrom, Carolyn, 44, 224, 226, 244
normalcy, the return to, 223–29
Norwid, Cyprian, 31
November Uprising of 1830, 31
Nowy Świat, 174
Nuremburg Laws, 92, 257n1, 257n2

Oberlangen (labor camp), 202, 222
occupation. *See* German occupation of
   Warsaw
occupation of the body, 87–91
occupation of memory, 107–9, 260n7
occupation of the mind, 91–101
occupation of place, 75–87
occupation of the spirit, 101–7
Ochota neighborhood, 204, 260n7
Ogrodowa Street, 150
Old Town, 6, 165, 177–80, 184–88, 260n10
Old Żoliborz neighborhoods: Civil Employees' (Żoliborz *Urzedniczy*), 7–8;
   Journalists' (Żoliborz *Dziennikarski*),
   7–8, 121; Officers' (Żoliborz *Oficerski*),
   7–8, 35; Workers' (Żoliborz *Robotniczy*), 7–8
Olesia, 153–54
Olgierd B. (journalist): on the conspiracy,
   110; description of Żoliborz, 9; and the
   Fall of Warsaw, 203–4; on helping Jews,
   144, 259n4; and the return to Warsaw,
   216–17; and secret schools, 98
Olgierd Z. (doctor): background information on, 13, 27; on conditions in the
   ghetto, 83–85; and conspiratorial acts,
   116–19, 129–30; example of social
   solidarity, 137–38; experiences as a displaced person, 212–14; and the Fall of
   Warsaw, 203; on helping Jews, 147, 148;

and the importance of culture, 123–24;
   memories of the exodus, 211; memories
   of the Siege of Warsaw, 50; memories
   of the uprising of 1944, 170–71, 173;
   narratives of death, 192–93, 196–98;
   narratives of destruction, 191–92;
   and occupation of the mind, 91–92;
   on the PRL, 236–39; on repression
   of religion, 105–6; and the return to
   Warsaw, 214–15, 219, 220, 222; and
   secret schools, 95–98; on treating the
   wounded, 4, 175–77
Oliga (Society of International Students), 51
Oliner, Pearl M., 151, 259n8
Oliner, Samuel P., 151, 259n8
Operation A-B *(AuBerordentliche Befrie-
   dungsaktion)*, 75
Opoczno, 208
Organization of Women's Military Service,
   128
Osóbska-Morawski, Edward, 232
Ostawków, 261n2
Oświęcim (Town of Auschwitz), 21
Ożarowa, 233

participant observation. *See* fieldwork
Paskievitch, Ivan, 256n2
Patkowska, Pani, 210
Patrons for the Care of Prisoners *(Patronat
   Opieki nad Więznami)*, 133
Paulsson, Gunnar, 147
Pawiak Prison, 99, 100, 115–16, 150, 156,
   159, 215
Pawiak Prison Museum, 245, 247
Peasants, The (Rejmont), 255n1
People's Army. *See* AL
People's Party (Stronnictwo Ludowe), 47
"personal fable" (Elkind), 53–54
Pianist, The (Szpilman), 80
Pietruszka, 198
Piłsudski, Marszal Józef, 28, 34, 35, 40, 42,
   47, 76, 255n5
Piłsudski's Legions, 12, 27, 28, 34
Pińsk, 58